HOW TO ENJOY BALLET

HOW TO
Enjoy Ballet

by Don McDonagh

DOUBLEDAY AND COMPANY, INC.
GARDEN CITY, NEW YORK
1978

Library of Congress Cataloging in Publication Data
McDonagh, Don.
How to enjoy ballet.
Includes index.
1. Ballet.   I. Title.
GV1787.M26   792.8
ISBN: 0-385-12690-5
Library of Congress Catalog Card Number 77-82958
Copyright © 1978 by Don McDonagh
All Rights Reserved
Printed in the United States of America

9 8 7 6 5 4 3 2

For my mother and late father,
both of whom encouraged me to experience
new things, as they did themselves

Contents

CONTENTS

Foreword

This is a book about classical ballet, not folk ballet, modern dance or any of the other serious forms of theater dance. There are hundreds of ballet companies scattered throughout the world, from Peking to Atlanta, of varying sizes and skills. The general comments within apply to all of them with regard to the basic vocabulary of steps, teaching principles, and the roles of the dancers and the choreographers. It was obviously impossible to discuss all of these companies in any detail, so a selection of eight major companies, of international reputation, representing as many distinct stylistic approaches, was made. Among the American companies which had to be omitted were the Pennsylvania Ballet, the Boston Ballet, Dance Theater of Harlem, the San Francisco Ballet and the Eliot Feld Ballet, as well as a substantial number of regional companies. The selections throughout Europe and Russia were as stringent.

Similarly, with an eye on the introductory nature of this book, the glossary of ballet terms was kept to a workable size. No attempt was made to describe all of the steps of the vocabulary, a job done quite thoroughly in a variety of stylistic manuals. The chronology of events in the world of ballet and in the Western Hemisphere is offered as a general framework upon which to relate parallel occurrences to an art form which is at least two centuries older than the founding of our own country.

FOREWORD

The photographs included represent a selection from the private collection of Michael Truppin, a friend of twenty years' standing. We met first under circumstances totally outside the world of ballet and only later discovered that we shared a similar passion for the art. Mike, in his role of obstetrician-gynecologist, delivered our four children, and it is a pleasure to share another project with him now.

CHAPTER ONE

What is ballet?

Ballet, as we see it today, is the product of four centuries of refinement and experimentation and is most readily defined in terms of its technique. That technique is based on the five classic positions of the feet from which all of the steps in the balletic vocabulary proceed and terminate. It is a performing art which creates a mood or tells a story using combinations of these steps, most frequently to musical accompaniment. The most striking feature of the technique is the turnout of the legs from the hip. It enables ballet dancers to move to either side as well as forward and back with equal ease, giving them command over a full circle of movement. Completely "turned out," the dancer can stand with heels pressed together and toes pointed to the side, forming a 180-degree angle. There are corresponding positions of the arms, but these are not identical from one school to another, though there are considerable similarities. These starting positions are the same for men and women, though each sex specializes in the execution of certain families of steps. Women tend to stress balance, and men, air work associated with leaps.

Ordinarily one stands with the feet parallel to one another, ankles facing and toes pointed straight ahead; and, at one time, so did dancers. From this position it is easy to move forward and backward, but the range of steps to the side is limited. With training, the leg can be rotated so that it becomes possible to develop movement to the side as easily as to the front and back. The result is that, looking at a ballet dancer in the first position, the torso and head face forward and the legs are seen in profile. This unusual conformation of the body is an essential part of the art and, in a way, is reminiscent of Egyptian wall painting. There the whole body was drawn in profile except for the eye, which was shown staring as it would appear if the person were looking directly forward.

FIRST POSITION: KIRK PETERSON

The ballet is the product of European civilization and its roots lie deeply in the folk dances of the area. It is almost impossible to trace the changes and refinement of those early dances as they were taken over by the nobility and incorporated into the life of the court during the Renaissance. We are aware, though, that the position of dancing master was an important one in the courts of Italy and that these men staged entertainments that were a mixture of song, recitation, music and movement that involved the members of the courts themselves. The ballets of the day were very much a participational art, and it was regarded as part of the accomplishments of ladies and gentlemen to be able to enter into them. The dancing master was a professional, as was any artist attached to a court, but the performers were amateurs.

SECOND POSITION: KIRK PETERSON

Dance spectacles were most highly developed in Italy and it was an Italian, Balthasar Beaujoyeux (né Baldassare di Belgiojoso), who prepared *Le Ballet Comique de la Reine,* which is widely recognized today as a major forerunner of present-day ballet. It was given at Paris in 1581 under the patronage of Catherine de Medici as part of the wedding festivities of the Duc de Joyeuse and Marguerite de Lorraine. The dancing in the production consisted of movements intricately arranged in geometrical patterns and did not feature any soaring jumps or turns in the air, which are familiar parts of ballets now. It was, however, clearly structured and depended on dance movements to advance the progess of the pageant. These spectacles were very popular with the court, and it soon became necessary in France as well as in Italy to have dance training if one were a member of the nobility.

Italy continued to produce ballets, ballet dancers and ballet masters in great quantity through the late nineteenth century, but increasingly the focus of ballet began to concentrate on France. To a great extent the French relied on Italian dancing masters to devise spectacles and to train them for their performance, but French teachers began to emerge. During the time of Louis XIV, who was a very active performer, the form received a great subsidy from the court and began to develop in complexity. The king himself ceased performing in 1670, which lessened interest in the art among courtiers, but he had handed the fledgling art form over to professionals by founding the Royal Dance Academy and granting a charter to found the Paris Opera. The result was that ballet left the privacy of the court and entered into the popular theater.

Pierre Beauchamps was the first ballet master of the Paris Opera, and in 1700 he described the five positions of the feet as we know them, which were essential to the ballet dancer. He was a choreographer and devised a system of notation by which he could record dances. At this time various of the steps were beginning to be codified by the names we have for them today. The words used to describe the steps were of course French, and when ballet spread to other countries the vocabulary used to

THIRD POSITION: COLLEEN NEARY

describe the steps went with it. The splendor of the French court
had set an example to the rest of Europe and the nobility of various lands adopted many of its customs and entertainments, one of
which was ballet.

As an aristocratic occupation ballet had some influence on
other traditional pursuits of the well-born. To this day the bodily
conformation and movement of the fencer bears traces of it,
as does the vocabulary, and the sport of dressage reflects a
dancer's posture as well as some of the floor patterns of court
dances. The influence of the court had both a good and a bad
side to it. It certainly encouraged the development of ballet, but
on the other hand held it back from a professional commitment.
When professionals began to take over the ballet the nobility became its audience. The art, which had emphasized geometrical
patterns sweeping along the floor, now began to exploit the air

above it more and more, and today the terms which are used (in French, naturally) to point out the difference are *à terre* and *en l'air*. Many steps are executed both while maintaining contact with the floor and while leaping up from the floor. The aristocratic dancers did not have the turnout, which was increasingly developed by the professionals, and the art form was dominated by the male dancer. Women in their large, long dresses glided about to a great extent with their feet and legs decorously hidden.

When ballet entered into the Paris Opera the parts that would have been danced by women were danced by men, in the same way that men or young boys acted women's roles in Shake-

FOURTH POSITION (FRONT): COLLEEN NEARY

FOURTH POSITION (SIDE): COLLEEN NEARY

speare's plays. It simply wasn't nice for women to exhibit themselves onstage. Even after women were admitted to the stage the ballets continued to be dominated by men, who alone were permitted to perform the more spectacular leaps and turns. Louis Dupré, one of these early stars, was styled "the god of the dance" by his public. Marie Anne de Camargo, the first woman to challenge male supremacy, had her skirts shortened to slightly above the ankles to permit herself easier movement. She was soon rivaled by Marie Sallé, and both were eclipsed by the striking virtuosity of the Italian dancer Barbara Campanini (affection-

FIFTH POSITION: KIRK PETERSON

ately called "La Barbarina"), who executed steps that were beyond their abilities.

The days of the court ballet were at an end and the new *ballet
d'action* (ballet with a story), which emphasized dramatic development of plot, began to gain ascendancy. The court ballet was
performed by amateurs and gave a strong place to recitation, song,
mimed passages and processions. Performances were given in private homes, sometimes of great size and richness, but they were
essentially private affairs, and selected incidents from Greek and
Roman mythology were chosen for thematic material. They had
a feeling of pageantry and sometimes even played a political role
when the theme selected from classical antiquity had some bearing on a current political confrontation. This aspect of the court
ballets still crops up in twentieth-century ballets presented in the
Soviet Union or the People's Republic of China.

8

CHANGING POSITION: COLLEEN NEARY

CHANGING POSITION: KIRK PETERSON

JETÉ: COLLEEN NEARY

WHAT IS BALLET?

When the ballet transferred its activities to the public theater many things changed, including the place and concept of the audience. The latter no longer participated, and the ballet was presented on a stage framed by a proscenium arch which the audience sat or stood in front of. In court ballet spectators sat around the spectacle. While still selecting subjects from classical antiquity, the choreographers tended to emphasize the narrative progression in the *ballet d'action*. Spectacle was retained but costuming was modified to allow the dancers greater freedom of movement. This eventually dictated the abandonment of the heeled shoe, masks, and the heavier aspects of court costume which would have impeded the dancers. Choreographers in several countries were developing this new type of theatrical dancing, including John Weaver in England, Franz Hilverding in Austria, Gasparo Angiolini in Italy, and in France Jean-Georges Noverre.

These men knew of one another and in several cases worked together on productions, but the one who is generally regarded as the most significant was Noverre. There were differences in approach among them all, but essentially they wished to take a court divertissement and transform it into an artistic vehicle capable of artistic expression on its own terms. Despite the fact that while the music of these ballets is often available and librettos exist, we really don't know what they looked like in terms of presentation. What we do know is that at this time, the middle of the eighteenth century, Noverre published his *Letters on Dancing and Ballets*, which pressed the case for the new type of ballet most forcefully and intelligently. It expressed in words the principles behind the new development in ballet.

Noverre was an excellent dancer himself and performed or choreographed in many of the major cities in Europe, including Vienna, where he had his greatest successes and where he also instructed Marie Antoinette in social dancing. Later, as Queen of France, she was his generous patron. He was variously engaged by the court of Frederick the Great of Prussia, where he became acquainted with another French expatriate, Voltaire, and spent several productive years in Stuttgart under the patronage of the

Duke of Württemberg. He danced and staged a ballet in London, and toward the end of his career he became the director of the Paris Opera. To a great extent, work in Paris did not satisfy him, and he carried out his most ambitious projects abroad. The development of ballet as a dramatic instrument of expression received an impetus that removed it forever from the conventions of court ballet by increasing emphasis on sheer movement, whether pure dancing or mime gesture.

While the *ballet d'action* indicated a new direction for ballet, it still looked mainly to classical antiquity for its subject matter and was influenced in this choice by the manners and whims of its royal patrons. The generation of choreographers that followed Noverre—men like Salvatore Viganò, Charles Didelot and Jean Dauberval—began to select themes for ballet from popular legend and folk sources. They continued the dramatic development of ballet as they had received it, but broadened the scope of its subject matter to include tales celebrating the doings of people who were recognizably from another strata of society. They maintained their delight in the use of spectacle, but slowly shifted the focus of ballet from the remote past to the more recent past. It was a period that declared its independence from the classical world of gods and goddesses and began to celebrate national heroes and folk characters.

Italy was still the fountainhead of dancing talent due to its early development of danced spectacle and continued interest in the dramatic possibilities of dancing. Several of the leading theatrical families developed in Italy, then flowered elsewhere in Europe. For three generations the Vestris family of Florence sent talented dancers to appear at the Paris Opera, and indeed all over Europe. The Taglioni family, originally from Milan, also gravitated to Paris, where Filippo Taglioni taught and choreographed his most important ballets and where his daughter, Marie Taglioni, set the tone for ballerinas through the end of the nineteenth century. Marie Taglioni was the embodiment of the Romantic ballet, which succeeded the *ballet d'action* definitively after her father created *La Sylphide* for her.

The primacy of dancing and the special use of mimed gesture

to tell a dramatic story had been well developed by the choreographers who created the *ballet d'action* of what had been the divertissement of court ballet. Subsequent ballets had been freed from the necessity to choose classical models for their subject matter, and the Romantic ballet went even further and deliberately chose stories that were calculatedly vague. It exalted the passionate, emotional side of personal expression at the expense of logic. It told stories all right, but stories of magic, exoticisms and unexplainable events which affected the here and now. It sought out the material of folk legend where spirits, elves and other ethereal creatures were celebrated. It did not reject mystery which resulted from the free play of the imagination, and would not be bound by the dictates of objective reality.

ATTITUDE: COLLEEN NEARY

Filippo Taglioni, in creating *La Sylphide*, established a pattern that was to be followed by major choreographers until the beginning of the twentieth century. It mixed the spirit world with everyday reality, and generally ended in tragedy. His daughter, whom he had trained himself, possessed an exceptionally fluent technique and was known for her lightness and delicacy of movement. She was not the first woman who danced on point (i.e. the toes), but she took what was a somewhat new, flashy technical feat and made it an artistic asset. By rising to full point she was able to give an air of ethereality to her characterization of the otherworldly spirit of the sylph. The effect on audiences was astounding and she became the most acclaimed ballerina in Europe. Everyone sought to produce a similar effect, and the result was the eventual domination of the ballet by the ballerina, although this took several decades to be accomplished.

Another Italian dancer and teacher who was extremely active at this time had a profound effect on the teaching and codifying of ballet technique. Carlo Blasis had performed in France and Russia before settling in Milan to concentrate on teaching, but once there he contributed extensively to the development of dancers from all over Europe, and even the United States, who came to study with him. He was a serious student of anatomy and formulated principles of instruction that eventually influenced the creation of the Russian school through Enrico Cecchetti.

The Romantic ballet spread throughout the countries of Europe with incredible rapidity and completely banished the *ballet d'action* with its strict emphasis on classic form and logical unity. The most widely known ballet of the era is Jean Coralli and Jules Perrot's *Giselle*, which is performed by many contemporary companies. It tells the tale of a young peasant girl who is deceived by an aristocrat and who persists in her love even beyond the grave. She ultimately saves him from the vengeance of the Willis, the spirits of young maidens who die before their wedding day, by the force of her own passionate and faithful love.

JETÉ: KIRK PETERSON

ARABESQUE: COLLEEN NEARY

High emotion causing logical dislocations beyond the dictates of the practical or even the forces of life and death, was a theme that occurred in myriads of variations and is reflected in the work of choreographers as different as Marius Petipa (*Swan Lake, Sleeping Beauty*), Arthur Saint-Léon (*Coppélia*), August Bournonville (*La Sylphide*), and Lev Ivanov (*The Nutcracker*). In each case some magical force interferes with the normal course of events. Whether it resulted in humorous consequences (*Coppélia* and *The Nutcracker*), tragedy and death (*Giselle, Swan Lake* and *La Sylphide*), or a temporary setback of the forces of love (*Sleeping Beauty*), it made an impact on the everyday world of the living. Flesh-and-blood people had their lives changed in some way by forces beyond their control.

During the nineteenth century there was a great exchange of dancers, choreographers and teachers between various European cities, and even with the United States. Fanny Elssler toured the East Coast with enormous success; students in Boston unhitched the horses from her carriage and dragged it back to her hotel; and Congress recessed so that its members could see her perform in Washington. Native-born George Washington Smith of Philadelphia became a member of her company and later had a successful career in the United States, as did Mary Ann Lee, who was his partner. The latter made her debut in 1837 with Augusta Maywood in Philadelphia, and while Lee remained in the United States after a period of study in Europe, Maywood became a member of the Paris Opera Ballet and performed widely in Europe, where she died. Aside from a few such talented exceptions, there was little in the way of ballet in the United States except that which was provided by touring Italian and French dancers, for the most part.

The ascendancy of the ballerina in Paris became total by the latter half of the century, and male dancers, who had dominated the stage earlier, were relegated to the subordinate position of lifting and supporting their ballerinas at the appropriate times. Italy continued to produce talented male and female dancers who toured regularly, and in Russia the schools in Moscow and St. Petersburg were beginning to produce gifted dancers. The Royal

Danish Ballet had developed under the directorship of August Bournonville, who had taught and preserved the tradition of the Romantic ballet as it had been in 1826 when he was in the Paris Opera Ballet. There were a great number of ballet performances, and ballet companies also regularly danced the divertissements that were included in opera productions. In Paris it was an unwritten rule that every opera had to have a ballet, a rule boorishly enforced by patrons, belonging to the fashionable Jockey Club, who interested themselves in the comings and goings at the opera. When Wagner created *Tannhäuser* without a ballet, he was told that it couldn't be performed. Angrily he acquiesced but put the ballet in the first act, which inconvenienced the Jockey Club members, who normally arrived only for the beginning of the second act.

Ballet at the Paris Opera became little more than a decorative plaything in the latter half of the century, and the energy that had once emanated from France was largely dissipated. But the art, which was languishing in the country that did so much to give it grace and discipline, was growing in strength in Russia. There, both French elegance in deportment and Italian virtuosity were being formed into a distinctively national style by the teachers and students in the Imperial schools. The most important of these was the Maryinsky in St. Petersburg, presided over by Marius Petipa. He himself was French, and his staff included a Swede, Christian Johansson, who was a brilliant pupil of Bournonville, an Italian, Enrico Cecchetti, who was a product of Blasis' training, and native-born Russians like Lev Ivanov. The pattern of ballet's adaptability was to be repeated in Russia, where the steps of the standard vocabulary were molded into a national style that expressed a dramatic and lyrical character.

During the age of Petipa the ballet was supported generously by the czar. Its glamor was unmatched anywhere else in the world, and in a few years it produced the artists who were to revivify the art of ballet throughout Western Europe. The political troubles that plagued czarist Russia erupted in a series of individual upheavals which finally resulted in the end of the Romanov line. In the Imperial Ballet there were rumblings that

ARABESQUE PENCHÉ: COLLEEN NEARY

eventually caused Petipa to live the last seven years of his life in enforced retirement and saw the development of an innovative choreographer, Mikhail Fokine.

The latter felt that the ballet had grown stale and lacked dramatic cohesion. He wanted to create ballets that had a unified story in which all of the gestures used were appropriate to the time of the ballet and that its decor and costuming were historically accurate. He was invited by Serge Diaghilev, a vigorous and tasteful admirer of the ballet, to choreograph ballets which would be performed in Paris by a company which Diaghilev would engage. He assembled a powerful group, among whom were Anna Pavlova, Tamara Karsavina, Vaslav Nijinsky and Adolph Bolm.

Fokine's ballets were praised, as were the dancers, especially the men, who were a revelation to the Parisian public, which had forgotten the power of great male dancing. Fokine eventually went on to form his own company and then to create ballets for a variety of companies, including American Ballet Theater. Diaghilev toured his Ballets Russes throughout Europe and the Americas for twenty years, during which he introduced dozens of new productions and an unmatched group of choreographers, starting with Fokine and including Léonide Massine, George Balanchine, and Bronislava Nijinska (Nijinsky's sister). After Diaghilev's example and because of the unsettled conditions in Russia, a flood of dancers and teachers chose to live in Western Europe or the United States, where ballet companies began to appear under their influence.

Mikhail Mordkin's small company became the core around which American Ballet Theater was formed, and Lincoln Kirstein invited George Balanchine to the United States to form a company which eventually became New York City Ballet. Ninette de Valois, who established England's Royal Ballet, studied with Cecchetti when he was teaching in London and she performed with Massine's own company as well as with Diaghilev's Ballets Russes. Various companies were formed in France around one or another of the choreographers, and eventually Serge Lifar, a notable dancer with Diaghilev's company, was appointed artistic director of the Paris Opera Ballet. Expatriate Russian dancers opened studios, among which those of Mathilde Kchessinska, Lubov Egorova and Olga Preobrajenska were the most noted in Paris. The balletic tradition which had been preserved in Russia was beginning to spread once again through the West.

When Balanchine arrived in the United States he also worked in the popular theater and movies as well as in the ballet proper. In 1936, Broadway first saw the word *choreographer* on a marquee when he designed the dances for *On Your Toes*, featuring the ballet *Slaughter on Tenth Avenue*. The word and the job have become a part of musical comedy, where previously the "dance arranger" reigned. The ripples from Diaghilev's era continue to radiate outward, and the major changes that he inaugurated, following the time of Petipa, govern much of what we see today. The standard length of a Petipa ballet or that of any of the nineteenth-century ballet masters was a full evening. While these ballets still exist and are still the norm in Russia, they have been supplanted to a great extent by shorter works which are clustered to form whole programs. Three and even four ballets, by the same or different choreographers, may be seen in one evening. Diaghilev also stressed the importance of collaboration between the composer, the designer and the choreographer. He himself was none of these but had an animating sense of urgency which drew first-rate work from the artists he brought together. He did not abandon the idea of ballet as a storytelling instrument or delineator of mood; he merely tightened the presentation.

Several of the choreographers who worked with him, however, experimented with ballets which were plotless in the ordinary sense. The first of these was Fokine, whose *Les Sylphides* creates a world of relationships without elaborate character studies. Massine worked on developing "symphonic" ballets which developed out of the plotless symphonic music that they were danced to. Balanchine has produced the largest number of these works, which evolve their meaning from the relationships of the dancers and tell their tales in close affiliation with the accompanying music. They are in a way, balletic equivalents of Mendelssohn's *Songs Without Words*.

CABRIOLE: KIRK PETERSON

While many choreographers still create story ballets, most of them also choreograph plotless ballets in which one's attention is drawn primarily to the quality of the dance movement without any passages of mimed action to advance a definite story. Without specific characterizations to worry over, designers have dressed such ballets in simple costumes that may suggest a point of historical time in some slight way or, even more basically, in neutral practice clothes that give no clue to any specific time or place. In such a case one assumes that time and place are of no special importance and that the ballet is in effect the essence of many situations and encounters which could be set in a variety of historical contexts. This "abstracting" quality of many contemporary works is merely the extension of a tendency which has existed in ballet almost as far back as one cares to look.

In every great classic ballet there is always a moment when the heroine and the hero take the center of the stage, either alone or with others in attendance at the edges, to dance their major *pas de deux* (duet). At this point almost all of the storytelling is suppressed by the choreographer and the pure steps of the classic vocabulary are used to show the relationship and the feelings they have for one another. When seen alone, outside the surroundings of the whole ballet, these abstracted bits lose much of their sense, since the dancers' characters have been created in the course of the production and they now are showing a climactic moment in the plot development. These dances are the great "arias" of full-evening ballets and should be seen in their normal setting for complete appreciation. Even abstracted as they are, though, they can be enjoyed for their technical display and also, with care, can be understood. Quite frequently, however, they are presented as "star vehicles" in a way that has little to do with artistry and much to do with display. Some audiences mistake this display for the ballets' meaning. No one has phrased it more clearly than the late dancer Robert Horan.

"It is not the business of an audience to be sophisticated in the matter of technique, but in the matter of meaning. One of the destructive emphases which ballet discipline has unwittingly encouraged in its audience is the recognition of technique as such.

Technique is professional; it is the artist's and at most the critic's concern. Knowledge about the intricacies of technical performance is a pathetic substitute for understanding of an art, as any studio full of dancers or musicians can well demonstrate."*

This is not to say that an appreciation of technique should be avoided but only that it take its rightful place in the viewer's attention. Ballet teachers exist to develop and correct technique and it is their primary concern. Frequently when they attend the ballet they hardly look at anyone else on the stage except the one dancer they are particularly interested in as a pupil. Of course they are aware of the others but reserve their real attention for the details of that one special person.

In a similar way the ballet master of a company whose job it is to rehearse the corps de ballet in a production is so concerned with them that he sometimes fails to "see" the principals. A ballet master with one of the major companies told me of his embarrassment when walking backstage just after a performance and encountering one of the principals. She asked him casually how he thought she had done that evening, and he really didn't know. He had certainly watched the ballet but his attention was focused elsewhere and it was not on her, so he was forced to cover with a polite neutral comment.

One can watch a ballet from many different aspects, but it is most rewarding to be involved in the whole sweep and thrust of the production rather than one narrow episode or facet of it. There is a kind of chat which one overhears in the theater occasionally which has a superficial gloss that sounds very knowledgeable but is mostly indicative of balletomania. The term originally described the emotional excesses of those who followed the Imperial Russian ballerinas of czarist times but covers all members of the audience with an obsessional rather than discriminating taste for the art. The talk may concentrate on technique or a personal favorite. "What about Svet in *Lac* sat mat!" is one of the choicer examples, but there are hundreds. It sounds intimidatingly intelligent but translates simply into a reference to

* Dance Index Vol. VI, No. 1, January 1947, p. 17.

one of the now retired Royal Ballet ballerinas, Svetlana Beriosova, who was dancing the principal role in *Swan Lake* (*Lac des Cygnes* in French) in a Saturday afternoon performance. The late Sol Hurok diagnosed the condition as "wanting new ballets and free tickets." By all means enjoy ballet, but be discriminating about it and be receptive to the best that all dancers and choreographers have to offer you.

JETÉ: COLLEEN NEARY

SHOULDER SIT: COLLEEN NEARY AND KIRK PETERSON

CHAPTER TWO

Dancers

The living, physical beauty of a stage full of trained dancers is overwhelming when first encountered. As one marvelously formed performer moves past, another comes into view. Their deportment is proud, graceful, almost an idealization of what the human form is meant to achieve in harmonious symmetry. The women are supported on long, powerful, pliant legs, their waists neatly trim, with arms finely extended and heads set delicately on still shoulders. Their hips do not waggle when they walk, their bearing indicates self-awareness in the best sense of knowing who they are, where their body's center of balance is located, and the security of being able to move with disciplined confidence.

The men are similarly proud in the upright strength of their carriage. Their shoulders are squared and their chests are high, the stomach flat and firm. Their arms are strong but the muscles are not highly defined. They do show great muscular development through the thighs and legs, the sort that would result from any regimen of concentrated, disciplined physical activity. Their feet spring from the floor when they walk, there is a sense of aliveness in every motion they make. Their carriage is obviously based on some ideal in which a secure blend of strength and grace was the model to be attained.

The dancer you see today in the major companies is the product of an intensive schooling that properly begins between the ages of eight and ten and continues every day in one way or another until the dancer decides to retire from active performing. Like any performing art, it takes an enormous investment of time and energy to achieve the first level of competence, and then constant attention to development after the basic skills have been secured. There never comes a time, even in the lives of the finest dancers, when they can abandon the regular discipline of daily dance class. Their physical skills are extraordinary, and they remain that way only through constant attention.

Once accepted into any of the major companies, the young dancer is assigned to the corps de ballet, a term that includes all of those male and female dancers who ordinarily dance as a large group. There are times when one or two of these male and female dancers will perform small solo variations in contemporary works, but in the classics they are the masses of dancers who frame the soloists. In a large active company they are very hardworking, since they will appear in several ballets during the course of an evening or several acts of one ballet during the program, while solo dancers appear at spaced intervals. The corps is the base of the pyramid upon which the whole company rests, and from its ranks in due course will emerge the solo dancers. The corps is the orchestration that gives that satisfying sense of developed spectacle to ballet.

In terms of historical development the corps has played an increasingly active part in ballet. When first devised, the corps to a great extent simply fleshed out the size and weight of a production without any special contribution in terms of expressive movement. They were there principally to show numbers. During Petipa's reign over Russian ballet he used them a little more actively, but essentially they were the decorative frieze against which he placed his solo dancers. Fokine animated the corps and drew it more into the action of the soloists, so that there was the feeling of an interchange between the individual and the grouped dancers rather than just the echo of soloists' movements. Balanchine has extended the animation of the corps even further, so that individual members in certain of his ballets perform as much as solo-level dancers in some classic ballets. The corps, which comprises the largest single classification of dancers in any company, will continue to be the secure base of the companies, but the opportunities for involvement in the action of the ballet have been enhanced, so that a corps member is no longer restricted in the range of dancing opportunities as was the dancer of a hundred years ago.

While the corps is the first stage to be achieved in any company, there is a whole range of other positions in the performing hierarchy. There is no more democracy in a ballet company than there is in an effective army. The company is structured according to ability, and the type of roles a dancer is assigned depends entirely on two standards. The first is proficiency in doing the steps; and the second by a less easily defined but definite consideration, the personality projected, whether essentially a character dancer, a demi-character dancer, or a classic dancer. The steps are the same for the most part, but it is the impression created, the coloration that they acquire from the individual's particular manner of articulating them, that classify the dancer into one of these three broad categories. A way of trying for yourself to see how this classification is made by the artistic director of a company, is to select any physical act such as walking or picking up a knife and fork, literally anything, and then observe how a variety of people perform the action. The first and most obvious thing you will observe is that no two people do anything exactly the same way, but you will be able to make broad groupings that describe several different types of approaches.

In classifying a dancer several things enter into the process. The first and most obvious will be physical characteristics. Those less ideally proportioned in terms of height (either too short or too tall) or in the balance between the length of the limbs and the size of the torso or head, will tend to be cast in character roles. Also, dancers who do not have the amplitude or the ultimate reach in performing the standard steps may find themselves better suited for character dancing. Generally a good character dancer is skillful in mimed action or has a certain acrobatic flair that is useful in dramatic portrayals or in divertissements that call for a "national" style of dance. In nineteenth-century ballets there were normally several of these, reflecting an indigenous dance from Poland (a mazurka, for instance) or the Hungarian czardas, or a tarantella from Italy. Many roles in contemporary ballets demand a high level of dramatic ability, which calls for the skills of the character dancer.

An intermediate category is the demi-character dancer who is adept in the performance of the classical vocabulary, perhaps even spectacularly so, and though physically favored in proportion, does not have the special lyricism and clarity of movement that is the hallmark of the pure classical dancer. These dancers customarily perform major roles in a company's repertory but are not given all of the roles that the top classical dancers regard as their special domain. This category of dancer, real though it is, remains very difficult to define exactly, since it depends on the level established by the classical dancer, which, in turn, forms the basis for comparison. Demi-character roles are all those which are located between straightforward character parts and classical roles but lie much closer to those of the top level. The "Bluebird" variation in *The Sleeping Beauty* is often cited as a fine demi-character role. The subjectivity that can enter into determining the demi-character dancer can be seen in the career of Mikhail Baryshnikov. Today he is recognized as one of the supreme exemplars of the classic tradition in the fullness and lyrical quality of his dancing. Yet in the Soviet Union, the directors of the Kirov Ballet were not convinced that he was a pure classical dancer and he found it very difficult to secure permission to perform the male lead Albrecht in *Giselle*, one of the great classical roles. He simply didn't fit the image of the type of dancer who was ordinarily cast in the part. He eventually performed the role, but it was by no means assured that he would be allowed to do so in the normal course of events.

Within these broad personality classifications there are degrees of competence based on the dancer's abilities to perform the academic steps as they are found in the various ballet roles. France, which so thoroughly structured ballet with its codification of steps, also has devised the most detailed gradations of accomplishment. These developed out of the experience of the choreographers and artistic directors who worked at the Paris Opera and are appropriate to that organization, though similar grading systems exist within every company. For the most part, however, the other companies have not made such fine distinctions between dancers.

To begin with, the dancer joins as a *stagiaire* (on probation) and becomes a member of the quadrille, or *corps de ballet* as it is generally known. The next advancement is to *coryphée*, which simply means that he or she moved to a position where he or she leads the quadrille in smaller or larger passages during ensemble dances. This could be thought of as advancing to corporal or sergeant from the lower ranks. The next grade is indicative of solo opportunities and is called *sujet*. To follow the military analogy, such a promotion would be equivalent to a company level officer, lieutenant or captain. A distinct advance is to *premier danseur* or *première danseuse*, which would be comparable to a field grade in the Army (Major, Lieutenant Colonel or Colonel), and in terms of roles would bring the dancer up to substantial divertissements or close to the center of the action in a dramatic ballet. The *Ètoile* is the highest gradation of dancer and is conferred when the performer is entrusted with the major ballets in a company's repertory. It is the top level attainable, although even so, distinctions are made in terms of special accomplishment.

Various nations have other methods of classifying dancers, but they are all based on a hierarchy in much the same way that orders of chivalry dictated who could wear what type of crown and how close each one could sit or stand next to the king or queen. Ballet has never relinquished its hierarchy, but it is a hierarchy based on achievement, not whim. The major ballet roles today are danced by those most qualified by training and artistry to do them. In the days of the court ballet the central role was always reserved for the king, and while the amateur dancer has been firmly replaced by the professional, the ordering system of the ranks is still very much alive.

The Royal Danish Ballet has four gradations in ascending order, from aspirants (those dancers 16–18 years of age who have just joined the company) through *ballet dancers* (in other companies called corps de ballet) to *soloists* and *principals*. The Royal Ballet does not have the *aspirants* level; dancers who join the company at the beginning level are termed *artists*. The ranking of *coryphée* is maintained for those whose proficiency brings them to the fore to a greater extent. Then *soloists* occupy the next rung on the hierarchy which is topped by the *principals*. Guest artists are listed with the principal dancers, since they have been invited to perform because of their special talents.

The Bolshoi as well as the Kirov Ballet lists solo dancers, which combines the categories of soloists and principals; all others are simply members of the company. There are, however, very significant distinctions within the Russian companies which all are aware of. There are titles of honor and decorations which carry significant weight in the Soviet Union. The highest of these is the designation "People's Artist of the U.S.S.R.," which could be thought of as a *premier danseur* or *prima ballerina*. If the dancer had additional honors to an extent greater than other "People's Artists of the U.S.S.R.," she might be thought of in older terms as *prima ballerina assoluta*. During this century, in prerevolutionary Russia it was Mathilde Kchessinska, and most prominently in postrevolutionary Russia Galina Ulanova. This would be a recognition that the artist was considered to be the best of a very fine group. The next highest category is to be called a "People's Artist of (a specific republic)." "Honored Artist" follows, and then there are the "Order of Lenin" and "Order of the Red Banner of Labor." The designations are quite strange and recent to ballet, but they do follow a definite pecking order and have meaning in terms of the roles that one can expect to see the person dancing.

American companies follow the traditional system, though it seems to gall them to admit it publicly. While they may not list their members by formal designations, they do cast their ballets with full recognition of the individuals' skills and pay them in terms of corps de ballet, soloist and principal. The practice of listing company members alphabetically in programs without any special regard to their contract ranking is one that is exercised notably by The Joffrey Ballet, though it preserves some semblance of tradition by listing the women in a block above the men. New York City Ballet and American Ballet Theater mix its men and women together alphabetically but list them in three clearly separate groupings, which they then refrain from characterizing with traditional terms of accomplishment.

Whatever the designation in the program, however, there is no mistaking a principal dancer onstage. These performers, above all, exude a sense of authority which they communicate to the audience. The principal dancer has mastered technique and has passed beyond glistening mechanical perfection to display a quality of personal assertion. The principal dancer has a resolute bearing which makes clear that timidity or hesitancy has no place at that level. A total, confident commitment of self through the discipline of a centuries-old technique is their special distinction. They demand attention, they get it, they deserve it!

Aside from performing excellence, one of the major contributions that principal dancers have made to the development of ballet in the course of its history, is to enlarge the vocabulary of steps. They are such brilliant technicians that they often experiment with classroom steps and develop exciting variations on them. One can never really be sure of all the specific contributions of these dancers to the standard vocabulary, but there are a number of developments which have become associated with one or another dancer. Anna Friedrike Heinel is credited with developing the *pirouette à la second* (a turn on the supporting leg, with the other bent outward at the knee with the foot near the supporting leg, from the second position). Pierina Legnani took the *fouetté* (a turn on the supporting leg while the other flicks out and back to the knee with each revolution) and strung thirty-two of them back to back before anyone else did. It is expected that dancers can now execute these steps in the normal course of performing, though they were once considered the property of outstanding virtuosos. One of the profoundest changes in the course of ballet occurred when an unknown female dancer began to move on the tips of her toes. This rise to the points has become so interwoven in the fabric of the ballet that there are classes given solely in point work, and many people think of ballet only in terms of point work. It's significant but by no means the whole story. Ballet originally developed into a popular art without it.

Marie Taglioni is credited with showing the artistic possibilities of the point steps, promoting them from a technical feat into an esthetic accomplishment. Many steps that were formerly performed off point became even more exciting when danced on point. At some time a dancer, probably Italian, copied a pose from classical statuary that showed the swift messenger god Mercury on one leg with the other extended behind him and his arm raised, extending the upward curve of the torso. No one knows his or her name, but the great teacher Carlo Blasis included it in his text on dance technique as the *attitude*. At times even an amateur like Louis XIV contributed to the balletic vocabulary. The modest crossing beats of the legs twice in the air have been styled the *royale* in his honor.

In traceable or untraceable ways dancers have continuously added to the expressiveness and excitement of the basic vocabulary, and the ease with which these additions have been taken up by other dancers attests to their effectiveness and suitability for the classic dance. Obviously it was simpler to add to the basic repertory of steps as the form was still emerging. Today, after so much experimentation, new contributions are less likely to occur and dancers to a great extent have concentrated on broadening the texture of the vocabulary by adding to the height, rapidity or repetition of the basic steps as techniques for strength and stamina have been developed.

Each day the dancer returns to the classroom to maintain, if not improve, those skills before anything else can transpire. With some differences, the day of a dancer in any of the major companies is the same. It begins in the morning with company class.

It is compulsory for the corps and soloists and elective by the principals, who may prefer study with a special teacher whom they find particularly helpful. Depending on whether the company is performing or preparing for a season, numbers of them could be rehearsing elsewhere, being fitted for costumes, or visiting physical therapists or doctors. But given a fairly clear schedule, the company will be more or less intact in class, which is given by one of the ballet masters of the company.

The class will be over by noon, and is followed by rehearsals for individual ballets in rehearsal rooms to which the dancers move in a casual but organized fashion. Throughout the rest of the day, with a small break for a light lunch, they will continue to move from one to another of these studios. The corps members appear in more ballets than anyone else, so they spend the most time moving. Choreographers will take a room to work on a new ballet or to develop and polish a familiar one that is being performed by a new cast. In late afternoon the regular day is over and the performance day begins after a short break. Dancers are at the theater early to attend to their makeup, get into costume, and prepare themselves with a warm-up before the start of the ballet. By the time the last curtain call has been taken, it is nearing 11 P.M., twelve hours after the start of morning class. It is a routine which will be repeated each day except on matinee days, when class will start a little earlier so that the dancers will have sufficient time to prepare for the afternoon performance. There is a break between the afternoon and evening performances, when they will again get into costume and warm up before appearing onstage. Between ballets, during the course of an evening while the curtain is down and the stage hidden from the audience's view, it is not unusual to see a choreographer explaining or demonstrating to a dancer fine points of execution in one of the ballets to be seen that evening. Training in one form or another continues from the time the dancer takes the first class in the morning until the last ballet of the evening is over. During their regular seasons American ballet companies give eight performances a week: six during the evening and two matinees. European companies normally intersperse performances with opera companies which share the same theater, and appear three or four times a week. When they visit the United States, though, they adapt to our schedule and seem to like it.

Dancers work very hard and in the early days of ballet were frequently treated quite harshly. During class it was not uncommon for a ballet master to correct a fault with a sharp blow from a stick. Though this practice has long since disappeared, dancers are still pushed very hard physically. They are being trained to move in a way that is not natural and to acquire instincts that frequently go against normal reactions. Dancers must have enormous trust and confidence in all of those who will be onstage with them, since there is no time to look around to see that everyone is correctly positioned. It has to be assumed that they are. This quality of homogeneous sympathetic movement is developed by regular performance and manifests itself in the smooth ensemble work of the corps with soloists, principals and one another.

Dancers have thoroughbred style and perform at the limits of speed and balance. The fraction of a second or inch that separates great from routine dancing is what distinguishes outstanding achievement in any physical discipline. With dancers, their superb conditioning is one part of their art, the other is the appearance of the body as it moves. Unlike athletes, they have to have a balanced and harmonious look; otherwise, the speed and balance are wasted. The art of great dancing is to conceal its muscular achievement in beautiful patterns of movement.

The youngest girl in the corps de ballet is physically very powerful no matter how delicately light she may appear onstage, and is capable of causing serious injury if her movement is not strictly controlled as she dances. The legendary Anna Pavlova, whose ethereal performances brought her world wide acclaim, once accidentally smashed her partner in the face and knocked out four of his teeth during a turn. The velocity required to give dizzying lightness to movement is also sufficient to produce a serious accident. The stage space is a rigorously controlled area in which each dancer must know precisely where every other dancer is going to be in relationship to the ensemble. To this end ballets are regularly rehearsed before each performance and especially carefully spaced before each appearance in a new theater when the dancers must accustom themselves to the exact dimensions of an unfamiliar stage. At times this may mean reducing jumps or extending them so as to achieve the same overall effect. The larger the number of people onstage the more complicated this process becomes.

The dancers in a major company may perform as many as forty ballets during a season. Since there is no commonly used "script" for these ballets they must remember them, a process which is aided by regular rehearsals. It is a remarkable feat for the dancers to be able to repeat these works exactly as they were created without changing them. It would be comparable for an actor to commit a dozen parts to memory and be able to play any three or four of them on call, or for a musician to memorize several orchestral works so that he could confidently play them as part of the ensemble during a concert. In a normal season dancers also learn new roles in ballets that are being created as well as maintain their roles in repertory pieces.

Because of cost, dancers ordinarily rehearse to music played on a piano rather than with the rich, dense tone of a full orchestra. They must, however, accommodate to this sound in performance and maintain the pace of the ballet as it has been set without changing its shape and accent. It demands a great deal of concentration and a great deal of energy. To maintain their level of strength dancers eat carefully but substantially, favoring high protein foods and avoiding fatty or starchy ones. They tend to be pared down to the muscles, though they appear to be heavier onstage. As a group they are compact rather than tall, and when encountered offstage appear to be thinner than one would have imagined. Stage lighting and framing create the impression of added bulk and height and pitilessly accentuates all physical traits. Deep-set eyes become spookily dark pits, the slightest bit of weight is magnified far beyond actuality, and facial irregularities become exaggerated to caricature. The normal way of dealing with the latter is through the astute use of makeup, which can compensate for stage lighting but can be quite grotesque when seen close up.

After a performance they are ravenously hungry and keyed up. Like athletes, they prepare both physically and mentally. They eat lightly before dancing but stoke themselves psychologically before appearing in front of the public. To present the ballet properly they must achieve performing pitch, which is a special state of sharpened execution and reaction. It is being "on," in the theatrical sense. Once "on," they cannot immediately switch to "off" but must regain normal everyday pacing gradually. A substantial meal is a great help.

Frequently, inept receptions are given to welcome companies after opening-night performances that take little account of the dancers' needs. Fussy hors d'oeuvres are offered when a steak is needed, and formal introductions are made when relaxed conversational banter is most wanted. The guests are happy but the dancers are prowling around waiting to escape. They handle it, usually without anyone noticing, as part of their professional duties. They are a youngish group on average, but considerably more mature than others of the same calendar age. They tend to be healthier, though with a higher number of daily aches and pains. Many judge the benefit of a class by the number of aches and pains, so that may not be a drawback. They are accustomed to the unusual through touring and cope with professional difficulties remarkably well. They tend to hate air conditioning and drafts and are comfortable in temperatures that would make the rest of us wilt, because that's when their highly trained muscles work most efficiently. They are an exceptional group.

In recent years one of the most remarkable demonstrations of their resilience and skill has been the performing of the Cuban-American ballerina Alicia Alonso. She rose to stardom in the American Ballet Theater while being plagued by injuries. At one time she was completely immobilized to correct detached retinas but recovered through her incredible determination. She founded the Cuban National Ballet in the middle 1950s, and while performing there experienced a steady deterioration in her sight.

ALICIA ALONSO AND JORGE ESQUIVEL IN *SWAN LAKE*

Eventually she could not read a menu in a restaurant; even corrective lenses were of no use. She grew accustomed to eating her meals as a blind person would, with the meat placed at one spot on the plate, vegetables at another, according to an imaginary clock face. She was, for all intents and purposes, blind, though she could still distinguish light and dark. She did not, however, give up dancing. She was thoroughly familiar with her own roles in the classics which had made her famous, the role of Giselle in the ballet of the same name being one of the most distinguished, and she was familiar with the various patterns of the corps in these ballets.

The music, of course, was her guide as to her own dancing, and she listened for the sounds of the other dancers so as to be able to visualize their exact position. She spaced the stage that she appeared on and was able to perform beautifully and artistically so that an audience unfamiliar with her condition, would not guess it. The only concession she made was to have small blue spotting lights placed at the edge of the stage in the center and in each of the wings at the sides. To appreciate the skill involved in dancing professionally with a stage full of people whom you cannot see, try walking in the dark through the most familiar room in your home without barking your shins. After a series of operations her eyesight began to improve so that it now approaches that of a normal person. She of course has continued to dance, and in her mid-fifties has had the pleasure of appearing in the same ballet with one of her grandchildren. She is an extraordinary woman and possesses to a special degree those skills which dance training imparts, in one measure or another, to all those who follow it seriously.

CHAPTER THREE

Choreographers

Dancers are the highly visible half of the team that makes ballet possible. The other half are the choreographers who design the dances that are performed. Dancers move so confidently and freely that it almost seems as if they are making up the steps as they go along. Nothing could be farther from the truth. The patterns they follow and the steps they use are all set by a choreographer. (The term is derived from combining two Greek words; the first means dance, and the second means to describe.) Choreography is a sequence of steps put together in a systematic way by an artist who uses human gestures in the way that a composer uses notes. From time to time a choreographer may devise a new step to add to the ballet vocabulary, but basically he organizes known steps into fresh new designs. As George Balanchine, our leading choreographer, has said: "Only God creates, I assemble!"

In a limited way, callers at a square dance function as choreographers. As the music plays they select the various steps which everyone knows and calls out the sequences to shape the final dance. As a matter of fact, the do-sa-do is derived from the French *dos-à-dos* (back-to-back), and the direction *allemande* right/left calls for a turn using the right or left hand (*à la main droit/gauche*), and a simple sidestep is a sashay, which in ballet is a *chassé*, so the terms have hung on even though changed to accommodate English speakers.

Choreographers may be active dancers with a company when they are young, but they retire from active performing in the normal course of time, and for the most part one does not see the choreographer onstage. Designing beautiful ballets is a full-time job, and it is a psychological as well as a physical strain to perform and choreograph. There are only so many hours in the day and night. Despite their retirement from the stage, choreographers never lose the sense of dance as expressive movement. They know what the trained body is capable of and they make only those demands on performers that can reasonably be met. One cannot imagine a choreographer asking for physically impossible movement, but one can easily see him designing a difficult part for a dancer in such a way as to extend the dancer's capabilities.

In preparing a ballet, what the dancer has learned in the classroom is now put to use. All the endless repetitions of basic movements have prepared the dancer so that he can work confidently with the choreographer. Of all the arts, ballet is unique in that its "script" is its performance. Musicians consult scores, actors read their parts, but dancers rely on memory alone. Until the development of film and videotape, dances were remembered by dancers and were passed on to others only in a direct teaching way.

Choreographers show their talent early, as do most artists. Painters paint because they have to, from some inner compulsion, as musicians are driven to compose music. All creative artists do what they do because they have never seen the world interpreted in the way that they feel is best—their way! They are restless people and never satisfied, and it is likely that if they should ever achieve a perfect work they would also retire; there would be no further challenge. Choreographers like to move people in composed designs—for the most part to music. There have been instances where a choreographer created a ballet without musical accompaniment, like Jerome Robbins' *Moves*, which is performed in silence. At times the choreographer prefers to work only with rhythmical accompaniment. Serge Lifar, who was director of the Paris Opera Ballet until the late 1950s, designed *Icarus* to percussion only. For the most part, though, choreographers prefer to work with music which they select from the concert repertory or which they commission from a living composer. George Balanchine worked in both ways with Igor Stravinsky during the latter's lifetime, selecting existing scores or choreographing to freshly composed music.

Ballet music covers an enormous range, from the oldest extant Medieval scores to the most advanced contemporary composers. It depends on the choreographer's interests at any given moment. At times popular music can be chosen and orchestrated for large ensemble, or a single piano may be used to play a sonata or a collection of short pieces. The variety is enormous: Lully, Mozart, Beethoven, Tchaikovsky, Verdi, Wagner, Massenet and Satie have all composed for ballet, and choreographers have selected scores from Bach, Brahms, Schönberg, Mahler, Chopin, Britten and Vivaldi among others. There are no limits except those which the choreographer's own taste imposes upon himself.

First-rank choreographers are rare, and there is no way to create them. Among the major companies discussed at length in this book, there are about twelve hundred professional dancers and only about a half-dozen first-rank choreographers. All of them have gone through the same type of training. At one point the budding choreographer starts to work on little dances with fellow dancers. If these embryo studies prove to have grace and beauty in the eyes of the directors of the company, they are shown to the public properly costumed and lit. Once established as a choreographer (having ballets presented to a fee-paying public), it becomes much easier to secure dancers and rehearsal time to develop further ballets.

Unlike the painter, writer or musician, the choreographer can work only in collaboration with other people, those highly trained and disciplined people who are professional dancers. They tend not to have a great deal of free time to devote to creating new uncommissioned ballets, since they are constantly going to class and rehearsing the pieces already in the company's repertory. In the beginning the dancers have to give their own free time to the budding choreographer so that he can realize his designs. It is entirely different when a choreographer receives a commission. Then he is paid a fee, provided with an accompanist, a studio, the number of dancers he requires, the services of a professional costume designer, a set designer and a lighting designer.

There is no known technique to detect choreographic talent among the pupils in a school. There is no question that an innate choreographer can benefit from courses that feature choreographic exercises, but there is no way in which he can be made into a choreographer if he is not already one potentially. It is a craft that can be learned but not taught. It is similar to the situation that prevails in music instruction, where all of the students take composition courses. Anyone emerging from such a course will be able to write a sonata or a fugue according to the rules they have absorbed, but only the rare student will write a piece that anyone would want to listen to.

Choreographers approach their task of organizing a ballet from a variety of different directions. Sometimes it is a certain movement quality that they wish to explore; at other times it is a literary theme that interests them or the personalities of various dancers. A piece of music that is particularly appealing will set them to thinking about how it would be possible to make a visual counterpart to it or they may have a particular composer in mind from whom they would like to commission a score. No matter what starts the process, the ideas will have to be shaped for the talents of the particular dancers available. Some choreographers prepare elaborate scenarios for themselves in terms of the characterization of the people in the ballets. Marius Petipa did a great deal of work, before coming to the studio, with little figures which he would arrange and rearrange in various combinations. When he found pleasing ones he made notes about them. Balanchine plays the music for the ballet, and when he has absorbed it thoroughly he is ready to encounter the dancers in the studio and create (Sorry, assemble; "Only God creates!") the ballet there. No matter what type of preparation is done, the ballet is made with the choreographer demonstrating the steps or describing them to the dancers. At this point there is little attempt to perform in the sense that one understands performing from the stage.

The dancers simply pay careful attention to what the choreographer is demonstrating and then sketch it out with their bodies, holding their arms in an approximation of their position or jumping in the right direction without full stage energy. This is called "marking" and it indicates the organization of the piece without the full orchestration of the movement. The process is a long one, since adjustments will have to be made so that the dancers will be able to accomplish the steps within the musical beat allowed for their execution. Normally at least two people are involved, if not also a whole corps de ballet, and each portion of a ballet must be set exactly. After an hour's work with the dancers, the choreographer will have set perhaps a minute or two of the movement that will comprise the final ballet. The rehearsal picks up again the next day and the day after until the whole ballet is completed.

During the creation of a new ballet it is not uncommon for a dancer to be given a particular movement and to develop it a little bit further for the choreographer's approval. If it is logical and in the spirit of the piece the choreographer may include it in the final version as is or change it a bit to make it conform as closely as possible to his idea of the "look" he wants to achieve. Dancers particularly like to be selected to work on new ballets because the finished work will reflect their own special movement skills; they may even be able to contribute to the creative process itself. When the ballet is "completed" (ready to be presented), the choreographer will frequently continue to refine and change small portions of it so as to polish it to its final form. The choreographer may offer verbal images to the dancers to give them a poetic insight into the tonality of the movement as well as the strict succession of steps themselves.

While work on the movement is progressing, the costume designer has been preparing clothes that will underline the quality of the ballet, and the scenic designer if one is required, will have prepared drawings of the stage settings and properties which will frame and enhance the action of the work. Since ballet needs a great deal of open floor space, the designer has to be bound by this limitation. Costumes cannot be made too heavy, since dancers have to be able to move freely, and the designer has to keep that in mind. Finally, the tone of the piece must be maintained even while illuminating the stage so that the movements are adequately visible. Lighting is one of the most complicated of skills, since one does not want to have a stage full of shadows or unsuitable light destroying a moody, melancholy passage in the choreography. The lighting designer also has to select effects that will realize the color values of the costumes and the set. By the time the ballet has emerged from the rehearsal studio it has been enhanced in many ways with various theatrical skills so that it presents a consistent image to the public.

The number of dancers selected by the choreographer depends entirely on his perception of the music. Ballets have been created as solo vehicles for dancers from time to time in response to an unaccompanied solo instrument or to a fully orchestrated score. The smallest number of dancers that choreographers work with ordinarily is two. There is really no limit to the maximum number of dancers except for the physical capabilities of the stage itself. Thirty-six dancers will fill any normal opera house stage for one of the full-evening classics or a modern work. When dealing with an especially large stage such as that of the Bolshoi in Moscow, as many as one hundred dancers may be present in one of the mass-spectacle scenes.

No matter what the size of the ballet presented, though, the process is essentially the same. It begins with the choreographer, who will transform an empty stage into a field of action with one or more dancers for a certain period of time. Like other artists choreographers have personal styles which are apparent when one has seen a variety of ballets. These personal styles exist within the various national styles of dancing in the same way that the work of one painter differs from that of another painter of the same country, although both are classified as being, say, of the "Flemish" or "Italian" school. The wider category indicates the broad limits within which each one works, but as always, the individual has a unique way of expressing a personal vision. The Impressionist school of painters included Manet, Renoir and Monet among others, and while each expresses delight in the surface beauty of things, each frames it in an unmistakably personal manner.

The choreographers of the *ballet d'action* were constrained to work with the mythology of the classic Greek and Roman world. They were intent on emphasizing the dramatic qualities of movement and the narrative power of dancing. Each found a separate approach to creating ballets which expressed these shared principles but allowed the individual choreographers to form personal artistic statements.

When the Romantic ballet swept through Europe in the early nineteenth century, choreographers turned to subjects far removed from classical antiquity and looked for themes and situations which did not have the classical balance and which expressed another, unconscious order, or seeming disorder, of life that could not be explained away entirely by logic. The generation of choreographers which followed them turned away from the exotic and found the idealized hero, a rustic or someone close to the soil who was important in national history or legend. The contemporary choreographer has had no difficulty in selecting a quite ordinary character as the hero of a ballet or in dispensing with the idea of a story altogether in order to allow the music to become his plot and the dancers to be his characters without any further elaboration.

A box of paints or a piano keyboard contain the elements for innumerable pictures and compositions, as does the large number of dancers in a company. It is simply a question of arranging the right elements in the right manner. Unlike the inanimate instruments of the painter and composer, dancers are a living and responsive group who set up a sincere interaction between themselves and the choreographer. For many choreographers the leading ballerina of the company will function as a particular challenge to his talents. One thinks of the special relationship of

Margot Fonteyn with Frederick Ashton, with whom she has performed and in whose ballets she has achieved the top level in her company. It would have been impossible for Ashton to have created his masterly *Symphonic Variations* for the young Margot Fonteyn whom he first encountered in the middle 1930s at the Sadler's Wells Ballet. But as she progressed in the strength and depth of her abilities, he was able to do more with and for her. It could be looked at the other way around as well—the ripening dancing talent of the ballerina inspiring the choreographer to his mature efforts. Whatever the case in any particular instance, the dancer and the choreographer are bound together in a way that no other artists are with the tools of their trade.

Another aspect of the choreographer's job, aside from creating ballets, is the development of the dancers with whom he has to work in terms of their performing skills. Since the chief choreographer of any company is usually its artistic director, it is his task to select the particular dancer for the particular role that needs filling. Since no dancer ever believes that he or she is truly understood by the director of a company, this is an impossible job. It is a job, however, which has to be done and redone for each generation of dancers and for each new dancer who joins the company. There are basically two possibilities: to select a dancer on the basis of proven ability and then assign a role from the standard repertory or a new work which is admirably suited to the dancer, or to select a role that will demand more from the dancer than is currently evident and hope for the best.

Whichever path is chosen, there will be successes and failures. The dancer who seemed just perfect for a given role will not quite match it and become frustrated, or perhaps will meet its demands too easily and become frustrated because it does not offer sufficient challenge. The dancer who's attempting a role seemingly beyond his or her present level of development, may find that its difficulties are largely imaginary and that with hard work mastery is achieved, or that no matter what the effort, the role remains tantalizingly out of reach. No dancer is suited for every role in the repertory, either because of training or temperament or both, and it is the job of the chief choreographer to see that each individual is pushed to the limit of his or her ability within the artistic dictates of the company. When the standard repertory fails to provide sufficient roles, the choreographer creates them.

The choreographer is limited in his own creativity by the skills of those dancers available to him at any given time. No matter how many good ideas a choreographer may have, there is nothing to be done with a company that does not have a sufficiently high level of technical polish. The great companies are therefore the performing tip of an iceberg of training that leads directly back to the school with which they are most intimately associated. The school exists to provide dancers with the skills and expertise that will be required when they are invited to join the company.

The yearly graduation ceremony of these schools becomes an event of major interest to those who follow the fortunes of any given company, for it gives an indication of the future of the company. These graduation exercises are handled in a variety of different ways, but basically they are designed to show the talent of the students through a combination of ballets selected from the standard repertory, and at times in new ballets specially commissioned for the occasion. In the Soviet Union these events are regularly filmed. There exists some exciting footage of a young dancer from the Kirov school performing the *pas de deux* from *Le Corsaire* who later achieved fame dancing throughout the West after he left the Soviet Union. The dancer was Rudolf Nureyev, who fulfilled the promise he showed in those early years.

Choreographers have to learn to work within the available time for new ballets. Some of them are extraordinarily quick, some are exceptionally slow, and most fall somewhere in between. No matter how quickly they are able to work, there is always the feeling that any ballet could benefit from an extra week of rehearsal before it is shown to the public. Most ballets are not seen to best advantage the evening they are given their premier performance, but no way has yet been found to start with the second. The final dress rehearsal in France is open to an audience, and the second performance before an audience is called the opening night. Audiences, being what they are, however, tend to want to go to the "second" night instead of the first, so the purpose of the final dress rehearsal is defeated.

Since dancers are professionals and have their own union to look after their working conditions, there is a limit set on rehearsal time. If the choreographer needs additional time, it becomes extremely expensive to the company, which must pay overtime rates to the dancers for the rehearsal. It is also terribly expensive to call a rehearsal for twenty dancers and then concentrate work on only a handful of them. Even those who stand and wait must be paid for it. At times choreographers come up with brilliant choreographic touches at the last minute. Some hours before the first performance of *The Prodigal Son* in May 1929, Balanchine was putting the finishing touches on the ballet and found that there was a gap in the choreography between one section and the next. Since there was music, he created a tableau out of the props already present in the scene. These consisted of tall trumpet-shaped forms, a long cape which was worn by the seductress of the Prodigal, and a banqueting table. He had the revelers overturn the table and stand in it like the crew of a boat making oarlike motions with the trumpets. The "Siren" bent outward from the head of the table like a ship's figurehead, while others of the crew held her long cape like a spreading sail. It remains in the ballet today.

More than twenty years previously, Anna Pavlova visited Fokine when both were living in St. Petersburg. She had been invited to perform in a charity concert that was essentially a musical evening. Fokine was playing "The Swan" from Saint-Saëns's *Carnival of the Animals,* and thought that the image of the swan and Pavlova were suited. Accordingly, he created for her a short variation which showed the graceful bird at the end of its life fluttering and finally subsiding in a graceful pose as its strength drained away. It called for particularly adroit use of the arms and no great feats of technical virtuosity, but it did make expressive use of the whole body. According to Fokine's memoirs, it was finished in "a few minutes." For a piece that took so little time to create, it has achieved a substantial performance record. Pavlova danced it until she died in 1931 and it became her trademark as "The Dying Swan." In our own time it has become an exceptional performing vehicle for the leading Soviet ballerina Maya Plisetskaya among others.

The process of creating a ballet does not always progress that easily or successfully. Several years ago when a company commissioned a ballet from a choreographer, it seemed to take an incredibly long time for anything resembling a completed work to emerge from the studio. As the first-performance date of the ballet approached, the head of the company advertised it in the newspapers and was promptly sued by the choreographer, who declared that it was not finished and that it did not fairly represent his conception. The strong-willed head of the company insisted on the premiere and won the court case. The ballet was duly given, with audience anticipation whetted by the controversy. The reception was cool and it was dropped from the repertory the following season. Some ballets have an exceptionally long life and others disappear after only a few performances. As a matter of record, most ballets do not remain in active repertory. Those that do have something exceptional to commend them.

Preserving a ballet is to a great extent not the job of the choreographer, who may or may not have a good memory. Most choreographers find it as easy to create a new ballet as to revive an old one. The amount of time and energy is about the same, and the satisfactions of creating something new always argue in favor of another ballet rather than the restoration of an existing one. The restoring is usually done under the direction of one of the former dancers in the work who has a particularly accurate recall of the patterns and individual steps. This ability is a gift like photographic memory or perfect pitch. When the sequences of steps have been demonstrated to the new cast, the choreographer will work with the dancers to achieve the right phrasing and tonality, so that the ballet has the impact it did when it was first

GEORGE BALANCHINE AND JEROME ROBBINS IN COSTUME
FOR *PULCINELLA*, EUGENE BERMAN AT CENTER
IN SUIT

created. All of this requires time in the studio, which is the chief
expense of most new ballets unless they have exceptionally elaborate and costly costumes and decor.

Work with the ballet does not stop after it has been created.
Each time a new dancer assumes one of the leading roles, minor
adjustments may be made so that it retains the smooth finish it
had with its originator. Such changes are minor and for the most
part unnoticeable to an audience, since they consist of small alter-
ations of balance or weight so that the dancer may pass to the

next step in a combination naturally and gracefully. Cast changes occur regularly in major ballet companies, which is one of the reasons why it is interesting to see the same ballet several times. Each new dancer brings a fresh and slightly different accent to the work, so that one becomes aware of different interpretations of the ballet as a whole, or of a particular role. As long as the choreographer is there to oversee the changes that are made, the process goes smoothly. When the choreographer is not present, changes sometimes occur which are not for the best. Most choreographers, when they work for a company not their own, teach the role to several casts and then have it written into their contracts that if the ballet is dropped from repertory for a season, the original choreographer or someone he designates must restage the work before it is again performed. It is a sensible precaution, since some dancers are prone to change things to suit themselves.

It is very rewarding to be able to design a pattern of movement for a score of dancers that has harmony and grace; it is the choreographer's chief reward. Performances alter from week to week and from season to season, so that he may not see a performance that has all of the elements in place more than once a season. The rest of the time there is always something slightly off which spoils the unity of the piece for him. In truth, he is probably the only one in the audience who notices, since such blemishes are relatively slight. But when it's your baby, and ballets are so regarded by their creators,* any blemish, even the

---

* Over twenty-five years ago Ashton had created a ballet for New York City Ballet called *Illuminations*. It was never mounted for his own company, the Royal Ballet, and was only seen in England when the New York City Ballet performed there in 1950. Subsequently, Ashton has had the opportunity to see it himself only when it was performed by the New York City Ballet at a time that he was in the same city. It last happened several years ago at Lincoln Center in New York when the Royal Ballet was presenting a season at the Metropolitan Opera House and New York City Ballet was performing it at the same time at the New York State Theater. After seeing the ballet Ashton commented: "It was like having a child grow up in a foreign country."

slightest, becomes highly magnified. Because dancers have injuries and illnesses that may prevent them from performing on any given evening, ballet roles must be "covered," that is, a second or third person who knows the part and can perform it. To provide these "covers," or alternate casts, the choreographer designates several people to perform the role. In fact, he may not be terribly happy with any of them, but the rules of practicality dictate that there be alternates, since the ballet would have to be canceled otherwise. The creator of a particularly beautiful version of *Romeo and Juliet* once muttered: "I have four Juliets and three of them aren't any good." He simply meant that one came very close to his idealized characterization of the part, and that the others showed an alternate approach to the role.

Choreographers are frequently frustrated people. They ultimately must depend on others to make their artistic conceptions visible to the public. Obviously they cannot dance all of the roles when they are performing, and when they retire from performing they cannot dance any of them. It turns some of them into martinets with their dancers; others, however, have the patience of Job. It's a matter of temperament. What the choreographer demonstrates to the dancers in the studio will never be seen by the public. The public only sees the dancers perform. Petipa summed it all up with one of his fractured Russian instructions. When he had finished setting the dances of one particular section during which he had worked with the group and the soloists individually with the little sketched-out movements he normally used, he sat back and instructed them: "Now show it nice."

Whatever the differences between good choreographers, they have one thing in common: they are extremely rare. It was no secret that as a young man Balanchine was attracted to and studied music very seriously, seriously enough to have considered a career as a concert pianist. Years later, his friend Stravinsky observed that the world was full of pretty good pianists but that Balanchine was one of the rarest of artists: a great choreographer!

CHAPTER FOUR

Watching and seeing individual ballets

Ballet, like any other art form, can entertain the spectator in a variety of ways. The choice is up to the individual. One can attend a ballet performance and be impressed with the physical prettiness of it. It is there to be enjoyed and it is not only a very important part of the appeal of ballet, it is basic.

There are those who go to opera for the enjoyment of a particular singer and don't really care much about what else goes on. Yes, they hear the other singers and the orchestra, but their main reason for being there is to enjoy the skill of one particular performer. It's a perfectly understandable desire and can be quite pleasurable. It's pleasant to walk through a museum and glance at all of the pictures on display, some of them with ravishingly beautiful colors or scenes. It is also possible to compare periods and styles, which deepens the appreciation of the immediately pleasant experience. One can speculate on the specific incident or scene more closely to see the details that the painter wishes to draw our attention to. A closer look can reveal the structural correspondences in shapes and colors which add to the rhythmic richness of the picture. All of these elements were present in the first appealing look but were not examined in any detail.

Ballet provides a delectable feast for the eyes, and great choreographers are expert at assembling ballets which have a variety of elements in them that appeal directly to the emotions as well as to the intelligence. The initial reaction should be an emotional one, for it is the basis of all the rest. One should be able to say quite simply, "I like it!"

In matters of taste there are no unchanging standards of good or bad. There are only preferences; these vary from age to age in artistic matters, and they change in individuals. It is commonly accepted now that the greatest poet of the English language is William Shakespeare, yet to the classically oriented taste of the eighteenth century, he was considered to have possessed a certain rude vigor but was lacking in literary refinement. According to their rules he was so lacking, but later generations have found great richness and subtlety in his plays. The plays haven't changed but the people have. The first ballet I can recall seeing was a light, diverting work by David Lichine called *Graduation Ball*. It seemed so joyous and lively that I totally overvalued it. I soon stopped thinking it was the greatest ballet ever made, but I have retained a special affection for it. The ballet hasn't changed, but I have after thirty years of attending performances. The reaction I had to that ballet, though, brought me back repeatedly to the theater to see more. It produced a thirst and a curiosity for further enjoyment.

The most important thing while watching any ballet is to pay careful attention to what the individuals do. It sounds quite basic and it is. It is also the key to the organization of the ballet. When a person crosses a road it is to get to the other side, and when a dancer crosses the stage to get from one place to another it is for a reason. The accumulation of these purposeful moves is the "script" of the dancer's role in that ballet.

Nothing happens by chance in a ballet; everything is calculated to fit together as a coherent whole. At first the sheer numbers of people on stage in many ballets offer almost too much for the eyes to follow. While you cannot see what every individual is doing at every given moment, you can concentrate on the most important dancers in the ballet. One of the clues as to who is important is the spotlight which follows certain performers around every time they appear. Lacking that clear indication, the program will tell you who is the most important person or persons in any given ballet. But of course, for that you must read the program, which many people do not do.

It is important to look for things actively rather than to just passively absorb a blur of movement. The person who looks is aware of what is going on, while the viewer who does not try to organize what he sees probably will not perceive more than the surface charm. If that is all that is wanted no further delving is needed, but delightful though it is, it is not the whole story. Ballet, like any art form, yields up its deeper harmonies to those who look for them but continues to entertain those who are absorbed in the pleasing surface sheen. People can go to the ballet for years because of the special excitement created by a stage full of beautiful dancers, though there is much more to it than that.

If a man continually approaches the same woman, it indicates a relationship between them. It may be simple infatuation, it may be a compulsive attraction that is rebuffed, or it may be a relationship that deepens with each encounter. In a ballet, one can only tell by seeing and evaluating what the dancers actually do. A particularly lovely ballet by Jerome Robbins called *Afternoon of a Faun* presents two people in an enclosed space who keep coming together yet stay emotionally apart. The music is a shimmering, dreamy composition by Claude Debussy whose haunting quality draws out images of a still, sunny landscape. The setting is a large gauze room suggesting a dance studio, since it has a barre running along the wall, and the side toward the audience is the wall which would ordinarily be mirrored. The program note identifies the place as a "Room with a Mirror."

A man with black tights and shoes stretches and turns his body from one side to another, peering forward as if into a mirror. His torso is bare from the waist up. He adjusts the belt of his costume and examines various body positions as one might in a standard class, but there is more self-involvement than one would find in an ordinary dance classroom. He is seeing himself as a person as well as a dancer practicing. Finally he curls up on the floor with his head down. A woman steps daintily into the classroom and goes to the barre to begin her warm-up. The man starts up and "sees" her in the "mirror." She continues calmly with her exercise but is aware of him. However, it is normal for several dancers to be together in the same room, each working privately.

He walks to her and slowly and smoothly lifts her in a long arc toward the center of the room in a classic way with his hands around her waist. It is perhaps unexpected but well within the normal boundaries of classroom exercise. He is attracted to her as a person, however, not just as a partner, and tries to stroke her hair. She twists deftly around and balances on his outstretched arm as if it were part of a *pas de deux* they were rehearsing. Each time he attempts to show his personal feeling she brings the situation back to the official vocabulary of the ballet and does not let her personal feelings emerge at all. As a trained dancer, he, too, is constrained by the conventions of the art until at one moment he leans over toward her and kisses her lightly on the cheek. That is not in the manual of style and cannot be "interpreted" in any other way except personally. She is staring into the "mirror" at the time and slowly, gently raises her hand to touch the spot and never ceases to stare at her reflection. She does not look at him, but the professional mood has been changed and she must leave. Still staring, she backs out of the studio and he curls up on the floor once again. Even without knowing what the specific steps of the classic vocabulary are, careful watching would show that she was much more reserved than involved in her bearing than he was, and that was the barrier between them. It is a lovely ballet and a fine example of the *pas de deux*, which is central to the understanding of classical ballet.

Ballet is an art which is based on the performing of men and women, and the special tensions that exist between them are explored in the relations of the *pas de deux*. It is the keystone of the art and at the heart of any of the classic ballets; *Swan Lake, Sleeping Beauty, Giselle, Coppélia, La Sylphide*, and even *The*

YURI SOLOVIEV AND ALLA SIZOVA IN *LE CORSAIRE*

Nutcracker. It may take some time for it to appear onstage, but the reason for the whole production flows out of the relationship of a man and a woman. Everything else is developmental and, no matter how beautiful it may be in itself, derives its reason for being from the essential relationship of the lead couple. Everything that happens either leads up to an event that will involve one of the principals or gives us some indication as to the plight, either joyous or sad, of the principals.

YURI SOLOVIEV IN *LE CORSAIRE*

WATCHING AND SEEING BALLETS

In the second act of *Swan Lake*, where the Prince encounters the Swan Queen for the first time, there is a very popular little variation for four of the enchanted maidens. It offers a capsule view of the fate of the Swan Queen, who is at the moment happy to have found a man to save her from the enchanter but who is still under the latter's spell. The four lock hands and prance prettily, but the physical shackling of themselves to one another is a reminder of the fate of the enchanted heroine and all those who inhabit Swan Lake. The Queen also preens beautifully but cannot escape by her own efforts.

In *Giselle* there is a charming little village in which a disguised nobleman, Albrecht, is wooing a peasant girl, Giselle. The local lord visits the village while on a hunt and among the party is Albrecht's official fiancée. Giselle is not so betrothed, nor could she be, in the feudal ordering of things. To please the aristocracy, who are seated at a table with refreshments, the villagers offer an entertainment. A young village couple dance a *pas de deux* for them. They are to be married, and this simple, straightforward and beautiful variation is an ironic commentary on the tangle that Giselle has unwittingly got herself into. She loves to dance, it is a passion in her life, and she should be able to dance such a duet with her admirer, but of course, it would be impossible to do so before the nobility, with the approved marriage partner already chosen and present. Albrecht is noticeably absent. The young couple's *pas de deux* is full of good spirits and expresses the tenderness that the rustic pair feel for one another. In itself it is very beautiful, but the reason for its existence is to offer further development to, and a comment upon, the less happy relationship of the principals.

One of the most haunting *pas de deux* ever created by Petipa occurs in the second act of *Sleeping Beauty* while the young Princess is in an enchanted sleep. The Prince, who is unaware of her existence, has left a royal outing in the country and is led on by a vision produced by the Lilac Fairy, who is the protector of the sleeping Princess. He is first permitted to catch a small glimpse of her, and then she appears before him glowingly beautiful. He lifts her, but when he attempts to embrace her the spirits, who have accompanied her, intervene and set themselves between the two. The Princess is on one side of their line and he is on the other. When he darts through to the other side she emerges on the side he has just left. Baffled, he pauses momentarily to look around when she lightly touches his shoulder to indicate her continued presence. The pattern of the spirits is at times a circle, a broad arc, or a diagonal line, and each time the Princess is able to escape into it just when the Prince is about to embrace her. Finally she disappears and the Prince demands to be taken to her. His command to the Lilac Fairy is the culmination of the enticing duet which has almost but not quite been consummated. It will only be resolved when he awakens the Princess from the enchanted sleep with a kiss and they celebrate their wedding *pas de deux*.

The symmetry of these duets and the balance of the supporting corps are hallmarks of the classic ballet. The *pas de deux* follows a development that first shows the principal couple together, and then each of the individuals dances a variation, the male first ordinarily, followed by the female, and they join together again in the coda for the final portion of the duet. When this pattern is violated, as it is in this vision scene, when there is no final coda, there is a sense of something missing. It is not by chance. The conclusion can only occur when the Princess has been freed from the spell. The breaking of the formula is an indication of a barrier which separates them. The classic *pas de deux* is like the classic sonata form in music with its alteration of tempos leading to the final climactic statement.

A contemporary use of the vision device is to be found in Balanchine's *Tchaikovsky Piano Concerto No. 2*, a ballet that was originally called *Ballet Imperial*. Unlike *The Sleeping Beauty*, it does not have a specific story, but the development of the ballet quite clearly draws out the relationships of the principals. They are introduced in the first movement, which is flashing and brilliant. Then the lead male finds himself, in the slow second movement, accompanied by eight women of the corps de ballet. Four extend out on either side of him linked like chains. The first one in the line holds onto his hand, and as he twists his body to the right the whole line sweeps around behind him, and so do the others when he does the same with the other arm. The women form a tether, holding each of his arms extended behind him as he leans back. With another move he sweeps them forward as one would crack a whip, but there are so many of them they encumber him and none of them is the one he is looking for. When he moves to the front stage they release him and form two columns at the head of which appears the woman he is seeking. The women lean to the right and left, parting before her as she runs down to meet him. Happiness returns as he finds her, and the *pas de deux* is interrupted again when the corps of women obscure his vision of her and she slips away, shielded from him. The device of using the corps as a shield is beautifully worked out. In this case the metaphor is not one of enchantment, because the situation is more like that of a ballroom where lovers seek one another through the crowds of other people. It is never specifically placed in time or locale, since there is no formal stage set, but one could easily imagine the search occurring in such a crowded, festive situation.

Balanchine's *Apollo* has four principal dancers—a man and three women plus three subsidiary corps dancers who enact a birth sequence in which the male is introduced. He is the young god and is attended by his three muses. At first uncertain and a bit hesitant, he grows in strength as the ballet develops. He guides them around like a team of horses eventually. First, each one dances a solo variation, then he dances his own. The favored muse is Terpsichore (muse of dance) and he dances a duet with her that shows his pleasure with her grace and restraint and concludes with a "swimming lesson" in which she lies face down on his back and the two part the air with outward sweeps of their arms as if propelling themselves through water. The selection of the favorite has been made and confirmed with the *pas de deux*, although he has danced with each of the others at one time or another and all three at times. Here the duet is the seal of judgment and approval. Balanchine created the ballet fifty years ago when he was choreographer for Diaghilev's influential Ballets Russes, which restored serious ballet to Western Europe. Diaghilev observed the progress of the ballet with the comment: "What he is doing is magnificent. It is pure classicism such as we have not seen since Petipa."

One excellent guide to the importance of the individual dancers or to climactic moments in any ballet is the music. Ballet is unique in that it exists as an art form of spatial movements in a set time. It is the only art form which combines the use of three-dimensional space in rhythmic time for its final realization. Fine art is pure space, either that of a painted flat surface or the three-dimensional space of a sculptured object. Music is an art of time and does not occupy space, only demanding our attention to a succession of moments. Ballet has both, and in its expression tends to share a sense of time which is related very strongly to musical time.

In ordinary day-to-day affairs, events occur in a more or less efficient, pedestrian way. It takes so many seconds to open a door or to pick up a glass, and that is the end of it. When speaking, it takes a minute or so to give directions or to explain something to someone. The time alloted to do or say anything is quite precise and tailored to accomplishing a specific task. Time in dancing is not the same at all; it is extended or contracted for artistic effect with repetitions that reinforce the impression the choreographer wants to make. This is similar to the use of repetition in a musical composition, where a song uses the same phrase over and over again with slightly different musical settings in order to achieve its desired effect. It is necessary and enjoyably enriches the expressiveness of the song. It is boring when someone repeats the same story or phrase over and over again in ordinary conversation. Only with the introduction of rhythm is it possible to use repetition creatively. Ballet takes a familiar gesture and repeats it in a variety of ways to make its point.

Repetition occurs in the *pas de deux* as well as in the interplay between principal dancers and the corps de ballet. It happens in varieties of ways as obviously as in the woman's variation and coda of Petipa's *Don Quixote pas de deux*, where the woman executes a series of fast whipping turns (*fouettés*) and is succeeded by the man, who amplifies the woman's whipping turns (with the flicking motion of the working leg) by turning even more rapidly with his leg fully extended out to the side as he whirls to an accelerated beat (*tour à la second*). Or it can be as subtle as the final movement of Balanchine's *Symphony in C*, during which the principal couples are in the center of a broad three-sided formation of the corps de ballet spread out around the sides and back of the stage. The women are supported by the men as they execute their turns, and the corps women perform a standard barre exercise (*battement tendu*) to the front, to the side, and to the back, which echoes the more spectacular movement in the center. The intent is to emphasize the quality of the basic steps and to add an accelerated excitement to it.

The standard steps exist for all choreographers to draw upon, and each one uses them in a personal way, as do musicians and painters with the materials of their art. They all work with basic elements from which they shape individual structures that bear the imprint of their personality. A choreographer like Antony Tudor, whose sensibility inclines him toward dramatic subjects, finds greater use for emotional gesture in carrying the artistic burden of his ballets. He, of course, employs the recognized families of movements in accordance with their various functions of transporting the dancers from one spot to another, or enhancing their mood once they have reached a certain place, or heightening an effect by lifting a dancer up into the air in a jump. The impetus of his ballets, however, derives from the acting depth of the individual performers, who convey their inner states of feeling by the length of a glance, a significant pause in the presence of another person, or an everyday gesture such as folding a woman's hand firmly and expertly into the crook of her companion's arm.

One of his most moving ballets is *Jardin aux Lilas* (Lilac Garden), which takes place in a darkly green garden with boughs of weighted lilacs. One can almost feel the scented atmosphere of this moonlit garden through the opulent foliage. A trapped young woman is about to marry a man she does not love, and we are present at a party to formalize the event. There is a more complicated side to it, however, in that the man she really loves is one of the guests, as is the former mistress of her intended. The costumes indicate a Victorian time setting and the music (Chausson's *Poème*) is lushly romantic. The ballet is, in essence, a series of stolen moments when true lovers, or former lovers, seize the opportunity to be with the person most important to them. The guests function as interruptions to these precious encounters. They always seem to burst in at just the wrong moment or whisper something behind a gloved hand. The times when the couples are together are so brief that there is no opportunity to dance a formal *pas de deux*. Everything is fragmented and one feels the hasty incompleteness of their moments together. At one dramatic point, time is frozen as everyone stops still in a set pose. The intended bends over to kiss the young woman's hand, and all of the guests are arranged decoratively about.

As the music continues the young woman leaves her place in the tableau and walks over to her lover, who stands like a statue, as do all the others. She is the only living person in a garden of manikins, and it seems as if we are able to see her thoughts as she regards the situation. When she returns to her spot the whole party becomes live again. It is just as she feared, there is no way out and the intended assists her on with her coat, places her hand in his curved arm and pats it the way an adult would comfort a worried child: "There, there!" It's a very simple sequence of movements but full of a kind of stifled horror as society closes in on the individual. She will marry him whether she wants to or not and will learn to live with it. The use of time is extremely varied, for in addition to the accelerated tempos of most of the dancing, there is the complete suspension of motion and then the naturalistic time it takes to leave the party and walk offstage. Tudor's mixture is brilliantly effective.

In the amusing ballet *Donizetti Variations* Balanchine also uses a time freeze but for purposes of humor. Again it is a situation in which a young woman steps out of a crowd and allows us to see what she is thinking. The ballet is light in tone and the music bubbles along as do the lead couple, who dance a classic *pas de deux*. They are attended by three other men and six women, with whom they also dance from time to time. At one moment the lighthearted music almost begins to sound serious, and all of the dancers run out to assume prearranged places with their heads bent forward and an arm shielding their faces. They stand stock-still. Then a bleary solo horn is heard in the orchestra and one of the women, not the lead, stands upright and looks around at everyone else frozen in position. In the original version she walked around to peer curiously at them all and with a shrug of humorous resignation elegantly resumed her place, then started dancing with all the rest as if nothing had ever happened. In a later emendation Balanchine altered the role so that it became a small solo for the girl, and during the horn playing she did a fast little dance, hogging the whole stage to herself while the others were immobilized, before returning to the group with her secret, to continue the ballet. It works well either way, but the cessation of movement is very effective when used as judiciously as it is here.

Choreographers have two major concerns: how to fill the performing space, and the management of time within that performing space. If a choreographer is faced with a full-evening ballet, he will approach the work differently than if he were going to do a short one-act ballet. In a full-evening ballet a great deal of time is available to develop and elaborate the basic theme. In a short ballet, as in a short story, there is little time to dwell on nonessentials; every moment must be used to the maximum.

A typical full-evening Romantic ballet like *Swan Lake* is divided into four acts. Two of these acts, the first and the third, transpire in a naturalistic setting; the second and fourth, in an enchanted lakeside by night. These acts are referred to as the white acts because of the costuming of the corps de ballet and the leading female dancer. They wear a calf-length, diaphanous skirt which is white, as is the top of the costume, which is ordinarily made of white silk. The length of the skirt is referred to as Taglioni length, since it approximates that worn by the great Romantic ballerina. The first act is normally devoted to laying out the beginnings of the story and acquainting us with the principals. There is an unhurried, almost leisurely pace to the proceedings, and we find ourselves beginning to move at the same timed pace as that of the dancers and becoming involved in the action of the ballet. It is far too early for any of the central drama to begin; the audience must be steeped in the locale and its ambiance before they can respond to any of the more serious action.

Since this is a Romantic ballet, the next locale we move to is the enchanted area, where the action will be advanced further on another level, the spiritual. There is always a great symmetry to these ballets, which alternate between the naturalistic and supernatural realm, and often back again. But the balance is kept between the natural and the spiritualized areas.

During the Romantic Era it was thought suitable for tragic ballets to have an even number of acts and comic ballets to have an uneven number. It was never strictly adhered to, and contemporary full-evening ballets, which do not follow the conventions of that era, may easily have a tragic ballet in three acts. There was, however, a satisfying balance in the old practice of presenting first one and then the other aspect of the story, the real and the surreal. Once this interplay of influences was no longer the basis of the story, the convention lost its meaning.

At the beginning of the full-evening ballet there is much character dancing to set the realistic situation, and only as the ballet develops does full-blown classic dancing begin to make its appearance. The major *pas de deux* are always done in the full classic style. National dances and comic variations appear in the naturalistic acts of the ballet, never in the white acts. There they would be inappropriate and violate the illusion of the ethereal nature of the inhabitants. Some of the characters in these acts will dance variations, but they are of the same elevated and unworldly nature as those of the principals.

The shorter ballets are, of necessity, constructed quite differently. The time the choreographer has at his disposal is very restricted and there is a premium on each moment. The luxury of casual digression into supportive but nonessential variations is severely limited. The rhythm of a long ballet is like that of a novel, leisurely and elaborate, while the short ballet is compressed and more intense. It must make its points rapidly with fewer low-key connecting passages. Shorter ballets have always existed in the ballet repertory, but until the twentieth century they were the exception rather than the rule. The program of short ballets as we know it was popularized by Diaghilev's Ballets Russes, which began to offer seasons of dance in Paris in 1909.

Brought up on the full evening ballet as it existed in Russia at the time, Diaghilev felt that some basic changes had to be made in the format for classical dancing. It appeared to him and his first great choreographer, Mikhail Fokine, that the older ballet had reached a point where ballets were being put together according to a formula that was no longer appropriate. In effect, Fokine wanted to take the formula padding out of ballet and include only those elements that were organically part of the story.

He wished to have all of the parts of the production—dancing, costuming, music and sets—reflect a unified conception. He was strongly opposed to the older and somewhat careless attitude which allowed choreographers to include national variations that were not historically consistent with the period of the ballet. He disliked the idea of having a Spanish dance turn up in a ballet set in ancient Egypt, no matter how beautiful the variation might be. He wanted the costumes to be historically valid as well, and he certainly wished to eliminate the old-fashioned mime passages of hands and arms in favor of comprehensible full-body gestures, which would be considerably less stylized. In all of these desires he was strongly seconded by Diaghilev, who presented his first four seasons in Paris showing Fokine's new ballets almost exclusively. It was a time when *Les Sylphides*, *Firebird*, *Carnaval*, *Le Spectre de la Rose* and *Petrouchka* made their impact. These ballets had a unified look in their various elements and confirmed Fokine's essential vision. Though he produced a full-evening version of *Sleeping Beauty* later, Diaghilev and the choreographers who subsequently worked for the company adhered to the short ballet as their favored form.

When the Diaghilev ballet dispersed after his death in 1929, all of the companies which were formed presented shorter ballets as a matter of course, even though they created or remounted the longer, full-evening ballets from time to time. The shorter, denser pacing of these one-act ballets appeared to be more congenial to the temper of the times and has continued to exercise its sway. All of Fokine's ballets that were mentioned are performed today by various companies more or less as they were first presented.

In certain essential respects, Fokine pointed the way to the development of the so-called "abstract" ballet, which can be seen in major company repertories. His *Les Sylphides* was a suite of dances in which there was no specific story but merely a succession of danced episodes in which the corps de ballet took an extremely active part. There was a single male dancer with three principal female dancers and the corps, but the patterns of the corps were of an exceptionally poetic nature. The ballet begins with all of the dancers onstage deployed in quiet, reposed groups. The man and the three principal women are toward the rear of the stage. The setting and the lighting suggest a romantic scene with a ruined castle in the background, the women are costumed as in a *ballet blanc,* and the man is in black and white. The mood conveyed by the individual and the group dances is that of a meditative, dreamy state. The women appear to be poetic extensions of the man's thoughts as they perform their solos, or alternatively the ballet could represent a poet seeking his muse; and at the end they cluster in the formation that opened the ballet. Chopin's piano music was performed in orchestrated form and contributed considerably to the romantic effect of the ballet. It was a piece that in mood owed much to the nineteenth century and in its imaginative structural design spoke directly to the twentieth. The dancers were not characterized in the program and the corps de ballet actively participated in the development of the ballet to a degree that was unknown up to that time. There was a central *pas de deux* that represented a world of romantic feeling, but it remained nonspecific, almost as if it were the essence of all such ballets and all such moonlight encounters. Although the encounter was there, the choreographer did not tie it down to one special incident, but allowed it to stand for many.

The abstract ballet is one that hews most closely to the pure elements of dancing without the support of an overt story. In effect, it presents what is implicit in a story in the most open and direct terms possible. Since the beginning of ballet as an art form there has been a distinct subdivision of it which has remained outside the specifics of story and literary plot, concentrating on pure dance incident. For example, the climactic and incidentally the most spectacular *pas de deux* of *Swan Lake*, *Sleeping Beauty*, *Giselle* and the like are abstract in that their expressiveness comes from the strict use of the classic vocabulary with a minimum of mime or dramatic gesture.

Some of the most famous ballet masters of the eighteenth century went to exceptional lengths to emphasize the dramatic potential of ballet and distributed extensive program notes to their audiences which verbally amplified the story development they were about to see presented onstage. Contemporary choreographers are reluctant to include anything but the briefest notes in the program, feeling that what is presented onstage should speak clearly for itself and should be allowed the maximum freedom to do so. The notes that are included merely indicate direction, in the way that a good road sign prevents you from taking the wrong turning. The trip itself, like the ballet, has to be experienced on its own terms.

When considering the various types of ballets it can be useful to think about the assorted forms of serious music. The fusion of staged drama, orchestral resources and singing represents the most narrative of musical structures: opera. The full-evening ballet with its libretto, spectacle and enhanced forces resembles opera in its approach. Music designed for instrumental presentation on a large scale, the symphony orchestra, or little ensembles like the chamber orchestra, wind octets and solo instruments, dispense with dramatic elements and song to present the composer's ideas in instrumental form only. While these compositions, without words or conventional plots, are all abstract, they offer enormous differences in approach.

"Abstract" is not a very apt word for the ballets we are trying to describe, since it implies something nonhuman and machine-like, which is not appropriate to these ballets at all. They use the same beautifully shaped and balanced vocabulary of movement as do the story ballets, although they tend to use mime gesture very sparingly. Since mime is used as a narrative device and these are not narrative ballets, there is little need for mime. *The Four Temperaments,* as designed by Balanchine, is an example of one type of plotless ballet. The idea is based on the four "humors" of the body which determine individual personality according to the proportion of each. There is a theme in the first movement, which is danced one at a time by three individual couples, each of whom has a distinct character, a character determined by the particular mix of the four "temperaments." This introduction is followed by four variations, each of which emphasizes one distinct side of the theme. The dance illuminates the quality of character featured in each of the variations. The first is "Melancholic" and quite logically features a single dancer, in this case a man who tosses himself back and forth and seems thoroughly dragged down by the weight of gravity. The "Sanguinic" variation features a couple, since they are more likely to be happy and cheerful, having one another to complete a relationship. The third variation examines the theme from the "Phlegmatic" aspect and again has a single male soloist, though backed up by a small corps of four women. He is sluggish and a bit listless, though not as desperately unhappy as the melancholic man. In fact, he is able to dance a short little happy variation when sufficiently perked up by the women. The final variation is "Choleric" and features an angry woman, furiously making an entrance, who is so difficult to approach that the men stand at the four corners of the stage as she turns and steps in a quiet but obvious rage. All of the dancers return for the finale, where couples pass from side to side between two lines of individual dancers and the women are lifted and carried along by the men as once more the humors are blended and no longer exist as pure states, as they did in the individual variations. It is a ballet without a "story," but it has a very clear beginning, middle and end, as stories always do, and can be appreciated quite easily without a conventional plot line.

This particular piece of music has no special dramatic line, but it does portray a collection of characterized moods which together add up to a small portrait of a society of men and women. It is far from being "music visualization," which is a form of

GLORIA GOVRIN AND JOHN CLIFFORD IN
PIANO-RAG-MUSIC, IN WHICH A SMALLISH MAN
HUMOROUSLY PARTNERS A JUNOESQUE WOMAN

dance movement in which various dancers echo the instruments with gestures. This type of ballet can be rather mechanical, although in the hands of a talented choreographer, like Jerome Robbins in *Fanfare,* dancers can take the parts of various instruments in and create humorous incidents based upon their themes.

Benjamin Britten's orchestral piece *A Young Person's Guide to the Orchestra* was designed to be given with a short text by a reader who explains the roles of the various instruments in the orchestra individually and then together as an ensemble. Each of the dancers is identified as a piccolo, viola, trumpet, etc., but Robbins then creates little situations for them which partake of the essential character of the instrument without following its melody note for note. For example, the flutes and piccolo have a little flutter variation that suggests rapid birdlike movements, while the blustery tuba is depicted as a military martinet with other horns as his squad of "Soldiers." The harp picks her way carefully and is very grand and elevated, while the double bass for all its deep sound, is portrayed as a comic, bouncy stringed instrument. The blare of trumpets, with their outthrust arms, is taken to be slightly menacing by the strings, who hover protectively around the harp in the way the little swans in *Swan Lake* cluster about the Swan Queen at the entrance of the hunters. It's a kind of in joke, but it shows how far from slavish note-by-note imitation Robbins has conceived the ballet. It's funny and beautifully crafted, while remaining true to the character of the programatic music.

Designating a piece of music as programatic simply means that the composer has taken an idea or a character or a situation and has composed a score which is more descriptive in musical terms than a less particularized piece might be. In Tchaikovsky's *Romeo and Juliet,* for example, a lovely singing theme characterizes the lovers, but there are also crashing chords which suggest the flashing swordplay of the contending houses of Montague and Capulet.

There are hundreds of ballets to choose from when selecting a program to attend, and they include a variety of approaches. There are those which feature humor, others which emphasize the story development of the ballet, still others which create a mood or show a series of danced incidents that may be thought of as abstract. Whatever the approach, some ballets are delightful on first viewing the way some pieces of music are immediately appealing or some pictures strike the eye and evoke an instant positive response. The following short list of "starter" ballets by no means exhausts the possibilities, but it does contain some that have proven readily accessible.

One's tastes change and sometimes ballets receive poor performances so that they don't make the favorable impression they can when performed well, which makes any list subject to personal correction. The ballets which are suggested as "starters" tend to have either spectacle, humor or a good story that is clear and readily understood, and they don't demand of the viewer a great deal of familiarity with the ballet. Some of them are classics from the nineteenth century and some of them were choreographed quite recently, but they tend to have good musical scores and a certain accessibility in their organization.

Beyond these ballets there is a world to choose from. Many ballets do not have a strong immediate appeal and demand a little more from an audience for full enjoyment. Of course new ballets are being prepared all the time by the companies, so the ones suggested here are drawn from that group which have had some exposure and durability. They are listed alphabetically for convenience. There is no particular merit to being on the first or second list, but merely a matter of the individual ballet's immediacy. Both lists could be added to but would become cumbersome as a result and could never really be complete as long as new ballets are being choreographed. The selections offered are merely a sampling, by no means the whole story, and are characterized by these abbreviations: H–humor; St–story; A–abstract (that is, without overt story); and S–spectacle.

The companies discussed in this book which have these ballets in their active repertory are indicated by the following initials: ABT–American Ballet Theater; BB–Bolshoi Ballet; JB–Joffrey Ballet; KB–Kirov Ballet; NYCB–New York City Ballet; RB–Royal Ballet; RDB–Royal Danish Ballet and SB–Stuttgart

Ballet. Some ballets which are now in the active repertory of the companies may be retired for a season or two, but there is no way to determine this in advance. The companies listed offer the suggested productions, though many companies present other versions under the same name. This is especially true of classics like *Swan Lake.*

STARTERS

Cakewalk	(H, St)	JB
The Concert	(H, St)	NYCB, RB
Coppélia	(H, St, S)	ABT, NYCB
The Dying Swan	(A)	BB, KB
Façade	(H, St)	JB, RB
Fanfare	(H, A)	NYCB
Fancy Free	(H, St)	ABT
La Fille Mal Gardée	(H, St)	ABT, RB
Gaîté Parisienne	(H, St)	JB
Giselle	(St, S)	ABT, BB, KB, RB, SB
Graduation Ball	(H, St)	ABT, RDB
Jeu de Cartes	(H, St)	SB
Jewels	(A, S)	NYCB
The Nutcracker	(H, St, S)	NYCB
Pas des Déesses	(H, A)	JB
Les Patineurs	(H, St)	JB, RB
Pineapple Poll	(H, St)	JB
Rodeo	(H, St)	ABT, JB
Sea Shadow	(A)	JB
Secret Places	(A)	JB
Stars and Stripes	(H, A)	NYCB
Swan Lake	(St, S)	ABT, RB
Le Spectre de la Rose	(St)	ABT, BB
La Sylphide	(St, S)	ABT, RDB
Les Sylphides*	(A)	ABT, BB, KB
Symphony in C	(A, S)	NYCB
The Taming of the Shrew	(S, H, St)	SB

WATCHING AND SEEING BALLETS

STARTERS

Tarantella	(A)	NYCB
Three Virgins and a Devil	(H, St)	ABT
Vienna Waltzes	(S, A)	NYCB
Viva Vivaldi	(A)	JB
Western Symphony	(H, A)	NYCB
The Whims of Cupid and the Ballet Master	(H, St)	RDB
Who Cares?	(H, A)	NYCB

In addition to the ballets listed above, there are many spectacular little *pas de deux* performed by stars of the various companies. To a great extent these are extracts from longer ballets, though not necessarily. Some of the better known of these are *Black Swan, Le Corsaire, Diana and Acteon, Don Quixote, Grand Pas Classique* and *Tchaikovsky Pas de Deux*. They are performed by the finest dancers in the companies and always add a special element of excitement, displaying as they do the classic vocabulary pushed to the extremes of virtuosity.

THE NEXT STEP

Afternoon of a Faun	(A)	NYCB
Allegro Brillante	(A)	NYCB
Apollo	(St)	NYCB, RB
At Midnight	(A)	ABT
La Bayadère	(A)	ABT, KB, RB
The Big City	(St)	JB
Billy the Kid	(St)	ABT
Chaconne	(A)	NYCB
Cinderella	(St, S)	RB
Concerto Barocco	(A)	NYCB
Dances at a Gathering	(A)	NYCB
The Dream	(St)	JB, RB
Eugene Onegin	(St, S)	SB
An Evening's Waltzes	(A)	NYCB

THE NEXT STEP

The Four Temperaments	(A)	NYCB
The Green Table	(St)	JB
Les Illuminations	(St)	NYCB
The Invitation	(St)	RB
Konservatoriet	(A)	RDB, JB
Jardin aux Lilas†	(St)	ABT
Ma Mère L'Oye‡	(H, St)	NYCB
Petrouchka	(St)	ABT, JB
Pillar of Fire	(St)	ABT
Prodigal Son	(St)	NYCB, RB
Romeo and Juliet	(St, S)	ABT, BB, JB, KB, RB, RDB, SB
Serenade	(A)	NYCB
The Sleeping Beauty	(St, S)	ABT, BB, KB
La Sonnambula	(St)	NYCB
Scotch Symphony	(A)	NYCB
Symphonic Variations	(A)	RB
La Valse	(A)	NYCB
Tchaikovsky Piano Concerto No. 2**	(A)	NYCB, RB
Union Jack	(H, A)	NYCB

* Called *Chopiniana* in U.S.S.R.
† Lilac Garden
‡ Mother Goose
** Called by original title, *Ballet Imperial* in England.

Theater- and opera-goers do not stop after seeing one *Hamlet* or *Carmen* but go to see a variety of artists in these productions. So when you have run through the list, look forward to seeing the productions again with other casts. Or if you like something particularly well, return to see it before bothering about other ballets. Though the choreography will remain the same, individual artists will develop the roles in different ways, and it is rewarding to see as many interpretations as possible.

CHAPTER FIVE
Company histories

UNITED STATES

Ballet in the United States is a relatively new art form and its most impressive development has come in the past thirty years. There were, since the beginning of the republic, some ballet dancers and troupes in the country, but more often than not these were individuals or companies making a single tour of the country and then departing. During the eighteenth century these dancers came from France for the most part, although Italian companies also made periodic visits. From time to time members of these companies would stay in the country, and frequently they would open up a dance school. These schools were quite simple in their aims, which were to prepare young boys and girls to become properly accomplished young gentlemen and ladies at social dances. Every once in a while an exceptionally talented student would emerge to make a career on the performing stage, but that was infrequent.

Such indigenous ballet as existed tended to concentrate in and around Philadelphia. It was there that John Durang was brought up and produced some of his large pantomime productions. Augusta Maywood, George Washington Smith, Julia Turnbull and Mary Ann Lee also worked in Philadelphia; Lee and Smith eventually formed a company which gave the first performance of *Giselle* in the United States. While in the very earliest days of the country all ballet talent came into the United States and none was exported, there was a slight shift in the nineteenth century. At this time talented young dancers were sent abroad to study, mostly in Paris; one of them, Augusta Maywood, was given a soloist's contract by the Paris Opera Ballet and remained in one European country or another until her death. She was the only American dancer to achieve a principal position in a European company until American dancers began to show up in Europe after the Second World War. The native companies that were established were short-lived and hardly ever survived the death of their founders. There was, in effect, no continuity or training ground from which could spring a living tradition of classical dancing.

Around the time of the First World War members of that exceptionally talented generation that emerged from the Maryinsky and Bolshoi schools visited the United States with touring companies, and some eventually settled down to form small ballet schools and teach. Mikhail Mordkin, who had been Pavlova's partner, founded his school in New York. Pavlova herself maintained a home in London but traveled and performed almost continually. Her contribution to the development of ballet was probably greatest in terms of audience development and as an inspirational force to a generation of young women who followed a dancing career after seeing her. Agnes de Mille was one of them. Adolph Bolm, who toured with the Diaghilev Ballets Russes when the company appeared in the United States, left it to join the Metropolitan Opera House and create ballets for its opera productions. The image of the ballet dancer as a Russian national started to become fixed in the American consciousness.

The process continued and received reinforcement in the 1930s. After the death of Diaghilev in 1929, his own company dissolved totally and some of the dancers and choreographers formed companies that were related to the style of Diaghilev's enterprise. These companies drew largely on Russian émigrés who were resident in Western Europe, or on other Europeans who discreetly changed their names so as to appear Russian. This practice, like so many others, had been started by Diaghilev, who took an excellent dancer of Irish extraction, Patrick Kay, and first renamed him Patrikayev, then Anton Dolin, and Hilda Munnings, who was the first of these "foreign" dancers that Diaghilev accepted, became Lydia Sokolova. One of her companions in the Diaghilev Ballet was born Edris Stannus and danced as Ninette de Valois. In her own company Pavolva took Hilda Boot and made her Butsova. The practice was resorted to because audiences had become accustomed to Russian dancers. They didn't believe in the skill of any others, but since the flow of good dancers from Russia had been cut down severely by war and revolution, Diaghilev took the best of the local talent who auditioned for him and passed them off as Russian. Audiences never knew the difference, because there wasn't any! The trained technical dancer possesses a skill that transcends national boundaries.

The Ballets Russes companies of the thirties totally dominated the public's imagination and they did so by carefully trading on the exotic and exciting repertory that had been formulated originally by Diaghilev and by cultivating the Russian "temperamental" image. It was hinted that only those who possessed the "slavic soul" could truly dance ballet. Practical necessity, however, dictated that more and more dancers in the Ballets Russes companies would not be Russian because of retirement, and local dancers were incorporated to take their places These dancers were frequently thought of by those of Russian descent as "foreigners," despite the fact that they were dancing in their own countries. The myth died hard, but before it did many dancers found that they could dance in these companies only as unpaid volunteers, since they would not be hired. They were allowed to appear, gain experience and mature as performers, but it wasn't until years later that they were actually hired. When they were, it was an immense step forward. When our own Fred Astaire was cast as a ballet dancer in *Shall We Dance?*, he answered to the name of Petrov! Richard Rodgers, who composed the score for *On Your Toes* in 1936, expected a moody, broody genius when informed that George Balanchine was going to choreograph the show and was pleasantly relieved to find an intelligent, efficient collaborator who knew how to work on union time. The myth gave way slowly, but eventually audiences came to realize that Americans could dance the classic vocabulary as beautifully as anyone would want it performed, and could also have pronounceable names.

New York City Ballet

The fluent visual music of George Balanchine's ballets has established the style and pattern of growth for the New York City Ballet. It is a style marked by velocity and intricacy which pushes dancers to the limits of speed and balance in ingenious patterns of human encounter. It realizes in space those musical designs which are its accompaniment and tends to dispense with the traditional use of plots, mime or sumptuous production values. It cleaves to and celebrates the core element of ballet, which is the expressive quality of the pure classical vocabulary in its endless combinations and traces its lineage back to the Russian school of Petipa in the clarity and beauty of its designs, to which it has added a twentieth-century urgency.

George Melitonovitch Balanchivadze (the name was changed to George Balanchine by Diaghilev) is of Georgian extraction and was born in St. Petersburg. His father was a composer and collector of Georgian music and his brother Andrei followed in the father's footsteps. Several uncles who were military men put the idea of a military career for him into his parents' heads. When he was of suitable age, ten, he was taken to the Imperial Naval Academy to be enrolled as a cadet. The same day his mother was taking his sister Tamara to the Imperial School of Theater and Ballet (Maryinsky) to audition for entrance. The first stop was the Naval Academy, where it was learned that the incoming class

EDWARD VILLELLA AND VIOLETTE VERDY IN *PULCINELLA*

had already been selected. At the Maryinsky school, where Tamara had been turned down the previous year, there were two hundred applicants for the twenty positions available. (Today there are two thousand for a like number of positions.) An official at the school who recognized Mrs. Balanchivadze suggested that her son audition as well as her daughter. She agreed, and he secured one of the favored positions while his sister did not. The audition, then as now, consisted of a medical examination, then an inspection by the admitting board of the school. Poise, carriage and natural grace were looked for; the students were not expected to have any specific dancing skill. The Imperial Ballet like the present-day Kirov Ballet, preferred to take the unformed child with no bad habits and shape him or her into its image of the polished classical dancer.

It might seem odd at first that a child who was intended for military school should end up auditioning for the ballet, but it was quite understandable in the Russia of that time and is so in the Soviet Union today, where the career of a professional ballet dancer is one of acknowledged merit and one that brings honor to the country through its expression of native artistic talent. The student uniform which was worn by those boys in the Imperial Ballet school was very similar to those worn by naval cadets, except that the little insignia on the collar was a lyre instead of a naval device.

When accepted, the applicant remains at the school as a border and is permitted visits home only at selected times. It was quite a shock to the young Balanchine when his mother left him and took Tamara to the little town outside of St. Petersburg where the family had moved. He was miserable and ran away to an aunt in St. Petersburg, who brought him back to the school, where he continued to be unhappy for the early part of his training. It was August 1914 and the guns of war in distant Western Europe were to have a profound effect on him as they did on the rest of society.

For three years he learned the classic vocabulary, as had generations preceding him, and in moments of relaxation he played the piano, at which he was quite proficient. His mother had been his first teacher. He was asked by some of the senior students to accompany them when they were preparing for their graduation exercises, which was a genuine acknowledgment of his ability. Russia's disastrous entry into World War I eventually brought the revolutionary ferment in the country to a head, and in 1917 Bolshevik troops closed the Maryinsky school as a despised aristocratic plaything. The students were left in the street to fend for themselves. They turned to anything that would give them food, which was in short supply, and Balanchine was a messenger, a saddlemaker's assistant, and among other things provided piano accompaniment to silent movies. Through intervention at the highest levels the school was finally reopened and the instruction went on in the old manner. He graduated in 1921 and was taken into the company. He had begun as a member of the Imperial school but emerged from the State school. Nothing had changed except the name.

While in school he had created his first ballets and continued to do so after graduation. These were presented at charity affairs or evenings given over to the efforts of the younger ballet dancers and choreographers. They were not the official expression of the school or theater. In point of fact, the officials in both institutions had found some difficulty in accepting the early work of Balanchine, and it was seriously suggested that he be expelled from the school. This was not done, but the "Evenings of the Young Ballet" were suppressed after only two performances. The system was dictatorial under the czars and was equally authoritarian under the revolutionary regime, but Balanchine found some opportunities to work in theater and opera productions where he could exercise his own taste. For the bulk of the time, however, he appeared with the official State company and outwardly conformed to the dictates placed upon him. His interest in music continued at a high level, and after graduation he enrolled in the academy as a music student majoring in piano and theory.

In 1924, Vladimir Dimitriev, a singer at the opera who admired Balanchine's talent, proposed that a group of singers and dancers from the ballet and opera make a tour of Western Europe as the Soviet State Dancers to show the artistic skills of the new regime. Such permissions to travel were exceptionally difficult to obtain, but the group was allowed to go abroad during the summer vacation period when the theaters were closed. They took a boat to Germany and traveled to Berlin, where they were almost immediately summoned home by an official telegram. The conductor and the three singers returned, while Dimitriev, Balanchine, Tamara Gevergeva (Balanchine's wife, who later changed her name to

ANTHONY BLUM AND ALLEGRA KENT IN *DUMBARTON OAKS*

Geva), Alexandra Danilova and Nicholas Efimoff elected to remain in the West.

They spent the remainder of the summer making a tour of the vacation spots in Germany, and then were engaged for a music hall production in London. There they came to the attention of Diaghilev, who summoned them to Paris for an audition. He was impressed with Balanchine's choreographic gifts and made him the official choreographer of the Ballets Russes. The others were engaged as dancers. At the tender age of twenty, Balanchine found himself in the most important choreographic post in the world. There were difficulties with the older dancers, who resented him but Diaghilev insisted, and for the next four and a half years until Diaghilev's death, Balanchine was the official choreographer. From being the slightly suspect purveyor of new ideas in the Soviet Union, he became the celebrated center of attention in the West.

This period was to mark his maturity as an artist. He had learned his craft in Russia, with the Ballets Russes he was encouraged to develop and refine it. The most profound influence on him was Stravinsky. When he began to work on *Apollo*, a ballet which is in the repertory of several companies, including that of the New York City Ballet, he learned to channel his choreographic energies and include only essentially related gestures in the ballet, not every fresh idea that occurred to him during its composition. He credits this discovery to the qualities of the music itself, which showed similar restraint and taste. The ballet itself was a success, and the pattern of his future artistic career was set.

During the time that he was chief choreographer for the company he created eleven ballets and firmly established his reputation in Europe. When Diaghilev died, so did his enterprise and the shelter it provided for Balanchine. He had several offers of work but contracted pneumonia and eventually tuberculosis, which sent him to a mountain sanitarium in Alpine France. When he was able to leave the sanitarium the only job open to him was offered by an English producer, Charles Cochran, who wanted Balanchine to do sketches in his productions. He worked for Cochran and later for Oswald Stoll, doing much the same thing, and also was engaged for a season by the Royal Danish Ballet. He mounted several of his ballets for them, but the latter period was not successful. He was a choreographer without his own company.

In 1932 the Ballet Russe de Monte Carlo was formed and Balanchine was made the artistic director. At this time the first students of the Russian emigrant teachers in Paris were emerging from the studios, and Balanchine took three of them into the company. They became famous as the baby ballerinas, since none was older than fifteen, but Balanchine had a falling out with the administration of the company. Seeking a company once again, he encountered a rich Englishmen, Edward James, who offered to back a new company to be organized along the lines Balanchine wanted. It was called Les Ballets 1933 and lasted for just one year. When it collapsed Balanchine was again looking for a company with which he could work.

Since 1924, when he was first engaged by Diaghilev and began to show his work in the West, he had been watched by an American a few years younger than himself who was infatuated with ballet and the idea of establishing a major performing company in the United States. Lincoln Kirstein approached Balanchine at the end of the short-lived experiment of Les Ballets 1933. He proposed that Balanchine come to the United States to found a school patterned on the Imperial Academy that Balanchine himself had been educated in, and later form a performing company to present his works. It was ambitious, adventurous and risky. It meant exchanging the Europe he knew for an America he did not, and placing his future in the hands of an intelligent and good-willed amateur who had had no professional theater experience. For reasons that may never be clear, he accepted.

He asked that Vladimir Dimitriev accompany him to be the administrator of the proposed school. Dimitriev had been astute enough to get Balanchine out of Russia when that was nearly impossible, and had shown generally good business sense thereafter. The two sailed on the *Olympic* and arrived in New York on October 18, 1933. Kirstein and his friend Edward Warburg had to post a bond to prevent Balanchine and Dimitriev from being sent to Ellis Island by the Immigration authorities. It was not the warmest welcome to America. It had been Kirstein's plan to establish the new School of American Ballet in a small city (Hartford, Connecticut) outside of New York away from the theater world. Balanchine announced that he was returning to Europe when informed of the plan. The plan was modified and studio space was arranged for in New York. The school opened in Jan-

LINDA YOURTH AND HELGI TOMASSON IN *SYMPHONY IN C*

uary 1934, on Madison Avenue at Fifty-ninth Street, in studios
that had once been used by Isadora Duncan.

Students of varying abilities were attracted to the school, and
by summer Balanchine felt confident enough to offer an invitational performance on the Warburg estate in White Plains. It
rained and the outdoor performance was canceled. It was given
the next evening. The first public performances were given in
the fall at the Avery Memorial Theater in Hartford and were
received quite well by the knowledgeable audience, most of
whom had traveled from Boston and New York. In March 1935,

the American Ballet, as it was then called, performed for two weeks at the Adelphi Theater in New York. That summer it performed at Robin Hood Dell in Philadelphia, then at Lewisohn Stadium in New York. It was after the Lewisohn Stadium concert that Edward Johnson, director of the Metropolitan Opera, asked Kirstein and Balanchine whether they would like to be the resident ballet company of the Opera. It was an undreamed of offer after they had been in existence for such a short period of time, and they accepted eagerly.

The dancers would be on regular salary and would perform in the ballet interludes of the various opera productions. Balanchine also wanted to be able to produce full evenings of ballet, but this was not possible in the beginning. Eventually it became possible, but Balanchine's advanced ideas of staging and his assertive choreography did not please the director of the Metropolitan. Other irritations such as inadequate rehearsal time, no orchestral rehearsals, and poor dressing-room facilities further strained relations between the Opera and the American Ballet.

To demonstrate its artistic standing the American Ballet staged a Stravinsky Festival at the Metropolitan in the spring of 1937, but had to rent the house in order to do so. Stravinsky came to the United States to conduct and assist in presenting three of his ballets: *Apollo, The Card Game,* and *Le Baiser de la Fée.* The two-evening festival was a great artistic success but did not really increase the standing of the ballet company in the management's eyes. The contract was not renewed and the American Ballet was again on its own. Balanchine, who is normally reserved and collected, permitted himself a few harsh words in public about the dispute. "The tradition of ballet at the Metropolitan is bad ballet. That is why I cannot stay."

He had started to work in the movies with the *Goldwyn Follies* in 1938; and on Broadway with *Ziegfeld Follies, On Your Toes, I Married an Angel, Cabin in the Sky,* and *Song of Norway,* to mention a few. It was a way of keeping his dancers employed and available when needed. Kirstein had decided to explore the Americana strain of artistic development, which was popular at the time, and had formed a small ballet company,

Ballet Caravan, which toured extensively in smaller cities. The school, under Dimitriev, continued to flourish while these other activities went on and was beginning to turn out new, younger dancers. Later, Balanchine was to remark that it took twenty years to get the sort of company that he wanted, but at this time he was well along the way. The Second World War interrupted everything.

Just prior to the outbreak of war in Europe there had been a mammoth World's Fair at Flushing Meadows in New York, and the Ford Motor Company pavilion hired Ballet Caravan to provide a ballet, six times daily, on the passing of the horse-and-buggy era. The production was called *A Thousand Times Neigh* and played hundreds of performances, affording many visitors to the Fair their first view of ballet. It wasn't the same as what could be seen in the theater later on, but it was a beginning, as were the tiny little television sets which were first seen that year. When the Fair closed, the members of Ballet Caravan joined with members of the American Ballet to tour South America under the sponsorship of the government. At that time the Administration was trying to improve relations with the other American states under the Good Neighbor Policy, and it was thought that an artistic expedition by a ballet company would be very helpful. The four-month tour was moderately successful and the company returned to the United States in October 1941. In December we were at war. One by one the men in the company were drafted and Kirstein gave up the administrative work. Ballet Caravan was disbanded, the American Ballet was inactive, but the school moved along steadily.

In addition to uprooting young men and women from various parts of the country, the war had also done much to loosen old attitudes toward almost everything from food to popular entertainment. When he was discharged from the service in 1945, Kirstein began to formulate new plans to provide ballet and opera entertainment to the public. He conceived the idea of Ballet Society, which was to be made up of a solid group of individual patrons whose yearly membership would entitle them to receive tickets to performances, books, records, and films on ballet and opera. The reception was reasonably good, and the Society's five productions a year were well attended. No attempt was made to have seasons in the ordinary sense; each program was presented at a specific time and did not have an extended run. The company played in a variety of auditoriums, including the Shriners' auditorium on Fifty-fifth Street, called the Mecca Temple, which had been taken over by the City of New York and renamed the New York City Center of Music and Drama.

The building of pseudo-Moorish design was, and is, vast, but the demand for tickets to Ballet Society productions had risen

KAY MAZZO AND PETER MARTINS (CENTRAL COUPLE)
IN *SYMPHONY IN C*

steadily, so that the house was not oversized. The 1948 production of *Orpheus* was particularly successful both with the general public and with Morton Baum, who was the guiding director of the City Center complex. It had begun as an organization to present drama and opera at popular prices, and Baum asked Kirstein if he would like to convert Ballet Society into New York City Ballet. It was an unexpected request, as had been the summons from the Metropolitan Opera thirteen years previously; and although the answer was the same, the result was different. New York City Ballet accepted its new name and has continued its association with the City Center for thirty years. It found the performing base that it needed to give it continuity and to enable it to build its audience. It attracted leading dancers and the choreographer Jerome Robbins, who ultimately became one of the artistic directors of the company.

Now that the company had a home of its own, it sought to assemble financially secure backing. Ballet, like any large-scaled performing art, is an enormously expensive undertaking, and can never adequately pay for itself. At best it can sustain current operating costs out of box office receipts if it does near-capacity business in a large (2,500-seat and over) house, but the operation that lies behind what is seen onstage consumes large sums as well. The money for new productions, without which a company cannot attract a public, must be raised elsewhere, since there are limits to what the public will pay for a ticket. Ticket prices, like college tuitions, pay only a portion of the actual cost. The company faced its financial problems in its earliest days through the private patronage of Edward Warburg and Lincoln Kirstein, among others. These sums, privately and generously dispensed, enabled the fledgling art of classical ballet to find a new home outside of Europe. As in the past, the process was the same. Foreign ballet masters, dancers and teachers choreographed, performed and taught until local students were able to fill their ranks. The expense was borne, not by titled aristocracy or the crowned heads of state, as was common in Europe, but by interested individuals and later by interested charitable foundations. The subsequent establishment of a National Endowment for the

Arts and local arts councils has helped to take up the burden, which has now exceeded the individual capabilities of private sources. The classic ballet could not have become established without private money, and now cannot be sustained without public assistance, as it is in Europe. A serious part of the operation of New York City Ballet was increasingly devoted to finding the means to maintain the artistic atmosphere in which the ballet could be available to an increasingly interested public.

Balanchine continued to create new ballets throughout the boom-to-bust activity of the various companies that were the predecessors of the New York City Ballet, and in 1954 he mounted a production of *The Nutcracker* that was to prove both an artistic and financial success. The length of the ballet's run has steadily increased until it presently occupies five weeks of the winter season annually and barely meets the demand for tickets. This production, and others like it by ballet companies all over the country, has become the production most people are likely to see when they first begin to attend ballet. It has been produced on television and is now part of the Christmas season.

It was the last of the three ballet scores that Tchaikovsky wrote and has exercised an appeal both on a purely musical level as *The Nutcracker Suite* and as a seasonal ballet spectacle. Over 150 productions of this ballet are now performed in this country by large and small ballet companies, and most of them tend to follow the traditional setting of a first-act party at the children's home, followed by the spectacular divertissements in the fanciful Land of Sweets in the second act. Not all of the productions are exactly the same, and some of them take a psychological view of the story. It depends on the company. All ballets called *The Nutcracker* are not the same, any more than all ballets called *Swan Lake* are the same. Though the music is familiar, the choreography is different.

In the case of New York City Ballet, when they announce *Swan Lake* it means the Act II setting by Balanchine. The music is the same as that act in any other full-length production of the ballet, which includes the full four acts. These abbreviated versions of the full evening ballets have been given quite frequently

GELSEY KIRKLAND AND CONRAD LUDLOW IN
CONCERTO BAROCCO

and generally tend to dispense with the mimed portions or the character-dance sections of the longer works to concentrate on the pure classic dance elements. *Aurora's Wedding*, given by many companies, is in reality the final act of *The Sleeping Beauty*.

95

THE CORPS HUMOROUSLY OUT OF SYNCHRONIZATION
IN *THE CONCERT*

Pure classicism has always been of primary interest to Balanchine, who year after year has exhibited a high level of creativity, presenting new ballets of subtlety and refinement that demand the utmost from their performers. Several broad lines of development in his work are discernible, all of which relate directly to the music. Foremost of these has been the series of ballets inspired by the music of Stravinsky. These ballets have tended to be those that stretched the choreographer's imagination furthest in reshaping the classically trained dancers' body. Primary emphasis has been on complementary visual development of the complex rhythmic structures offered by the music. Ballets such as *Apollo, Orpheus, Agon, Symphony in Three Movements, Violin Concerto, Movements for Piano and Orchestra*, and *Variations*, are the central line of this development. Traditional glitter and passion with contemporary impetus has characterized many ballets to Tchaikovsky's music: *Ballet Imperial* (now *Tchaikovsky Concerto No. 2*), *Suite No. 3* (which included his earlier *Theme and Variations*), *Allegro Brillante* and *Diamonds* (the final portion of his full-evening *Jewels*). Popular music has inspired *Stars and Stripes* (Sousa), *Who Cares?* (Gershwin), *Western Symphony* (Traditional arr. Kay) and *Vienna Waltzes* (J. Strauss, Sr., Lehár, R. Strauss).

Ballets which have been set to run-of-the-mill music have also tended to be run of the mill, such as the ill-fated advertising jingle for an airline that inspired *PMTGG*. For Balanchine, music is the "floor" on which he sets his ballets. For that "floor" to be in top-notch shape he has always worked most comfortably with first-rate musical directors. The first was Leon Barzin, who saw the company through its first ten years of existence as it changed from the private Ballet Society into the public New York City Ballet. He was succeeded in 1958 by Robert Irving, who had been musical director of England's Royal Ballet (1949–58). Irving's awareness of the musical needs of ballet is unmatched among contemporary conductors. Not only is he called upon to rehearse and conduct a variety of scores that would be worthy of a first-rate symphony orchestra, but he must be aware of and remember the slight variations in tempo that are congenial to different interpreters of the major roles. The musical values, however, are never distorted by slowing or accelerating tempos excessively but are subtly modulated. The music is played at the pace one would expect to hear in concert performances, which is the way the composer wrote it. Because of Balanchine's extreme sensitivity to music, it occupies a central position in the concerns of the company. It is for this reason that the collaboration of Irving and Balanchine has been so close and obviously full of respect on both sides.

HOW TO ENJOY BALLET

After the company had settled in at the City Center Theater on Fifty-fifth Street, it began to lengthen its seasons and think about the possibility of overseas touring. In 1950 Balanchine set his *Ballet Imperial* for the Royal Ballet (then known as the Sadler's Wells Ballet), and its success facilitated the visit of New York City Ballet to London in July. Many of the critics were unprepared for the lack of Americana ballets about cowboys and the Wild West, which were thought to be the proper subject for an American ballet company. Despite mixed notices, the company was invited to return two years later for another season at Covent Garden. The public had reacted enthusiastically and warmly.

In 1952 the company toured the Continent before performing at the Edinburgh Festival and in London. The reception was excellent except for a dispute about Jerome Robbins' *The Cage*. It was, and is, a beautiful but grim ballet about the mores of an insect society in which the young female kills her male companions. In Holland the company was asked to drop the ballet or forfeit its season. It didn't. Local authorities backed down; the ballet was presented and judged to be chilling but not pornographic. The tour left the company with an international reputation and enhanced standing at home. The new production of *The Nutcracker* contributed to its financial stability and it began a decade solidifying the support of its growing audiences. Among the new ballets created were the amusing *The Concert* by Robbins. It was a ballet that spoofed music lovers, ballet conventions, shoppers and the individual's natural vulnerability. At one point the dancers walked across the stage with umbrellas—some of them furled, others open. The contrast threw doubts into their minds, and eventually all ended up huddled in a large moving mass under one tiny umbrella before departing on their individual errands. A standard corps of six women, attempting to perform a unison variation, continually suffers from one individual's inability to keep to the count, and while listening to the music a man dreams of murdering his wife but ends up wounding himself. It was a surreal collection of incidents that retains its humor even after repeated viewing. Robbins left the company to form a small concert touring group called Ballets: USA, which appeared in several European festivals in 1958 and again in 1959 and continued performing until early in 1961, after which time he worked on Broadway and in Hollywood for several years.

The appearance of *Agon* in 1957 was the final section of the Balanchine-Stravinsky triptych that included *Apollo* and *Orpheus*. It was athletically lean and spare, with a casual elegance of bearing that marked it as one of the most successful of their collaborations. The music was commissioned for the ballet, and Stravinsky participated in rehearsals as well. Literally the title means a contest, but it is not so much between the men and women of the ballet as between the choreographer and the restrictions of time imposed by the old French dance forms that served as the basis for the ballet music. It was courtly and also contemporary and holds a high place in the company's repertory.

A historic collaboration occurred in the spring of 1959 when New York City Ballet and the Martha Graham Dance Company jointly presented *Episodes*. The music comprised all of the orchestral compositions of Anton von Webern. Approximately half of them were used by Graham, and the other half by Balanchine. Each created a complete ballet, and they were performed back to back. Several of the ballet dancers were used in her production, and Balanchine created a solo for Paul Taylor of the Graham company which was included in his ballet. The work is still carried in New York City Ballet's repertory, but the solo has been dropped. *Episodes* is performed to uncompromisingly spare music that almost seems beyond the scope of dance use, but has proven to be eminently danceable and is witty and noble by turns.

Story ballets like *The Seven Deadly Sins* and *Night Shadow* were revived, and a full evening *A Midsummer Night's Dream* received its first performances in 1962. In addition to its own merits, the production served to provide further performing opportunities for the children of the School of American Ballet. Dozens of children had the chance to appear onstage in annual productions of *The Nutcracker*, and with the introduction of *A Midsummer Night's Dream* two dozen more opportunities were

99

opened up. The first appearances that Balanchine himself made onstage were as a student in the Maryinsky school and was well aware of their usefulness in the training of young dancers. Three years later, in 1965, after the company had moved to the New York State Theater, he created another long, elaborate production, *Harlequinade*, which involved children as well, and further enlarged the performing opportunities for them with a production of *Coppélia* in 1974.

As part of the World's Fair in 1964–65, New York State undertook a substantial building program which included highways, a Fair pavilion, and a new theater. The architect Philip Johnson designed the festive pavilion at the Flushing Meadows site and the New York State Theater, at Lincoln Center. After the Fair, the building was operated under the direction of the New York City Center, which had moved its opera and ballet companies to the Lincoln Center house. The company opened in its new quarters in the spring of 1964.

During the preceding December, the Ford Foundation made a substantial grant of $7.7 million to "strengthen professional ballet." Of this money $2.0 million was given to New York City Ballet and $2.4 million to the School of American Ballet. The money was distributed on a staged basis during the course of a decade and enabled the school to offer many more scholarships than it had previously. As with most private schools, it relies on tuition payments, but has been able to offer complete support to talented children in increasing numbers with the aid of this grant.

Among those dancers recruited for the school scholarship program was Suzanne Farrell, who was found in a local audition in Cincinnati. Her progress in the company was rapid and fulfilled the expectations aroused by her early promise. She has been featured prominently in a series of new ballets as well as repertory selections. Coincident with its arrival at State Theater, the company began to participate in school programs sponsored by Lincoln Center designed to introduce ballet to children as part of their general education. Dancers of the company visit local schools and demonstrate ballet technique as well as perform excerpts from ballets and are available to answer questions that may arise. The increasing scale of the company's activities and the ris-

VIOLETTE VERDY AND ANTHONY BLUM
IN *FOUR TEMPERAMENTS*

PHOTO BY LOUIS PÉRES

JACQUES D'AMBOISE IN *CORTEGE HONGROIS*

ing expense of presenting ballets necessitated the institution of a subscription policy with regard to its performances. This was begun with the spring season of 1966.

Traditionally, tickets had been sold on an individual basis, but this did not permit the company to project its income in any but the most general way. Accordingly, many performances were designated as subscription performances and could only be bought as part of a series of other performances, usually three in all. The policy was undertaken reluctantly but necessarily and has become a regular means for the dispersal of tickets. For similar reasons the subscription policy has been assumed by other domestic companies and managements who offer foreign touring attractions. There are still performances which are not sold on subscription for which tickets may be purchased individually. Insofar as possible, managements have designed these subscription series so as to offer a wide variety of different ballets to patrons, including particularly sought-after productions as well as those of equal merit that might not attract as much attention. The subscription policy has been traditional with older cultural institutions such as the major symphonies and opera companies for many years and has helped to assure their financial stability. The subscription is a way of helping these institutions plan their operations in advance, and until something better comes along will remain in effect.

With the enlarged stage and technical facilities of the New York State Theater the company undertook the production of several full-evening ballets, including Balanchine's *Don Quixote* and *Jewels*. Both have become regular features of the company's seasons. The former is based on Cervantes' hero who is driven by chivalric idealism to awkward encounters with prosaic, everyday matters. When it was first performed at a benefit preview the role was danced by Balanchine himself, who has occasionally performed it but usually unannounced, as he used to appear from time to time as the mysterious Drosselmeyer in *The Nutcracker.* Both are character roles requiring dramatic ability but little pure dancing. *Jewels* is a most unlikely three-act ballet in that it does not have a story line, as is customary with full-evening ballets. It is more in the nature of a three-part suite of dances grouped together by the theme of glittering gems. The three countries in which Balanchine has spent most of his creative life and in whose languages he is fluent are France, the United States and Russia. The ballet celebrates aspects of all three, and though the sections could be given separately, and occasionally have been, they are presented most satisfactorily together.

Jerome Robbins' work with the company, which has produced many fine ballets, resulted in one of his most popular works, *Dances at a Gathering*, first shown in 1969. It was set to a selection of Chopin mazurkas, waltzes and etudes, played by a pianist seated onstage as the ten men and women of the piece danced alone or together, evoking a feeling for a friendly society in a country ambiance. The ballet has no explicit setting and the costuming only hints at European peasant dress. Robbins' fondness for Chopin's music was demonstrated in his earlier *The Concert* and subsequently in *In the Night*, a dance for three couples using a selection of nocturnes.

One of the significant departures from the company during this time was its outstanding principal dancer Arthur Mitchell, who left to found Dance Theater of Harlem, a company which was modeled on New York City Ballet. Its purpose has been to provide performing opportunites for black, classically trained dancers, whose presence in major ballet companies has been minimal. Starting with the premise that a school was the first necessary building block, Mitchell established one and waited several years before starting to perform regularly. The pace and development of the company have been sure and systematic, and in 1971 it appeared with New York City Ballet at the State Theater in a production choreographed by Balanchine and Mitchell: *Concerto for Jazz Band and Orchestra*. Since then the company has toured abroad and offered seasons in New York and elsewhere in the United States.

The company reached a logical crescendo of activity in 1972 when it celebrated The Stravinsky Festival, a week of performances from June 18 to June 25. It contained thirty-one ballets with music by Stravinsky, twenty-one of which were newly mounted for the celebration, and nine by Balanchine himself. The occasion marked what would have been Stravinsky's ninetieth birthday and was a special homage from Balanchine to Stravinsky, whose music had changed his choreographic outlook.

It was a monumental undertaking which no one who participated in would ever forget. It attracted world press coverage and inspired other, considerably reduced, Stravinksy festivals throughout Europe.

SUZANNE FARRELL IN *CHACONNE*

The logistics of mounting a ballet entail rehearsal time, fitting for costumes, dress rehearsals, and private rehearsals, along with the normal business of performing and taking daily class. The Stravinsky Festival preparations started the year previously when Balanchine discussed the possibility with members of the company and his board. As the specifics were added, the pace of the preparations picked up until the final week before it was to begin, when all normal operations were suspended so as to devote the entire energies of the company to the festival. Total dedication replaced any other concern as dancers, musicians, stage hands, costumers and the administration worked overtime to meet what looked like an impossible deadline. The usual task of mounting one new ballet can consume enormous amounts of time and attention, and here the company was attempting to mount and rehearse twenty-one new ballets as well as polish ten that were in repertory. John Taras, one of the company's ballet masters, commented, "We're all strangely calm." On the opening night, which began with a playing of Stravinsky's *Greeting Prelude* and included the scherzo from a newly discovered piano sonata, which was included at the last minute, Balanchine presented *Symphony in Three Movements* and *Violin Concerto*, which were among his finest creations. It was evident that this was not to be a misty look to the past but a continuing collaboration of great music with great choreography.

The rhythm of the festival dominated one's life, as each evening's return to the theater became part of a ritual. One participant likened it to a crossing on a transatlantic liner where one met the same people again and again. Evening after evening of new and repertory ballets were presented, costumed, rehearsed and, beautifully accompanied by the orchestra under the leadership of the company's musical director, Robert Irving, or associate conductor Hugo Fiorato. Arthur Mitchell returned to perform his original role in the seminal *Agon*, which was presented as the third ballet in an evening which consisted of *Apollo* and *Orpheus*. On the final evening after the ballets had been presented, the festival concluded with an orchestral and choral rendering of the *Symphony of Psalms*, during which the members of the company and administration sat onstage and listened along with the audience. Before the performance began, Balanchine and Kirstein, the company's chief administrator, drank a vodka toast onstage to Stravinsky and invited the audience to join them afterward in the promenade of the State Theater. When the final selection had been played, the audience filed out to find hundreds of little jiggers of neat vodka arrayed for the individual toasts. The Stravinsky Festival concluded with a celebratory drink; the company had presented an incredible series of performances and morale was high. The performing world was astonished at the accomplishment. Balanchine remarked simply, "No other company could have done it." It confirmed his own dedication to Stravinsky's music, to its special pertinence in the stream of twentieth-century cultural life, and his own choreographic development of its cadences through the classic dance.

Slowly, during the following fall season, the company introduced the works performed during that remarkable week into the regular repertory, and then, in 1973, began to prepare new ballets at the usual pace. Seasons continued in the spring and in the fall, and in July the company repaired to Saratoga, New York, where it had had a month-long residency at the Performing Arts Center for ten years. The next year the company celebrated its twenty-fifth anniversary as New York City Ballet, after it had changed its name from Ballet Society and joined the performing family of the New York City Center. A lingering taste of the recent past was reawakened by the appearance of *The Stravinsky Festival of the New York City Ballet* by Nancy Goldner, an excellent book detailing the events before and during that momentous week.

In 1975, to commemorate the centennial of Maurice Ravel's birth, the company decided to launch another festival. This one would be spaced over three weeks of its regular spring season. The scope of the celebration was more modest than the Stravinsky Festival, yet it produced more new works during its short span than other companies show in several years. Balanchine led the way with six of the thirteen new ballets but chose to revive only one of the ballets which he had previously created using

Ravel's music. The festival was greeted with particular warmth by France, which proposed an exchange of principal dancers from the Paris Opera Ballet with New York City Ballet. New York City Ballet has shown great reluctance to accommodate guest stars, preferring to develop its own or simply to incorporate other dancers permanently into the fabric of the company. On this occasion, though, an exchange did take place which was well received by audiences on both sides of the Atlantic.

During the bicentennial year the company did a paradoxical thing and mounted a production celebrating England. Called *Union Jack*, it scored an immediate hit with audiences. Balanchine, who choreographed the ballet, saw it as a companion piece to his friendly celebration of the United States, *Stars and Stripes*, a ballet which had been in the repertory for nearly twenty years. Both of them are obviously patriotic but also express some of the funnier aspects of the respective cultures. In its next season (1977) it celebrated the great Danish choreographer August Bournonville by mounting extracts from five of his ballets under the title of *Bournonville Divertissements*. The production was the work of Stanley Williams, a former member of the Royal Danish Ballet and a teacher at the School of American Ballet.

The rise of the company from a simple conversation between Kirstein and Balanchine in London in 1933 to a national institution has been the product of Balanchine's incredible productivity, unmatched in our time, and the energetic organizing ability of Kirstein. The latter has been unfailingly generous with his own private means to support his vision of the classic dance which has taken root and flowered in the United States. That vision has now, in part, become recognized by the national government, which in the past decade and a half has moved to protect its cultural heritage as it has begun to recognize the necessity of the arts in civilized living.

American Ballet Theater

The story of American Ballet Theater is the story of an idea or perhaps an ideal first put forth by Richard Pleasant. It was stated in bold type on the posters which announced the first American Ballet Theater season in 1940: THE GREATEST BALLETS OF ALL TIME STAGED BY THE GREATEST COLLABORATION IN BALLET HISTORY. It was brash, ambitious and exciting and reflected the youthful, visionary side of the times. The country was just emerging from a severe depression that had scarred all those who had endured the difficult thirties. It was the start of a new decade with new opportunities, and the country was more than ready for a change. The New York World's Fair of 1939–40 offered a glittering promise for the future in terms of sleeker automobiles, planned cities, and even novelties such as television, which made its first broad public appearance at the Fair. The country was eager to entertain new ideas, and the sweep of the American Ballet Theater concept fit right in with the spirit of the times.

The development of the company went back several years to the arrival of Mikhail Mordkin in the United States. He had graduated from the Bolshoi Ballet school and had joined the company in 1899. He later became the ballet master of the company, and he had also been noticed by Serge Diaghilev, who was intending to present a series of Ballets Russes performances in Paris. Mordkin was invited to be part of the first season in 1909 and was the leader of the Bolshoi contingent, which was joined with St. Petersburg's Maryinsky dancers for the occasion. Mordkin's handsome bearing caused him to be named the "Greek God" in Paris, and Pavlova was delighted to have him as a partner. When the successful season was over, the two of them were invited to London for further appearances. They decided not to return to Russia or to Diaghilev; instead, they formed a small company and toured together for several years. Mordkin formed his own company for a year in 1912 but then returned to the Bolshoi. He

CYNTHIA GREGORY IN *GRAND PAS CLASSIQUE*

stayed for five years and left in 1917 after the Revolution to direct a company in Lithuania. In 1924 he again came to the
United States and formed the Mordkin Ballet in 1926. It was
short-lived, and in addition to his school, Mordkin staged ballets
for opera and worked in the musical theater for the next decade.

In 1937 he decided to re-establish the Mordkin Ballet, using the
students of his school as the nucleus of the new company.
Among these were Lucia Chase, present codirector of the American Ballet Theater with Oliver Smith, and Leon Danielian, the
present head of the American Ballet Theater School. For the
company, Mordkin revived his productions of *Swan Lake* and
Giselle and staged a new production of *La Fille Mal Gardée* as

well as created several smaller ballets. The company enjoyed a success, so much so that a permanent administrator was needed the following year. Dimitri Romanoff, one of the dancers in the company, suggested Richard Pleasant, whom he had met when Pleasant was running a dance studio in Hollywood. In due course, Pleasant was asked to join the Mordkin Ballet and accepted.

In many ways Pleasant was an unusual choice for the job. First, there was his background, which included a degree in architecture from Princeton in 1932, and the fact that he had never run a ballet company before. He did have some experience in regional theater, having directed one in his home state of Colorado, and his dance studio in Hollywood was successful, which weighed to his advantage. The company began further touring in the Midwest after having performed in and around New York. The reception was substantial enough for the company to think of enlarging and reorganizing itself on a very ambitious scale. This was made possible through the generous support of Lucia Chase and the innovative ideas of Pleasant. In 1939 the Mordkin Ballet ceased to exist and Ballet Theater was born as an organization, the dancers of the Mordkin company providing the core around which the new company was formed. (It started as Ballet Theater and officially changed its name to American Ballet Theater in 1956.)

Pleasant envisioned the troupe in the widest possible terms. It was to embrace all, literally all that was best from the extant classical repertory and contemporary productions. It would also commission new works from choreographers of merit. As the social observer Lucius Beebe noted in an essay printed in the first season's souvenir book, Ballet Theater was after excellence whether it was traditional, contemporary or even controversial. Pleasant conceived the company as a "museum," with different wings in which the classics would provide one section, contemporary productions from abroad another, and a complete American wing. The company was in rehearsal for four months before its spectacular opening in January 1940.

The first three-week season at the Center Theater in Manhattan was an unquestioned triumph both artistically and by virtue of public response. The huge 3,500-seat theater was packed night after night as the public saw the mixture of old, new and controversial that had been promised. The choreographers represented were Agnes de Mille, Antony Tudor, Eugene Loring, Mikhail Fokine, Andrée Howard, Adolph Bolm (who had also participated in Diaghilev's first Paris season in 1909), Mordkin, Bronislava Nijinska (Nijinsky's talented sister) and Anton Dolin. The latter restaged *Giselle* and, along with Tudor and Howard, represented the contemporary English wing of the company, as well as being an outstanding solo artist. The controversial ballet by Eugene Loring, of the American wing of the company, was *The Great American Goof*, which had a libretto by William Saroyan, who was enjoying the first flush of his literary celebration. The classics were, in addition to *Giselle*, Act II of *Swan Lake* and Nijinska's restaging of *La Fille Mal Gardée*, which incorporated aspects of Mordkin's earlier setting. Fokine presided over the revival of two of his most popular ballets: *Les Sylphides* and *Carnaval*. There was even a children's matinee piece in Bolm's ballet to the enjoyable Prokofiev score for *Peter and the Wolf*.

The audacious formula devised by the young and ambitious Pleasant had convinced the public of its worth, and plans were made for the following season. Pleasant went even further in his concept of a dance museum with various wings. The first year had featured a company of eighty-four, including sixteen dancers in the Negro unit and seven dancers in the Spanish unit. For the next season Pleasant intended to have the various wings operate almost independently, in the way that curators of special collections might in a fine arts museum. There would, of course, be an overall director, but essentially the heads of the various wings would be completely responsible for mounting, rehearsing and putting their works onstage. The wings were to be called "Classic," "American" and "New English." Pleasant even had in mind a project in which a contemporary modern dancer, the late Doris Humphrey, would stage a work for the company. There were, however, internal problems over priorities and costs, and Pleasant resigned. The company which continued was considerably

smaller in size, forty-eight dancers, and the concept of the wings
was quietly abandoned.

The company was invited to stage the opera ballets for the
Chicago Civic Opera and to give evenings of its own for six
weeks and again had a winter season in New York. Tudor, De
Mille and Loring continued to revive their ballets and Dolin
created one of his most widely performed pieces, *Pas de Quatre*,
based on the legendary performance of the four famous Romantic ballerinas (Taglioni, Grisi, Cerrito and Grahn) in London
in 1845. During the wartime years of 1942–45 the company

MIKHAIL BARYSHNIKOV AND MARIANNA TCHERKASSKY
IN *LE SPECTRE DE LA ROSE*

drifted away from its original conception, featuring guest artists heavily, and began to tip its repertory toward that featured in the various Ballets Russes companies which had developed after Diaghilev's death. These ballets were unashamedly popular in design, light, humorous and full of performing brio. Despite the change in emphasis ("The greatest in *Russian* ballet by the Ballet Theater," proclaimed posters), Tudor continued to choreograph regularly and during these years produced a clutch of his most enduring ballets, including *Pillar of Fire* and *Romeo and Juliet*.

NATALIA MAKAROVA AND TED KIVITT IN *LE CORSAIRE*

Because of the special demands that Tudor made on his dancers, there grew up inside American Ballet Theater a small group of artists who were known as "Tudor dancers," since they were most frequently cast by Tudor in his new ballets. Hugh Laing was one and Nora Kaye was another, and both were included in *Pillar of Fire*. In actual fact, Kaye owed the development of her career to her success in this ballet. When the curtain came down it was apparent to the audience that they had seen the emergence of a supremely talented dramatic ballerina. The score selected was Schonberg's *Transfigured Night*, and the ballet told the story of a despairing woman whose unhappiness was also transfigured through love. The setting is a street with two contrasting houses facing one another; three sisters dwell in one, and the other is disreputable. The young man who frequents the house opposite exercises an attraction on the central sister, Hagar, who does not want to be a spinster like her older sister. She is driven into the designing young man's arms when the man she likes appears to be more attracted to her younger sister. She is filled with remorse. Naturally, the young man spurns her after their brief liaison. Ultimately the friend does return to her and they depart together, with the past a forgotten incident. As in his most significant works, Tudor tosses his characters into an emotionally fraught situation from which they must work to disentangle themselves, using the unique combination of balletic steps and ordinary gesture that is the signature of his ballets.

Among the other significant things that happened during this period in the company's development was the emergence of Jerome Robbins as a choreographer. In 1944 he created *Fancy Free* about three sailors on shore leave, and it was adapted into a Broadway musical the next season. Leonard Bernstein was the composer who did the original ballet score and the musical. A year later, Robbins created *Interplay*, another ballet that was taken into the repertory of American Ballet Theater. It was designed by Oliver Smith, who had also done *Fancy Free*. The latter had an immediate appeal to a wartime audience which recognized the familiar situation of men with limited time chasing after female companionship. The three manage to snare two young women and so must devise a way to cut their own numbers down to match. They decide on a contest and ask the women to judge. Each dances a solo variation, but before a judgment can be made they are brawling. During the fight the women leave, and the sailors are on their own. They make a pledge to forget about women, which lasts only until the next one comes into view, and the ballet ends with them frantically chasing after her. When seen today the ballet still retains its humorous freshness.

After the war the company turned once again to its original structure as a museum of dance which would incorporate new and old ballets from a variety of sources. The pattern of the year had settled into national touring, with spring or fall appearances at the Metropolitan Opera House. The transcontinental tour had emerged when the company had first associated itself with impresario Sol Hurok in 1941, and the new management of Oliver Smith and Lucia Chase, who appeared as codirectors in the 1944 season, continued the practice. The company was now offered a choice engagement at the Royal Opera House in London and gave a successful summer season there. It was the first American company to have been invited after the end of the war. Robbins' *Fancy Free* and *Interplay* were particularly praised.

The company returned home in more ways than one. It had turned once again to the ideal originally set down by Pleasant and it was eager to develop stars from within its own ranks rather than hire them from outside. It was engaged in building a "permanent institution, American in character and international in scope." As was customary, the company went on national tour and included Havana for its final engagements in the spring.

One of the chief activities of American Ballet Theater has been its sustained touring, whether domestically or abroad. It is unquestioned that the company has brought classical ballet to more communities in the United States than any other company. It has contributed strongly to the creation of an audience for ballet which would not have existed other than through its efforts. The results for the company, though, were mixed. While it undoubtedly was able to survive as a performing unit through touring, it also found that such incessant touring began to have a deleterious effect on the level of the company personnel after too long a period. Toward the end of the decade certain criticisms about the dancing standards of the company began to be heard. These criticisms were mainly in the domestic press and not from abroad, where the company began to appear with assistance from the State Department's Cultural Relations Division.

During 1950 the company spent five months in Europe, including an appearance at the prestigious Edinburgh Festival as well as a return visit to London. During the season there, De Mille's *Rodeo*, which she had restaged for the company, was an outstanding hit. During the next several years the company undertook to make several tours abroad to South America and Europe, frequently with assistance from the State Department. Given the eclectic outlook of the company, it naturally reflected some of the influences to which it had been exposed. For a while a distinct French influence was felt in the ballets of Roland Petit and the outstanding performances of Jean Babilée and Nathalie Phillipart, who joined the company for a couple of seasons. A long-delayed step was taken in 1951 when the Ballet Theater School was opened in New York under the direction of Nijinska.

By 1955, when the company was celebrating its fifteenth anniversary, it had danced in all (then) forty-eight states and had appeared in fourteen European countries. Touring seemed to consume almost all of the company's energies, and few new productions were mounted. Those that were did not last more than a season or two. Fortunately, the company still had a stock of excellent ballets available from its previously commissioned repertory. The company's appearances in New York, where it had first established itself, were increasingly rare, and in the season when it officially changed its name to American Ballet Theater it made only a single appearance in its nominal home city.

The lack of good new ballets was particularly felt, and the management established the Ballet Theater Workshop in 1956 to correct the situation. These productions were mounted with great care as to their performing but were not elaborately costumed or set. Those works which proved to have merit were

MIKHAIL BARYSHNIKOV IN *THEME AND VARIATIONS*

taken by the company and then more elaborately costumed and set. Two of the successful ballets were Herbert Ross's *The Maids* and Robert Joffrey's *Pas de Déesses*, but on the whole the concept failed to live up to expectations and was abandoned.

As a matter of fact, the company itself seemed to have reached a definite low point in its career, and after a season at the Metropolitan and a single outdoor performance in June 1959, it disbanded for nearly a year. The company which had been greeted with such acclaim in the early 1940s had wandered away from its original course into the world of the Ballets Russes in the mid-forties, but recovered its original path toward the end of the decade. National and international touring became all-consuming in the 1950s, with a consequent loss of roots and creative energies, and by the end of the decade the future was pretty bleak.

Once again with the aid of the State Department, the company was asked to re-form, to undertake a tour of the Soviet Union. It was to be the first American company ever to play there. Energetically, the dancers were recalled and the ballets remounted for a short season in New York before leaving for Russia. In general, the season was not highly thought of and complaints were heard about the poor quality of the various productions. It was felt that the haste with which the season had been put together showed. Maria Tallchief and Erik Bruhn, the international Danish star, were the leaders of the fifty-three-member company which arrived in Moscow in September 1960. The tour began in the capital and included Tiflis, Leningrad and Kiev before returning for the final performances in Moscow. The company, which had not appeared to best advantage in the United States, flowered in Russia and was highly praised. Its last performance in Moscow was attended unexpectedly by Nikita Khrushchev, then the most influential man in the country, which put the final seal of approval on the visit. The audiences were enthusiastic and the critics favorable, though a bit puzzled at times. The man from Isvestia misread De Mille's *Rodeo* as a "celebration of livestock breeders in the southwestern states of the USA." But there was no mistaking the rhythmic applause that shows Russian audiences' special favor.

HOW TO ENJOY BALLET

The tide began to turn slowly for the company when it returned home from the Russian triumph. Toni Lander, another Danish star dancer, joined the company and made the cross-country tour with it. In 1962 the company was the first ballet company to perform at the White House. President Kennedy invited the company to provide the entertainment for his guest, President Felix Houphouët-Boigny of the Ivory Coast. The Washington Ballet Guild offered to sponsor the company so that it would become the resident company of Washington, an offer that was subsequently limited to support of those performances actually given in Washington proper. Domestic touring along with a visit to a selection of South American countries, assisted by the State Department, brought the company up to the eve of its twenty-fifth anniversary.

It was a watershed for the company, and its season at the State Theater in New York was highly successful in terms of audience response and new works. David Blair, of Britian's Royal Ballet, staged Act II of *Swan Lake* in an authoritative version, and Jerome Robbins returned to create *Les Noces* for the company with which he had made his choreographic debut. The newly formed National Council on the Arts presented the company with a check for $100,000 to help continue its operations and later offered a matching grant for $250,000, when the company would undertake its next national tour. The opening night of the season had an added glamor, since the United Nations representatives of twenty-two nations in which the company had appeared were invited.

The following year the company undertook another tour of Russia and presented a complete version of *Swan Lake*. The production was so successful that Blair was asked to remount *Giselle*. It too proved to be a great success, and guest stars Carla Fracci and Erik Bruhn were celebrated for their partnership in it. From among the members of the company, Cynthia Gregory began to develop her distinctive and classical approach to the full-evening ballets. Japan received the company warmly for a tour in 1968, and the announcement was made that it would become the resident company of the Kennedy Center, which was

MIKHAIL BARYSHNIKOV, CYNTHIA GREGORY, ERIK BRUHN,
ALICIA ALONSO, JORGE ESQUIVEL, IVAN NAGY AND
ELEANOR D'ANTUNO AT A GALA PERFORMANCE

then under construction. Eliot Feld made his choreographic
debut with the highly acclaimed *Harbinger* in 1967 and followed
with a well-received *At Midnight* during the company's winter
season. In the course of the year the new repertory had been substantially strengthened with Feld's emergence.

For the next two years the company continued to tour regularly and again dipped into the Tudor repertory to revive his humorous *Gala Performance*, which contrasted the behavior of an
Italian, a Russian and a French ballerina. Seasons were given at
the beautiful opera house of the Brooklyn Academy of Music. In

RUDOLF NUREYEV, CYNTHIA GREGORY AND ERIK BRUHN
IN *LA VENTANA*

1970 American Ballet Theater Players, a smaller company, was formed to play in communities that could not support an appearance by the larger company. In London the company's production of *Swan Lake* was particularly well received by the public and critics. It was, in fact, substantially the ballet as it was first mounted for the Royal Ballet years previously, but had been superseded by another, less distinguished version. After the appearances in England, where the company had not been seen since 1956, it continued on to tour the Continent.

At this time it pioneered in making summer appearances at the State Theater in New York. Hallowed, but false, wisdom had it that the official theater season was over at the end of May and would not revive until after Labor Day in early September, if not later. Managements blindly assumed it to be true, forgetting the advent of air conditioning and the fact that the large majority of people remained in the city during the summer, not to mention out-of-town visitors. The success of the company's season in June 1970 prompted another in July–August of 1971 and was greeted with similar good houses. The news spread quickly and foreign touring companies found that performing in New York during June and July and part of August made box office sense.

While the company was in London, Natalia Makarova of the Kirov Ballet left her troupe and elected to remain in Europe when the company returned to Russia. She signed to make guest appearances with American Ballet Theater and has become a regular feature of its seasons. In the same year the Kennedy Center opened in Washington, D.C., and the company made its first appearance there in the winter. It followed quickly with a spring season in 1972. These appearances, coupled with performances of its smaller productions at the City Center Fifty-fifth Street theater in New York and its larger, more elaborate ballets at the State Theater, became the quadrants of the company year, though it still maintained some touring weeks.

Eliot Feld had left to form his own small company but did return to stage his dramatic and beautiful *Theater* in the winter season as well as *The Soldier's Tale* and *Eccentrique*. Paolo Bortoluzzi, of Maurice Béjart's Ballet of the Twentieth Century, joined the company, and in the summer Fokine's remarkable *Spectre de la Rose* was staged for him. The Ford Foundation came to the company's assistance with grants totaling $1,000,000 over a four-year period, to help it bridge a chronic cash-flow problem. As with all performing companies, it had to incur the expense of production and travel before receiving its agreed-upon fee. The gap was sometimes closed through receipt of subscription money for the following season, but frequently this was not the case and the Ford Foundation attempted to rectify the imbalance.

The ballets of Antony Tudor had been featured throughout the history of the company, but in the early seventies were featured even more strongly. Tudor himself was named an associate director of the company in the spring of 1974 and devoted much of his energy to supervising and polishing their appearance. The company achieved a long-cherished ambition by presenting the first part of a full-evening production of *The Sleeping Beauty*, when Act III was given during the summer at the State Theater. As in the past with *Swan Lake*, a portion of the ballet was given before undertaking the full work.

Another spectacular Russian dancer left the Kirov Ballet when Mikhail Baryshnikov decided to remain in Canada rather than return to the Soviet Union. He joined Makarova in choosing to perform with American Ballet Theater. His first appearances amply confirmed the substantial hearsay reputation that he enjoyed outside of Russia, and he has become a regular guest artist with the company.

In January 1975 the company held a gala celebration of its thirty-fifth anniversary at the City Center Fifty-fifth Street theater in which retired members made appearances as well as the current members of the company. The presence of the Russian stars with the company started a small Russian phase in the repertory. Rudolf Nureyev, who frequently appeared with the company, staged a full-length *Raymonda;* Makarova remounted a stunning production of *La Bayadère*, which showed off the company's corps de ballet to splendid advantage as well as its soloists; and Baryshnikov followed with his own production of *The Nutcracker*, which had psychological overtones, in 1977. The company also added a historically important piece of Fokine's when it presented *The Firebird* during the same season.

Several contemporary choreographers were asked to prepare new ballets, of which the most successful was *Push Comes to Shove*. In it the choreographer, Twyla Tharp, who had previously worked with the Joffrey Ballet on two productions, created a comic gem that received a particularly vivid performance from Baryshnikov, who was ordinarily not seen in such modern works. Herbert Ross, who choreographed several ballets for the company in the 1950s, had in the meantime turned to making films and combined both of his interests in *The Turning Point*, which featured members of the company as well as well-known film stars. His wife and former ballerina, Nora Kaye, was appointed as an associate artistic director.

The company was progressing along the path it had set for itself in the early years of its organization, staging traditional ballets and encouraging new talents. Its establishment rested on the commitment of Lucia Chase, its codirector, who supported it generously through its various trials and triumphs. The company is the product not so much of any one choreographer, though one thinks often of Tudor's contribution, as it is the embodiment of an idea formulated by Richard Pleasant and modified by the experience of close to four decades of performing. Through its touring the company has attracted substantial audiences to ballet and has shown major productions of classic ballets more consistently than any other American company.

The Joffrey Ballet

For a company that has a modern and even "pop" image, the Joffrey Ballet has been unusually sensitive to the revival of excellent works from the past. The past that it has cast its eyes on most frequently, though, has definitely been of the twentieth century, not of the Romantic Era. It has on occasion mounted works from the traditional nineteenth-century repertory of the Royal Danish Ballet, but for every one of those it has remounted twenty productions by contemporary masters like Fokine, Jooss, Massine, Balanchine and Ashton. It is a repertory company in the wide selection of its ballets and even in their casting. The company director has formed the ballet according to the model favored by great dramatic repertory companies. There are no stars listed as such, but an ensemble of dancers who may have the lead role in a ballet one evening and a supporting role the next. As a matter of policy, the Joffrey Ballet has deliberately restricted its roster to about forty, so that it has approximately half as many dancers as the other two major American companies. It is tightly and logically organized, as befits the highly focused ambitions of its founder, Robert Joffrey.

Abdullah Jaffa Anver Bey Khan was born in Seattle in 1930 to an Italian mother and an Afghan father. Professionally he changed his name to Robert Joffrey and as a child studied dance to help cure an asthmatic condition. His first influential teacher was Mary Ann Wells in Seattle, who subsequently had the satisfaction of presenting her ex-pupil with the Dance Magazine Award after his company had made a successful tour of the Soviet Union, though that was twenty years in the future. Miss Wells encouraged him to travel to New York for further study after giving his first program of ballets in Seattle in 1948. While studying at the School of American Ballet he auditioned for a touring French company, Roland Petit's Ballets de Paris and was taken on for its New York season.

In addition to his studies in classical ballet he also took class with the modern dancers May O'Donnell and Gertrude Shurr and appeared for one season with the O'Donnell company in 1952. That same year he gave a recital of his own works in New York and was invited to perform at the Jacob's Pillow Dance Festival in the summer. He was active as a teacher at the High School of Performing Arts in Manhattan as well as at the American Ballet Theater School and developed a substantial reputation as one with a particularly keen eye for spotting young, talented students.

In the following year he established his own school, the American Ballet Center, which, in enlarged form, continues to the present and is the official school for the Robert Joffrey Ballet. He continued to choreograph his own works and in 1954 presented *Pas des Déesses* on a program as part of the Ballet Theater Workshop series. It was well received, and the next year he was invited to mount it for the Ballet Rambert in England. The company carried it as one of its productions when it visited China two years later on tour. To date, it is the only ballet by an American choreographer which has been presented in mainland China since the mid-twenties when the Denishawn dance company toured the Far East.

The piece is an imaginative and witty retelling of an actual en-

GARY CHRYST IN *TRINITY*

counter between the reigning ballerinas of the Romantic Era in London. They were indeed "goddesses" of the dance with egos to match. There were four of them—Marie Taglioni, Carlotta Grisi, Lucile Grahn, and Fanny Cerrito—but Joffrey reduced the number to three, substituting Arthur Saint-Léon for Grisi. When the ballet opens, he is on one knee, with the three ballerinas posed standing behind him. He dances a *pas de deux* with each of them which emphasizes their special quality, the glamorous and lilting Grahn, Cerrito's perky and bouncy attack, and the gracious, floating Taglioni. The humor of the piece derives as much from the exits before each *pas de deux* as from the duets themselves. It is necessary that two of the three ballerinas relinquish the stage to the third, and it is something they are reluctant to do, putting it off until the last minute. Many polite but competitive glances are exchanged among the three before each *pas de deux* begins. Saint-Léon has his own variation after playing the long-suffering partner of the three ballerinas, and they assemble in the opening pose of the ballet to finish. The pose they assume is copied from one of the most famous dance lithographs of the nineteenth century commemorating the historic collaboration. It is one of Joffrey's best-known works and has been performed at the White House and in the Soviet Union as well as in other cities where the Joffrey Ballet has traveled.

In 1956 the Robert Joffrey Theater Ballet was formed, consisting of six dancers (three men and three women), four ballets (all by Joffrey), and one rented station wagon which carried the company on a tour of eleven states. Joffrey himself did not go on the tour but remained in New York to run his school. For the next ten years the pattern of the year was the same but on a slightly expanded basis, and eventually the company played in all forty-eight states. During the first six of those years the company existed by touring and by summer seasons at such places as Jacob's Pillow, Chautauqua and Seattle's Aqua-theater.

In 1957 Joffrey was asked to become the resident choreographer for the New York City Opera, and members of his company performed in the opera ballets that were needed during the regular season. They also performed in opera ballet productions in other cities as well. In 1962, the Rebekah Harkness Foundation offered to become the company's financial sponsor, and during that summer the company was invited for a residency at Watch Hill, Rhode Island, Mrs. Harkness' summer home. During the summer six choreographers were commissioned to produce works for the company, and these were shown to an invitational audience at the Fashion Institute of Technology in Manhattan during the following fall.

That November the company began its first overseas tour

under the sponsorship of the federal government and ANTA. The tour lasted nearly four months and traveled from the Near East to Southeast Asia. The following summer the company returned for its second residency at Watch Hill, and in the fall appeared as part of the outdoor dance festival, held in New York City at the Delacorte Theater each autumn since 1959, when it was established by the Harkness Foundation. In early October the company appeared at the White House to perform for the late Emperor Haile Selassie of Ethiopia. At the end of the month the company, which had now grown to five times its original size, began a tour of the Soviet Union which was to last two months. The company appeared in Moscow, Leningrad, Kiev and Donetsk with great success. A particular favorite of the Russian audiences was a humorous piece by Gerald Arpino, *Palace Music Hall*, which spoofed old-time vaudeville. Full of high spirits after the acclaim in Russia, the company started a two-and-a-half-month tour of the United States.

It had been a heady two years with substantial foreign and domestic tours in each, and a delightful summer residency at Watch Hill during which repertory could be rehearsed and new ballet productions mounted. In March of 1964 Joffrey announced his withdrawal from the association with the Harkness Foundation. It cost him nearly all of his dancers, who were under contract to the Harkness Foundation, and the performing rights to many ballets which had been commissioned by the Foundation, including his own and those of Arpino, his artistic collaborator. The dispute arose when the Foundation wanted the company name changed to the Harkness Ballet and intended to leave the future artistic direction of the company in an ambiguous state. Joffrey was not convinced that he would retain the authority that he had built since 1956 and preferred to resign rather than relinquish it. A month later, devoid of a company, he received the Dance Magazine Award for his achievements in what had been a remarkable decade.

However, what looked like the end of the road was converted into a new beginning. The school still existed and during the years with the Harkness Foundation he had met Alexander

CHRISTIAN HOLDER AND CORPS IN *TRINITY*

Ewing, whom he found to be a sympathetic and responsible company manager. In September 1964, the Foundation for American Dance was established, with Ewing as the head of the nonprofit corporation. The Ford Foundation granted the new group $35,000 on an emergency basis and pledged $120,000 in further support. The next summer the newly reformed Joffrey Ballet appeared at the White House Festival of the Arts and made its official debut at the Jacob's Pillow Dance Festival in August. Almost immediately after, it appeared in New York at the Delacorte Theater in Central Park with a cluster of new ballets, including Arpino's *Viva Vivaldi*, Anna Sokolow's *Opus '65*, Lotte Goslar's *Charivari*, and Joffrey's own *Gamelan*, which was seen in the United States for the first time. The latter was one of the productions commissioned by the Harkness Foundation whose performance rights had been returned to the choreographer. The company's reception was extremely warm and a great testament to Joffrey's resiliency. The triumvirate of Arpino, Ewing and Joffrey prepared for a spring season at the New York City Center.

The performances were notable for their sheer excitement, and attracted near-capacity audiences night after night. There was understandable curiosity about the company, a definite sympathy for its remarkable comeback and interest over anything newsworthy and somewhat controversial. Morton Baum, who had felt similar excitement when Ballet Society performed at the same theater twenty years earlier, invited the Joffrey Ballet to become the resident company of the City Center's theater on Fifty-fifth Street. The directors accepted the offer and in June announced a fall residency for the newly named City Center Joffrey Ballet.

That autumn the company presented a mixture of new works and revivals that would set the pattern for all subsequent seasons. Arpino, who was and is the resident choreographer for the company, prepared two ballets, *Nightwings* and a revival of *Incubus;* Eugene Loring was commissioned to do a new ballet, *These Three;* and the company revived Balanchine's *Donizetti Varia-*

tions. Ruthanna Boris's comic gem *Cakewalk,* a ballet that has become something of a tradition with the company, was revived, as were Gloria Contreras *Moncayo I* and *Vitalitas.*

Coincident with the reforming of the main company, Joffrey created an intermediate apprentice group of advanced students from his school. These young dancers were given intensive instruction under the direction of Lillian Moore, and several ballets were taught to them so that they could learn how to dance as an ensemble. Since there is no substitute for actual performance before a live audience, selected members of the apprentice group were regularly given public exposure in ballets that were being performed by the regular company. Subsequently many members of the apprentice group were taken into the regular company and their places filled by other talented students from the school. By the end of the fall season there was no doubt that the country again had a functioning ballet company under the direction of Robert Joffrey—a company that he had firmly based in a regular home with a fully operative school behind it.

Immediately after its own season the company went to Houston to participate in the opening week's festivities which surrounded the dedication of the Jesse H. Jones Hall for the Performing Arts, and then in the spring presented its second regular season as the resident company of the City Center. Again several revivals were made, one of which was recognized as a masterstroke, Jooss's antiwar ballet *The Green Table.* The piece was created in 1932 and presented in Paris at the Théâtre des Champs-Elysées where it won first prize in the first international choreographic competition organized by the International Archives of Dance under the sponsorship of Rolf de Maré. When Jooss's company was forced out of Germany by the Nazi government in 1933, it relocated at Dartington Hall in England and continued to tour from there. After the Second World War the company was disbanded and little was heard from Jooss except that he continued teaching.

On a tour of South America in 1941, two of his dancers had left him in Santiago de Chile to form a dance company which later became the Chilean National Ballet. Ernst Uthoff had danced the role of the Standard Bearer in *The Green Table*, and his wife, Lola Botka, had danced the Young Girl, and the piece became an important part of the repertory of the Chilean National Ballet. That company performed in the United States in 1964 and made a terrific impact with *The Green Table*, and Maximiliano Zamosa made a special place for himself in the principal role of Death. Zamosa subsequently joined the Joffrey Ballet, as did another member of the Chilean company, Michael Uthoff, the son of the director. When Joffrey decided to revive *The Green Table* for his own company he had the services of a completely coached central figure in Zamosa, and Michael Uthoff danced the Standard Bearer, as had his father before him. Michael was married to Lisa Bradley, who was also a member of the company, and she danced the Young Girl, as had her mother-in-law. Of course, the elder Uthoffs came to the United States to offer their support and expertise. *The Green Table* was a total success and has remained in the company's repertory for over a decade. The casts have changed but the impact of the work is still formidable.

The score was composed for two pianos, and the first scene opens with two groups of men, wearing masks that make them look like aging diplomats, facing one another across a green table that slants down toward the audience. They are all dressed identically in black suits, and gesture to one another in a menacing or conciliatory manner by turns, as the lilting pianos play a charming dance melody. Their "negotiations" are a form of deadly dance that ends with them drawing out tiny pistols and firing them. A low drumming is heard from the pianos as the lights go out, and when they come up they reveal a figure at the back of the stage marching in place with a deadly rhythm. His face is a death's mask and he wears a helmet so that he resembles Mars, the god of war. He makes gathering motions with his arms to indicate the feast of lives that will once again be his in wartime.

This is followed by a selection of scenes, each one separated by a blackout, showing the young men rallying to the standard, scenes of combat, an old woman dying because there is no point in living after everyone she has known has been taken from her.

A young girl is drawn into the world of casual sensual encounters and is carried off by Death; a profiteer who enriches himself from others' miseries is finally caught in the trap as well. Throughout, the figure of Death marches in all of the tableaus and takes his victims roughly or tenderly, but inevitably he takes them all. The final scene is the same as the first, with all of the "gentlemen" again facing one another across the green table. The cycle is about to be repeated and the green table of the earth will once again feel the tread of Death's pounding feet.

In addition to this highly dramatic work, the company revived Balanchine's *Scotch Symphony* with great success and then headed off to spend a summer residency at Pacific Lutheran University sponsored by the Pacific Northwest Ballet Association. In addition to the normal teaching and performing, Joffrey was much taken by the rock dancing he saw there when the formal class day was over and began to work on a ballet that would incorporate elements of popular "rock" music with the sort of lighting that one might find in a discotheque. He decided that the whole scene reminded him of a ritual of some sort and so shaped his ballet accordingly. It ended up with film projections of the live dancers on an eccentrically shaped screen, dazzling lighting effects, and a live rock group playing the accompanying score which was composed for the ballet. He called it *Astarte* and it became the most newsworthy ballet the company had ever done. *Time* magazine had a picture of it on the cover of an issue featuring a survey of the dance field, and it attracted media coverage from a variety of sources.

The ballet is a *pas de deux* which begins with a woman alone on the stage surrounded by a bluish glow. She is serene, removed and vaguely mysterious. Red and green spotlights play over the audience restlessly as if looking for someone or something. Suddenly both of them focus on a man in street clothes, sitting quietly in the orchestra among the other members of the audience. He rises, as if transfixed, and begins to walk down the aisle toward the stage. He climbs up to the stage and a battery of lights flash as he makes his way from the audience onto the stage. His eyes are fixed on the woman all of the time as he slowly removes his outer clothing until he stands naked except for a brief dance belt. He goes to her and they dance together; at first he twists and manipulates her, sometimes brutally, then she gains the upper hand and dominates him. At the end he turns and walks out an exit at the rear of the stage and onto the street as a film of him doing exactly that is shown on the irregularly shaped screen that was the background to their dance. The effect was startling for its use of mixed media and became a popular favorite with audiences.

It also helped establish the company's popular image in the minds of viewers. Other ballets using advanced means were mounted by the company but with less effect, and through it all Joffrey continued to revive works of merit which had been allowed to pass from other companies' active repertories. These included Balanchine's *Pas de Trois* and *Pas de Dix*. New works were regularly prepared by the company's resident choreographer, Gerald Arpino, including *Fanfarita* and *Partita for Four*.

With a solid three years of work at his new home, City Center, Joffrey was again ready to show his company abroad. In 1969 he was invited to Vienna, and *Astarte* proved a razor's edge dividing the critics. The more conservative were not at all receptive to the innovation, but others were, and the public gave it fifteen curtain calls to show its enthusiasm. Gerhard Brunner, at that time an active critic and now director of the Vienna State Opera Ballet, wrote that *Astarte* was "a product of that American world of today that will also be ours tomorrow." The company generated excitement and continued to do so in the United States when it showed a little nudity in *The Poppet* during its 1969 fall season. This piece proved a dead end, so to speak, and was dropped almost immediately.

The company entered the seventies and asked Léonide Massine to revive several of his ballets, starting with *The Three-cornered Hat* followed by *Le Beau Danube*, *Parade*, and *Pulcinella*. Unquestionably the most successful was *Parade*, which was praised not only for its dancing but also reviewed favorably by art critics for its execution of the original Picasso costumes and decor. It was precisely the sort of piece that Joffrey intended to re-es-

DERMOT BURKE AND DONNA COWAN IN *TRINITY*

tablish in the public's attention by his systematic program of selected revivals. Fokine's *Petrouchka* became a company standby after it was revived, and the strictly classical repertory was strengthened by the addition of Bournonville's *Konservatoriet* and *William Tell Variations* as well as Balanchine's *Square Dance*.

In the spring of 1971 the company again went abroad and enjoyed a good reception in London, although once again *Astarte* divided the critical commentators into two opposing camps. When the company returned home Joffrey was interviewed about the direction of his company. He affirmed that he liked new works but insisted that he didn't want to lose the older ones. To drive home his point he had presented a revival of *Le Beau Danube* that season as well as Jerome Robbins' early success, *Interplay*. He had also commissioned a new work from vanguard modern dance choreographer Twyla Tharp to be presented in his spring season. He played down his role as an active choreographer and asserted that he liked being a director as much as anything else. He said the pleasure he derived from seeing *Interplay* in his repertory was as satisfying as having one of his own ballets there. "I enjoy running the company."

The ballet produced by Tharp, *Deuce Coupe*, was an enormous hit. It featured the Tharp company as well as the Joffrey dancers and brought the music of the Beach Boys, a rock group, to the attention of a ballet audience. It was a raffish, riotous ballet that led Joffrey to ask her for another one a year later. This time she produced *As Time Goes By*, a classical piece with her own squiggly accents to a Haydn Symphony. It, too, proved successful. The revivals for the season included Frederick Ashton's *The Dream* and José Limón's *The Moor's Pavane*, both solid works. *The Dream* was as well received as his humorous *Façade*, produced two years earlier. Despite its artistic successes, the company faced severe economic problems as City Center cut its financial support to the company drastically, and the company in turn eliminated two weeks from its normal six-week season.

The Joffrey II company, which was a development of the apprentice program, received support from the government for touring outside New York and continued its existence preparing its dancers for performance with the larger company. Despite the financial pinch, a month-long tour of the Soviet Union was undertaken in 1974, a little over a decade after Joffrey had led his first company there. The success was repeated, but with a completetly different repertory of ballets. Arpino's ballets were again the most popular with the Russian audiences, and his rock work, *Trinity*, was singled out for special praise. Others of his ballets that were favorably commented on included *Viva Vivaldi* and *Confetti*. The company had proved itself in Russia a second time with new dancers and new ballets but the same artistic director.

In 1975 Joffrey again asked for and received one of Ashton's beautiful ballets, *Monotones I and II*, and revived John Cranko's *Jeu de Cartes*. The company had already enjoyed a popular success with his *Pineapple Poll*. In the bicentennial year the company decided to honor Jooss and also native choreographers. In the spring the company offered a tribute to Jooss, who had just celebrated his seventy-fifth birthday, by duplicating exactly the first complete program that he had presented in the United States with his own troupe. Joffrey offered *The Big City, Pavane on the Death of an Infanta, A Ball in Old Vienna* and *The Green Table*, with the musical interludes that were the custom in 1933.

In the fall the company presented a season of thirty ballets, all by American choreographers, with, of course, revivals and new works. Among the latter was a third ballet for the company by Tharp, *Happily Ever After*, done to country and western music, and Agnes de Mille's masterful *Rodeo* was restored with its original costuming. The formula of old and new ballets in a repertory format had served the company well for a decade and continued to do so.

Having had its share of fiscal woes and being especially sensitive to the loss of seemingly secure patronage, not once but twice, Joffrey was acutely aware of the thin fiscal line that arts organizations tread. Accordingly, he canceled his spring season at the City Center to avoid increasing his indebtedness. It was a radical, but considered, step. It is an irony of large ballet companies that they lose money when they perform and save money when they don't. Carried to its logical extreme, it would dictate concentrating on the school, which makes money, and abandoning performing altogether. Of course, there would be no point in educating dancers if there were no outlets for their acquired skill, so the argument ends up in a spiral. In this particular instance, though, Joffrey felt that the season was too expensive and it was canceled.

The company returned in the fall with three novelties, two revivals by Ashton, *Les Patineurs* and *Jazz Calendar*, and Oscar

Ariz' *Romeo and Juliet,* the first full-evening work that the company had ever performed. It was done to the familiar Prokofiev score that several other choreographers had used, but emphasized the dancing more than the storytelling aspects of the ballet. The company continued to be true to its preference for a blend of revivals and new works.

Though the smallest of the three big companies, Joffrey Ballet has achieved an international reputation in about half the time and has undoubtedly benefited from the trail-blazing efforts of the other two. If any confirmation were needed as to the establishment of a living ballet tradition in the United States, one might point to the Joffrey company and its development—from a rented station wagon twenty years ago to residence at a major New York theater and an international reputation.

RUSSIA

No nation on earth cherishes ballet more than Russia. It is considered on a par with other major art forms and supported sumptuously with government funds. After the awesomely destructive siege of Leningrad in World War II during which nearly half of the population was killed, a third of the buildings flattened, and the surviving citizens at the point of starvation, the government rushed in food to alleviate immediate hunger and started restoration of the Maryinsky Theater to refresh the spirit of the people. What would be the first public edifice restored in your city?

The Soviet Union is the only country in the world where a leading athlete could write to the newspapers and complain that his salary level was less than that of Bolshoi ballerina Maya Plisetskaya and should not be, because he was at the same level of proficiency in his field. Needless to say, it would be impossible to imagine a sports professional of superstar caliber in this country complaining that he was not paid as much money as a ballerina.

Within the Soviet Union there is a lively competition to develop dancers and companies and national competitions, and displays are held frequently. Dancers emerge from almost any-where. Mikhail Baryshnikov is from Latvia; Rudolf Nureyev is a Tartar; Vakhtang Chaboukiani, a star of the thirties and forties, was from Georgia (a region in Southern Russia), as is George Balanchine. The country is vast and the population disparate, but ballet is found everywhere, even in Siberia's Novosibirsk.

Nearly ten million adults and children are enrolled in the hundreds of ballet schools and worker's clubs scattered throughout the thirty-eight socialist republics, regions and districts, each one of which has its own large ballet company and opera house. Nearly four thousand professional dancers are employed by companies, all of whom can retire on a guaranteed pension after twenty years. Andrei Vosnesensky, one of the country's leading poets, has written verses in honor of Plisetskaya, and when dignitaries pay state visits to Moscow, an evening at the ballet is included in their official itinerary. Ballet tickets are always difficult to get and leading dancers are worshiped with the sort of adulation generally reserved for movie stars. Within the highly stratified system of work compensation, dancers are accorded privileges reserved for highly placed government figures. The Russians cherish ballet and in a proprietary manner often refer to it as "our ballet" in much the same way that the ancient Romans used to refer to the Mediterranean as *Mare Nostrum.*" They have strong claims and strong feelings about it.

While there are many ballet companies of substantial size in Russia, the two most important are the Kirov of Leningrad (the Maryinsky in Czarist days) and the Bolshoi of Moscow. Bolshoi in Russian means big, and the company is the largest in the Soviet Union, but its huge stage, which used to be first in size, now takes a back seat to that of the newer Novosibirsk in Siberia. Moscow and Leningrad are rival cities in the way that Los Angeles and San Francisco are, and represent the two major strains of ballet development in the Soviet Union. Leningrad, the city of the czars, tends to look upon the Bolshoi as slightly acrobatic in its approach, while the Moscow dancers cherish their dramatic emotiveness and speak deprecatingly of the Kirov's reserved coolness. The differences are subtle but real.

Despite the vast interest in ballet, there are no dance critics in the Soviet Union as we know them in daily or weekly periodicals, nor is there any single publication devoted to writing exclusively about ballet. Discussion of the performance of a new ballet or the debut of a performer in a new role often does not take place until weeks after the event—in an article in one of the newspapers. Then the discussion will often include the coach or teacher of the dancer as well as the dancer himself. New works are discussed as to their political suitability as well as interest of their overall style and the choreographer's skill in presenting the theme.

MAYA PLISETSKAYA IN *DON QUIXOTE*

Longer articles examining aspects of ballet development or appreciations of a particular performer appear in theater magazines, and writers will have studies or history volumes published by Novosti, the state printing house. All of this material is subject to official scrutiny before it is printed, as are any works authorized to be printed at all. For dancers and choreographers, then, there is a considerable delay in hearing assessments of their work. For them the first reactions are from friends who have seen the performance, discussion with their coaches, and a feeling of public response from the audience. There is not the immediacy of response that Western artists are accustomed to. Success and failure are taken at a more leisurely pace, as is the general approach to the art.

Ballet did not start in Russia, though the Russian's affection for it might make one think it did. The art came to Russia from Western Europe in the eighteenth century when foreign ballet masters were engaged to conduct dancing classes for aristocrats. The Russians chose to model themselves on the French school, and as a result imported the language of ballet, which was French, as well as the technical aspects of the art.

The traditional capital of Russia was and is Moscow, but ballet flourished first in Leningrad, then known as St. Petersburg. The city was comparatively young compared to Moscow, since it was founded at the beginning of the eighteenth century by Peter I, known as "The Great." His reign of thirty-six years consisted to a great extent, of warring with his neighbors on the south, the Turks, who controlled access to the Mediterranean through the Dardanelles, and with the Swedes in the north, who commanded the Baltic Sea. Peter was much impressed by the development of Western Europe and wanted to "Westernize" Russia, so he moved the capital of the country to the new city, which is on the Baltic, and gained unrestricted access to Western Europe after defeating the Swedes. His opening to the West, St. Petersburg, became the center of trade, government and the arts. One of those arts was ballet.

Empress Anna invited Jean-Baptiste Landé to give dancing classes to the corps of cadets, sons of the ruling class, and four years after his arrival founded the St. Petersburg Ballet School in 1738. A succession of foreign teachers and choreographers were engaged, and in 1756 Catherine II ("The Great") formally organized the Imperial Theaters system. The theaters, which presented both opera and ballet, were subsidized by the monarch out of private funds, and the artistic policies of the theaters were dictated by a director appointed by the monarch. The system remains the same in the Soviet Union today, with direction and funds supplied by the Ministry of Culture.

In 1806 the theaters in Moscow were brought into the Imperial system and the two major cities were joined into one large network with frequent exchanges of performers and choreographers. It must be emphasized, however, that the preferred appointment was to St. Petersburg. To be moved from St. Petersburg to Moscow was looked upon as a demotion, whereas the reverse move was considered highly desirable. The function of the Imperial Theaters was to provide entertainment for the nobility, since they comprised the core of the audience that attended opera and ballet productions. But while they attended the presentations, the nobility had no desire to appear in them; that work was best left to the less socially placed. In Moscow the students for the Imperial school were at first recruited from an orphanage, later from the general public. In St. Petersburg the examinations for admission to the school were taken by the lower strata of society. The advantages were obvious. Students who were accepted for study received a general education in music and literature as well as formalized instruction in the art of ballet. They graduated into one of the major companies and received a guaranteed pension after twenty years' service. It was a way for aspiring parents to advance their children.

The Bolshoi Ballet

For about two centuries after it was established in 1703, the city of St. Petersburg was the capital of Russia, although the czars faithfully returned to Moscow for their coronation ceremonies. At the conclusion of World War I and the overthrow of the monarchy, Lenin moved the capital back to Moscow officially, and in the years since then the Bolshoi, which is the major resident company of Moscow, has received a disproportionate share of favor in the eyes of the government. Since the development of ballet instruction was most advanced in St. Petersburg, the Maryinsky school consistently developed a higher level of graduating students than any of the other schools in the country. Systematically, during the nineteen twenties and thirties these graduates, including Galina Ulanova, Marina Semyonova and Alexei Yermolayev, were taken into the Bolshoi to provide it with the strongest level of principal dancers. With the appearance of Maya Plisetskaya during World War II, the Bolshoi school began to graduate an exceptional level of dancer under the tutelage of Asaf Messerer as the school's chief teacher, and has continued to do so. (Messerer, incidentally, is Plisetskaya's uncle.) There is now no pressing need to "borrow" dancers from other companies, although the outstanding individual may still find himself or herself directed to join the Bolshoi, as was Ludmila Semenyaka, a Kirov dancer, when she won one of the top prizes in a domestic ballet competition. The latest example of this enforced transfer was that of Nadezhda Pavlova (no relation to the late Anna Pavlova), who was taken from her home company in the Siberian city of Perm and attached to the Bolshoi. She is a dancer of exceptional accomplishment and promise, and with her husband, Vatcheslav Gordeyev, as partner, has become one of the favorites of Moscow audiences. Like Semenyaka, she also was a prizewinner in the All-Union Contest of Ballet Artists, which is, conveniently enough, held in Moscow.

Ballet in Moscow had an on-again off-again relationship with

YKATERINA MAXIMOVA AND VLADIMIR VASILIEV
IN *THE NUTCRACKER*

the czars, having been alternately encouraged and ignored. Even without royal patronage, however, ballet continued to be presented in the theaters in Moscow—at one time even by an English producer, Michael Maddox, who relied upon foreign ballet masters to choreograph the works and to teach the pupils. Interestingly enough, the man who was to set the definitive style for the St. Petersburg school and company, Marius Petipa, began his choreographic career in Moscow. He was part of a theatrical family from Marseilles and, while on tour in Russia during the middle of the nineteenth century, was engaged by the Imperial

Theaters, where he remained to become the most influential teacher and choreographer of the century. His first major success was *Pharaoh's Daughter*, which starred an Italian Ballerina, Carolina Rosati, and brought him most favorably to the attention of the Directorate of the Imperial Theaters. Seven years later, in 1869 when Arthur Saint-Léon retired, he was promoted to be the ballet master of the Maryinsky company in St. Petersburg, where he worked until his retirement in 1903.

In Moscow he was succeeded by a string of directors, none of whom had his talent, and the quality of the company began to decline seriously until at one point it was only required to give small divertissements in opera productions. It didn't help that the more talented of the dancers and the choreographers, such as Lev Ivanov, were summoned to St. Petersburg to please the taste of their imperial patron. Since the support of the ballet was still the private prerogative of the czar, his tastes were catered to.

What Moscow continued to do was produce a number of good dancers if not choreographers, and they in turn became teachers in the school and formed the style of the company. The most famous of these were Vassili Tikhomirov and Yekaterina Geltzer, both of whom were born in 1876.

Geltzer danced at the Bolshoi for forty-one years and died in 1962, having coached a whole generation of dancers. Tikhomirov, who died in 1956, was noted for his heroic bearing which he instilled into his pupils. The social and political restlessness in Russia at the turn of the century was reflected in the artistic work of Alexander Gorsky, who became the ballet master of the Bolshoi in 1902 and staged several ballets which showed the influence of the dramatic naturalism then being forged at the Moscow Art Theater under the direction of Konstantin Stanislavsky (who, incidentally, had taken ballet instruction as a young man). There was an increase in the use of pantomime in Gorsky's productions and a general interest in experimental work that increased the realistic aspect of his ballets. It was controversial but part of the questioning going on at that time in all aspects of Russian life.

Difficulties increased and for five years, between 1906 and 1910, the Bolshoi school did not admit any new pupils; when the doors were reopened in 1911 it was on a severely limited scale. Five years later they were closed again. The national mobilization for World War I and the years of civil war following the Revolution were extremely difficult for the Bolshoi, which was only able to begin admitting pupils again in 1920. At this time all elements of the classic dance were being questioned for their relevance to the Revolution, and assorted experimental approaches were tried, since the classic ballet was associated too strongly with the deposed monarchy. In the mid-twenties the Minister of Culture, Anatoli Lunacharski, even invited Isadora Duncan to open a school in Moscow for her style of expressionist dance. When the upheaval was over, the classic ballet remained first in the hearts of the government and the theater public, which had expanded far beyond the small circle of aristocratic patrons.

A new generation of dancers and choreographers, including Asaf Messerer and Igor Moiseyev, were in the company, and the teaching staff as well as the performing company was strengthened with transfers from the Kirov Ballet in Leningrad. Yelisaveta Gerdt, the leading ballerina of the postrevolutionary Maryinsky company and a strong exponent of the teaching methods of Christian Johansson, one of the shapers of the Maryinsky style, became part of the faculty. Victor Semyonov, also a principal dancer of the Maryinsky, transferred to the Bolshoi school, where he was a leading teacher until his death during World War II. With the assistance of these teachers and the young dancers produced by Leningrad's Agrippina Vaganova, the Bolshoi began to develop into the powerful performing ensemble that it is today. Now each decade the school produces talented dancers who replace those who retire from active performing and devote themselves to private coaching work with professional dancers or to the guidance of new pupils in the school.

The Moscow Choreographic Institute, which is the official

school of the Bolshoi Ballet, has over six hundred students who are selected on the basis of a physical examination to detect any abnormalities of bone structure, and then by a short rehearsal to observe their musical sensitivity. Pupils who are admitted receive a fully subsidized course of training, which includes expenses of costuming as well, and in their senior years at the school are eligible to receive a small stipend as well as their school expenses.

When they have finished their schooling they are taken into one of the many companies and ordinarily begin as members of the corps. Progress from then on is left pretty much to the individual. While in school, every aspect of their training is supervised, but once they have joined a company they are given a great deal of responsibility to see to their own continued development.

The repertory of dances which they perform includes the classics—*Giselle, Swan Lake, Sleeping Beauty* and *The Nutcracker* —in versions which differ for the most part from those given by companies in the West. The music remains the same, more or less, but various choreographers have had a hand in shaping the productions. These ballets are full-evening works and are the rule rather than the exception in the Soviet Union. New ballets are created also, in three or four acts, and are frequently based on subjects of contemporary history or on historic themes which underline the triumphant struggles of the common man against a ruling elite. The ballets are a collaborative effort between the librettist, who frames a suitable story; the choreographer, who devises the steps to present it; and the composer, who writes the score.

Since nothing is without political significance in the Soviet Union, it is not surprising that ballets are also judged to be suitable or not suitable on the basis of their attitudes toward the "class struggle." When in doubt, choreographers stage yet another version of one of the classic nineteenth-century ballets which are "safe," or select a theme from Pushkin like *The Fountain of Bakhchisaray* since his place in the pantheon of Russian poets is also "safe." During one of its more repressive moments the government classified all domestic ballets with a letter-grading system which indicated the ballets' acceptability, and some were judged not fit to be seen on the stage. Though this degree of severity is a thing of the past, the government still exercises control over what is presented to the public at large, even by those foreign companies which are invited to perform within its borders. For reasons of its own, the Soviet Government once refused to allow American Ballet Theater to perform *Billy the Kid* and *Fall River Legend*, which dealt with American subjects—an outlaw and a celebrated murder trial—and then relented on a second visit. The whims of the czars were replaced by the caprices of the commissars.

To see what the Bolshoi looks like in action let's examine one of their major current productions, *Spartacus*. The ballet has for its subject the slave uprising in the Roman Empire (73–71 B.C.) led by the gladiator Spartacus. It is full of spectacle, heroic dancing, artlessly tuneful music, and pointedly contrasts the struggle of the slaves for freedom and the cynical power-hungry masters whom they revolt against. The story is told in straightforward manner with little psychological subtlety. The major characters are all of a piece. Thus, the leader of the revolt, Spartacus, is strong, dedicated and brave, while the Roman overlord, Crassus, is cruel, arrogant, and cowardly. Aegina, his mistress, is devoted to accumulating power by manipulative means and is morally corrupt. Phrygia, Spartacus' wife, a legitimate status, as compared to Aegina and Crassus' exploitive relationship, is loyal, compassionate and without blame in her private life.

The music by Aram Khachaturian has proved attractive to several choreographers, each of whom produced a full-evening ballet using the score more or less in full. The version which has captured the favor of the Russian public is the latest one, which was prepared a decade ago by Yuri Grigorovich, the Bolshoi's chief choreographer. The ballet opens with the conquering legions of Rome under Crassus' direction subjugating the province of Thrace. The legionnaires' massed dances are done with verve and mechanical power as they join their shields in an overlapping pattern to present a machine-like and efficient face to their enemies. They even goose-step a bit, reminding one of Hitlerian

Germany.* They return to Rome bringing many slaves from their conquest, including Spartacus and his wife Phrygia. During the ballet the major characters step forward from time to time to dance solos, while the action of the ballet is frozen but visible behind a tinted curtain. Spartacus, in chains, dances out his defiance and then melts back into the mass of the other slaves, who are all driven off to Rome by the cruel exhortations of the slave master. Phrygia and the other female captives lament with arms over their heads, and spin with their bodies held as if they were dangling from a hook. The slave state is clearly demonstrated, though Spartacus has shown his own brave discontent.

In the second scene, at the slave market, the men and women have been separated for sale and there is a great deal of confusion and despair. Phrygia moves out to dance her monologue, which shows her in a state of blind panic, running helplessly and sinking down as a slave. In the third scene the action continues after the auction at Crassus' villa, where an orgy is in progress. Many of the revelers wear suggestive goat costumes and four men make a display of Phrygia. Crassus had bought her and drags her off to one side, stirring the jealousy of Aegina, who dances seductively to attract his attention away from the shrinking Phrygia. He is caught up with her and the orgy picks up in pace with leaps and passionate embraces. For the amusement of his debauched guests, Crassus has two masked slaves brought in and stages a fight to the death between them. Since they cannot see one another, their swords pass in the air without making contact at first, like boxers testing the opposition. Crassus is visibly bored with the preliminaries and wants to see blood, his body spasms sensually and he goes to his mistress Aegina. When the fight is over and the masks removed, Spartacus sees that he has killed a fellow slave and is filled with remorse. In the final scene of the first act he is taken back to the slave quarters, where he rallies his fellow gladiators. He turns powerfully and they spin away from him as if

---

* The Soviet Union lost an estimated 20,000,000 dead in World War II, which is customarily referred to there as "The Great Patriotic War" and still stirs strong feelings.

energized by his own force. He groups them into formations and they leap spectacularly around the stage like the Roman legions who captured them. Spartacus even leaps at their heads in the same manner that Crassus did when he was conquering Thrace. They force their way out of the prison toward freedom.

In the countryside beneath an open sky, where Act II begins, shepherds are having an innocent gambol, in contrast with the orgy under Crassus' roof. The newly escaped Spartacus enters at the head of his band and encourages the shepherds to join them.

MAYA PLISETSKAYA AND VLADIMIR TIKHONOV
IN *DON QUIXOTE*

HOW TO ENJOY BALLET

A series of character dances, indicating their rustic strength and good hearts, leads into an acceptance of Spartacus' invitation. In the next scene he finds Phrygia and dances happily with her after their separation. Spartacus now wears a red leader's cloak instead of a slave's chains. It is perhaps as much an indication of his future death as it is a noble-looking robe. The lifts in this *pas de deux* are spectacular in their acrobatic energy, and in one slow passage he greets Phrygia as a free man with a gesture reminiscent of those of the slave master who tore her from him. Phrygia and Spartacus obviously respect one another in a way that Crassus and Aegina do not. Their partnership is for mutual assistance and not manipulative gain.

In the third scene the patricians enter with their women, led by Aegina, who steps forward to dance her solo, which is characterized by languorous, seductive movements. The action continues with Crassus, as he sweeps Aegina into a *pas de deux* that is dexterous and showy but with little tenderness. All of the men and women come together, Crassus waves his sword, and the others join him in a fascist salute. But the advancing army of Spartacus causes them to flee, showing how cowardly they all are despite their militaristic bluster.

In the final scene of the act Crassus has been captured and brought before Spartacus, where he is offered the chance to fight for his life. In contrast to the degrading spectacle of two masked gladiators, Spartacus takes up his own sword and faces Crassus. The latter is bested and in cowardly fashion begs for life, which Spartacus spares contemptuously.

At the start of Act III Crassus is filled with a bitter hatred and a thirst for revenge. Aegina is with him and in a long mimed passage inflames his desire for an attack on Spartacus. Suddenly he grabs up his sword and reorganizes his legions and they goosestep off. When they have left, Aegina devises a plan to subvert Spartacus' army.

In the slaves' camp Phrygia is worried, and as she dances alone she is suddenly stricken in her light and airy movements with an invisible blow and reacts like a wounded bird. She is worried and Spartacus has been warned that Crassus and his army are approaching. He dances with her again trying to comfort her, and lifts her high above his head as he did when they were first reunited. He must, however, speak to his commanders and show them his plan of attack for defeating Crassus. It is daring and relies on their solidarity.

Aegina has stolen into the slave camp, however, with her own plan to undermine his. In the meanwhile, Spartacus, as he had done in prison when first leading them to revolt, tries to inspire them with his own formidable energy. They spin around him but there is something lacking in their commitment. He leads them off to do battle and Aegina enters with a band of women to seduce the slaves. Their sensual dance entrances many of the soldiers to desert the slave army for private pleasure. Crassus takes them by surprise and captures the betrayed slaves. He sees what Aegina has done for him and orders that she be borne off on one of the legion's standards.

Crassus now stands aside and dances a solo calling for vengeance, as he senses his imminent triumph. The battle scene between the two armies fills the stage with struggling masses of men swooping back and forth. The tide turns against the slaves and Spartacus chooses to die rather than surrender. He struggles on despite his wounds. Finally Crassus orders him killed but is not man enough to do it himself, though he raises his leader's baton in triumph. Spartacus is raised on their spears and Phrygia grieves over his body, which is draped in the symbolic red cloth. Together they suggest Michelangelo's "Pietà."

The ballet is a spectacle full of resounding action punctuated with individual encounters between the principals. The moral of the story is simple enough: heroism alone is not sufficient in the face of the rulers; co-operative action is necessary for a true victory of the oppressed. The actions of the patrician Crassus and his mistress Aegina are carefully designed to show that their victory is self-seeking and achieved by underhanded means, while Spartacus and Phrygia have mutual respect for one another and the interest of the oppressed at heart. The costuming is designed with historical accuracy, as are the settings for the individual scenes. The choreography combines mimed gestures such as the goose step and the fascist salute to characterize the actions of the evil-hearted, while a more expressionistic gesture is used between the hero and his companion. In the group dances a mechanical coolness in the movement of the Roman legionnaires is contrasted with the bounding bucolic gestures of the shepherds and the slaves when they are escaping from their captors.

In the various duets between the principals the soaring, almost acrobatic lifts of the Bolshoi school are seen to spectacular effect. It is a style which is cast in the heroic mold and given maximum impact by the emotional and dramatic intensity of the dancers. There are few subtleties in the presentation of the story or in the relationships between the individuals. Slaves are shown in chains, and masters in armor strut over their conquered foes. The lack of subtlety in developing such ballets gives them an old-fashioned flavor that suggests melodrama more than contemporary staging, with its awareness of the psychological complexities of motivation. The dictates of the Soviet system require that ambiguity be avoided in favor of direct purposeful expression so as to speak to the widest possible audience without misunderstanding. The ballet must, in its way, contribute to the achievement of governmental artistic and educational aims and not exist in a cultural vacuum. It must be relevant to the achievement of an ideal state in which the exploitiveness of the master-slave relationship will be banished.

These political necessities are felt and seen most clearly in the newer ballets. During the height of political fervor between the two world wars, choreographers were creating ballets about life on collective farms and similar intractable subjects, but they also skewed the direction of the revived classics to conform with political thinking. Thus the tragic *Swan Lake*, as re-created by the Bolshoi in some versions, introduced the proletarian figure of the wise Jester to comment on the action of the aristocrats, and indeed appended a happy ending to the story with the rescued Swan Queen, hand in hand with her hero, stepping into a glorious sunrise after the evil magician has had his come-uppance. Though not so violently mishandled, even the heroine Giselle, of that romantically perfect ballet, was shown to be the victim of a calculating aristocrat who exploited her innocence for his own selfish ends. While the newer Bolshoi choreographers are not as consistently heavy-handed in their treatment of thematic material, they are still conscious of the necessity to remain within certain guidelines of what is acceptable and unacceptable in a socialist state that controls every aspect of cultural life.

That control extends, of course, to the physical well-being of the dancers, where it is benign. The students of the Moscow Choreographic Institute are educated in a special group of buildings on the Moscow River, where they attend carefully supervised courses in the humanities comprising history, languages and literature, and the sciences, in addition to their work in ballet classes. They are exposed to art and they are encouraged to develop musical skill as part of their education. Great care is taken with the students. During World War II the school and its pupils were moved for safety to the town of Vasilsursk. During the war its work continued (Maya Plisetskaya, its leading ballerina, was graduated at that time).

The Bolshoi Theater, which seats about 2,000, is the home of the ballet company and where at least half of the company is in residence. The other half tours the major cities of the Soviet Union or makes appearances abroad. Since there are 300 active members of the company, there is no need to keep them all in Moscow all of the time. In addition to the Bolshoi Theater, the company also performs in the huge 6,000-seat Palace of Congresses, a newer building in Moscow.

Attached to the Bolshoi Theater is a five-story scenery and costume loft, which employs 2,500 people from shoemakers to costume designers and scene painters. This staff, which is also part of the government payroll, tends to the special needs of the company for all of its productions, from the manufacture of leotards to the creation of wigs.

Contrary to American practice where principal dancers perform several times a week during the regular seasons, the leading dancers in the Bolshoi appear infrequently—at most a half-dozen times a month, frequently less. The active repertory of dances to be performed is smaller, less than half the number maintained by

VLADIMIR VASILIEV AND YKATERINA MAXIMOVA
IN *THE NUTCRACKER*

major American companies, and the leading dancers work on perfecting perhaps a dozen roles. This concentration on a limited number of ballets in the course of a season enables the Bolshoi to add a richness of background texture to their productions which is ordinarily not seen in American companies that do many of the same classic ballets, like *Swan Lake, Sleeping Beauty* and *Giselle*. The crowd scenes, as they are set by the company's regisseur, contain many bits of individual miming passages that, in and of themselves, are slight but richly decorate the production and give it fullness.

Progress in the company from the corps to solo and principal status tends to be slow, and dancers tend to make the most out of the smaller roles which they occupy for years before being offered the chance to do the larger ones. This also contributes to the elaborate finish of these productions. The whole pace of the system is deliberate and is based on the concept of long-term evolvement rather than a spectacular rise to the top. The latter, of course, can happen, but it is the exception rather than the rule. The student enters the school with the full expectation of rising as quickly as talent and the system permits, and then being assured of a pension when his active dancing days are over. His skill is rewarded, as is that of others in entirely different fields, according to a fixed scale. Even Galina Ulanova, now retired but still active as a coach, who was the finest ballerina of the Soviet School, spoke as modestly as any blue-collar hand about fulfilling her work "norms."

The Kirov Ballet

The city of St. Petersburg did not evolve from reasons of economic necessity, as have major cities traditionally. It was the result of an imperial ukase resulting from a trip throughout Western Europe taken by Peter I in the late seventeenth century. When he returned from the trip he was resolved to bring Western trade and technology into his country to modernize it. For that he needed sea access to the West and decided that a new city built on the Baltic would be the answer. He invited Italian architects to design the city and it emerged with some of the qualities of a northern Venice, a city to which it has been compared because of its system of waterways and canals.

As it prospered it attracted an artistic class to serve the court, which was highly conscious of French culture above all others in Western Europe. French became the preferred language of aristocracy, and French ballet masters were the most frequently hired for teaching in the newly established school of ballet. Some of these masters remained in Russia for many years while acquiring only the most rudimentary knowledge of the Russian language, and yet they were able to function perfectly well. The limits of the society that supported and patronized the art were so narrow that nearly everyone they met was conversant in French.

In addition, all of the pupils they instructed had to learn enough French so that they could understand the various technical terms for the steps. Ballet had received the patronage of the French Court especially under the enthusiastic involvement of Louis XIV. Since the French thought so highly of it, the Rus-

IRINA KOLPAKOVA AND VLADILEN SEMYONOV
IN *THE NUTCRACKER*

ALLA SIZOVA IN *THE NUTCRACKER*

sians adopted it enthusiastically, and for nearly two centuries hired foreign ballet masters from Western Europe to be their artistic directors. Not all of them were French. Some of the most important ballet masters of the time from other countries presided over the ballet in St. Petersburg, among them the Austrian Franz Hilverding and the Italian Gasparo Angiolini. They also were part of the line that included Charles-Louis Didelot, Jules Perrot (*Giselle*), Arthur Saint-Léon (*Coppélia*), and Marius Petipa (*Swan Lake, Sleeping Beauty*). Petipa was the longest in point of service of all of these, and set his mark indelibly on the Maryinsky.

He first came to Russia in 1847 as a dancer and was noted for his skill at character delineation. He demonstrated ability at arranging divertissements and at creating spectacles that were extremely pleasing to the aristocratic audiences. He had an exceptional talent for bringing out the best in his dancers and creating for them roles that would display their strengths and conceal their technical weaknesses. He had the ability to work quickly to complete a ballet and also proved adept in reading the political winds in court circles.

He had the administrative acumen to organize the immense apparatus of the Imperial Theater and School and surrounded himself with a talented staff that included a brilliant Swedish teacher, Christian Johansson, who had been a pupil of August Bournonville, the shaper of the Royal Danish Ballet. Within Russia he elevated the native-born Lev Ivanov to be his assistant ballet master; Ivanov assisted in the creation of *Swan Lake* and *Sleeping Beauty* and choreographed *The Nutcracker* entirely. From Italy he engaged Enrico Cecchetti as a virtuoso dancer and teacher. The Imperial School system had as yet to produce the top-ranking virtuoso dancers that Petipa wanted for his major compositions, and he regularly engaged lead dancers like Cecchetti from abroad to appear with the Maryinsky. Among other famous Italian dancers were Virginia Zucchi and Pierina Legnani, whose legacy to us today is the series of thirty-two whipping turns (*fouettés*) in the Black Swan *pas de deux* which she introduced into the part.

Petipa strove to move his dancers as close to photographic perfection in the steps of the ballet repertory as he could. For him the deployment of the human form in harmonious arrangements of the legs, trunk and expressive arms was the ideal and he was greatly aided by his teaching staff, especially Johansson. The latter remained as an instructor until close to his ninetieth birthday and put extraordinary demands on his pupils for ever greater virtuosity. By the late nineteenth century a generation of Russian dancers had assimilated all that the West had to offer and were ready to show the West what they had made of the fledgling art form they had nurtured for two centuries. In a flood, talented dancers emerged from the Maryinsky school, including Nicolai Legat, Anna Pavlova, Mikhail Fokine, Tamara Karsavina, Mathilde Kchessinska, Adolph Bolm, Olga Preobrajenska, Vaslav Nijinsky and others. Petipa's hold on the Imperial Theater in St.

Petersburg was firm. He knew the taste of the court with regard to spectacle and always saw to it that there was a sufficient number of individual variations for his better dancers to keep his company and its audience contented. His task at times was complicated by extraneous matters such as the fact that Kchessinska had been Nicholas II's mistress and her wishes had to be considered. It was she, however, who as much as anyone else, broke the reign of the foreign ballerina in the Maryinsky when she became the first totally Russian-born and -trained dancer to match the technical feats of the imported stars.

With the variety of things plaguing him in his position, however, Petipa always asserted the supremacy of the classic dance in his productions and did not find himself, as a choreographer, diverted into dramatic or gymnastic gestures at the expense of the classical school of dancing. He organized his ballets according to a set pattern in which there would always be a climactic *pas de deux* between the male and female principals of the ballet, preceded by character dances of fairy-tale figures or visitors from exotic places. In the course of the ballet there were group dances among the attendants of the principals or the villagers who formed a background to the action of the ballet.

The subject matter of these ballets, of which he created over sixty, ranged from ancient Egypt to the never-never land of Cinderella, but tended to have a positive resolution. He himself wrote many of the libretti that formed the basic core of the ballets, and without fail he wrote detailed instructions to his composers. These instructions were precise down to the number of bars he wanted, the character of the music in terms of menace, joy, etc., and a suggestion as to the rhythmic measure of the section—$\frac{2}{4}$ or waltz, for example. It was a practice he followed with all the composers he worked with, from docile court musicians like Ludwig Minkus to an international figure like Tchaikovsky. The following is an example of his instructions to Tchaikovsky for the music to accompany the injury that sends Princess Aurora into an enchanted sleep of one hundred years in *The Sleeping Beauty*. "Suddenly Aurora notices the old woman who beats on her knitting needles a $\frac{2}{4}$ measure. Gradually she

ALLA OSIPENKO AND YURI SOLOVIEV IN *LE CORSAIRE*

changes to a very melodious waltz in ¾ but then suddenly a rest. Aurora pricks her finger. Screams, pain. Blood streams—give 8 measures in ⁴⁄₄ wide. She begins her dance—dizziness. . . . Complete horror—this is not a dance any longer. It is frenzy. As if bitten by a tarantula, she keeps turning and then falls unexpectedly, out of breath. This must last for 24 to 32 measures. At the end there should be a tremolo of a few measures, as if shouts of pain and sobs: 'Father, Mother'!"

One would think that this was unneccessarily restrictive to a composer of Tchaikovsky's stature, but *The Sleeping Beauty* has proven to be one of the finest ballets of the Maryinsky tradition and one of Tchaikovsky's finest scores. Ironically, after the first performance of the ballet when the composer was presented to the czar, the latter remarked noncommittally that it was "very nice." Tchaikovsky wrote only one more ballet score for Petipa, and that was done under the same restrictions. It was *The Nutcracker*. Before he could choreograph the ballet, however, Petipa fell ill and entrusted it to his assistant, Lev Ivanov, who worked with the libretto as outlined by Petipa and the music composed specifically for it by Tchaikovsky. It has endured both as an orchestral suite and in hundreds of productions of the ballet itself. *Swan Lake* was commissioned by the Bolshoi Ballet and first performed in 1877 and again in the 1880s, but was not successful until Petipa presented his vision of that score in 1895 with the substantial assistance of Ivanov.

These three scores are the only ones that Tchaikovsky wrote specifically for ballet, and yet their rhythmic inventiveness, colorful melodies and unified style of composition express the best of nineteenth-century ballet. Tchaikovsky worked to a formula, but in it found a way to greatness. It was not always the case with the composers who worked for the Imperial Theaters. Most of them were skilled at composing tuneful swatches of music that would then be put together by Petipa as he saw fit. The music was regarded as being of distinctly second importance, as was most every other element in the production with the exception of the dances. It was the custom to mix time periods in wildly improbable juxtapositions as well as styles of clothing and decor. There was no feeling that a production must be consistent in terms of time or setting. It was important to have so many dances for soloists, so many mass-spectacle dances, and a major *pas de deux* for the ballerina and her partner, and it didn't really matter if logic was stretched to achieve these ends.

Bits of music would be excerpted from one ballet and inserted into another, a particularly successful *pas de deux* or solo could find its way into another ballet, and costumes were sure to be flattering to the leading dancers even if it meant violating the historical setting. Ancient Greece could be suggested by the same costume that served for Egypt, except that one would have a lotus flower and the other a Grecian ornament. In some ways it was like the Elizabethan theater, where an actor wore his best clothes no matter what role he was playing, and settings were indicated by rudimentary stage props. As the Elizabethan accent was on the word play, so in Petipa's theater the emphasis was on dancing. Everything else was subordinated to it. The perfection of his dancers' technique was unmatched anywhere in the world. They had the finish of the French school and the vivacity of the Italian virtuoso approach interpreted in a uniquely Russian manner. Commentators refer to its "singing" quality, and the great Russian poet Pushkin characterized it as "soul-inspired flight." It was Petipa's legacy to his adopted land.

The final days of the master were spent in enforced retirement from 1903 till his death in 1910. He moved to the south of Russia and lived on his pension in the warmth of the Crimean sun. The restlessness that touched all parts of Russian life was felt very strongly in the Maryinsky as well in the years preceding the outbreak of World War I. Mikhail Fokine, one of the brilliant products of the school, began choreographing short works in which he called for a more cohesive approach to producing ballets. He wanted only dances that were appropriate to the epoch in which the ballet was set and wished to do away with the custom of introducing a character variation of another era just for the sake of the dance itself. He wanted costuming to reflect the historical actuality of the period in which the ballet took place and wanted to do away with the hand and arm, standardized mime passages of the "Me Prince–You Beautiful–We Marry!" variety in favor of more naturally evolved gestures using the whole body. He wanted to produce ballets that had a unified conception in all their aspects. Increasingly he found himself in conflict with the wishes of the directors of the Imperial Theater.

The discontent was generally prevalent, and in 1905 the dancers presented a petition demanding reforms and called a strike. They wanted to have more control over their performing

IRINA KOLPAKOVA AND VLADILEN SEMYONOV
IN *THE NUTCRACKER*

lives than the directors were willing to allow them. They even
wanted to recall Petipa from retirement to lead the company
once again. The insurrection was broken, but the restrictive artistic policies of the Imperial Theater had been challenged seriously
for the first time. In later years nearly all of the concerned
dancers, including the choreographer Fokine, left Russia to pursue careers in Western Europe or in the United States.

A group of artists and musicians, including Alexander Benois,
Léon Bakst, and Serge Diaghilev, interested themselves exceed-
ingly in the life of the Maryinsky and were increasingly involved

165

in various productions. Diaghilev soon emerged as the gifted organizer of the group and presented art, music, opera and ballet productions in Paris celebrating Russian achievement. These were well received, particularly the seasons of ballet which started in 1909. The presentations continued in succeeding years during the summer months when the dancers were on their official vacations from the Imperial theaters and eventually led to the formation of Diaghilev's Ballets Russes company, which had as its leading dancers Pavlova, Fokine, Nijinsky and Karsavina, among others. It brought back to the West the art of ballet as it had not been seen for over fifty years since the decline of the Paris Opera Ballet. Diaghilev felt that the old formula of full-evening ballets was no longer productive and introduced the evening of short ballets, which is today the rule rather than the exception that it was then.

VLADILEN SEMYONOV IN *THE NUTCRACKER*

With the success of the 1917 Revolution the Imperial theaters were shut for a time but opened again on a limited scale. A whole generation of dancers had left Russia, but an inspired teacher, Agrippina Vaganova, maintained the teaching traditions while actively developing her own approach, and in 1925 graduated Marina Semyonova, widely regarded as the first Soviet prima ballerina. As in Moscow, the existence of the classic ballet was challenged by other forms of experimental dance which claimed to be more relevant to the new emerging society. Despite this buffeting, the tradition won out and the company was reformed. While the instructional methods were modified somewhat, the largest change occurred in the subject matter of the ballets. These were frequently topical, such as *The Red Whirlwind* and *Partisan Days*, or satirical thrusts at prerevolutionary society, including a historical look at the French Revolution in *The Flames of Paris*.

In addition to new works, the traditional *Swan Lake* and *The Sleeping Beauty* were remounted with more or less fidelity to the Petipa original. The most artistically renowned production of the period was *Romeo and Juliet*, which had a distinguished score by Prokofiev and was choreographed by Leonid Lavrovsky. Despite the transfer of gifted dancers and teachers to Moscow, the Kirov Ballet and school continued at an exceptionally high level and produced dancers of equal stature to replace those who were lost. Among the most celebrated teachers was the late Alexander Pushkin, who was known especially for his skill in instructing male dancers. Among his pupils were Valery Panov, Rudolf Nureyev, and Mikhail Baryshnikov, all of whom were featured soloists in the Kirov Ballet before leaving the Soviet Union.

Despite the many changes which have been instituted since the Revolution in the proper subject matter for ballet, the productions which present the Kirov Ballet at its clearest are those traditional ones which have been passed down and date to Petipa's day. One of the finest of these is Act IV of *La Bayadère*, which is set in the underground Kingdom of the Shades. A version of it was mounted for England's Royal Ballet by Rudolf Nureyev, and another slightly different version was staged for American

HOW TO ENJOY BALLET

Ballet Theater by Natalia Makarova. Makarova, like Nureyev a product of the Kirov school and company, also chose to live and perform in the West. When the Kirov company made its first tour of the United States, in 1961, it brought with it Act IV of *La Bayadère*.

The ballet in its full production of four acts is set in India, where a young dancing girl (the *bayadère*), Nikia, is pursued by one of the temple priests but is in love with the warrior Solor. He has just killed a tiger, which he sends as a gift to the raja of the district while he goes to the temple to see his beloved Nikia. He swears his troth to her, but they are overheard by the priest. In the second act the raja is so pleased with the gift that he offers his daughter Gamsatti in marriage to Solor. The latter is overwhelmed by the honor and agrees, despite his previous vow to Nikia. The rivals face one another angrily and Nikia attempts to stab Gamsatti, but is restrained.

The wedding in Act III finds Nikia ordered to dance with the other *bayadères* in honor of the occasion, but a servant of Gamsatti's passes her a basket of flowers which contains a poisonous snake. During the dance she is bitten and the priest offers to save her life if she will renounce Solor and be his. Unlike Solor, she will not deny her vow, not even to save her own life and dances until she expires from the venomous bite—faithful unto death.

This portion of the ballet (Act IV) tells its story strictly in dance without any special decor or costuming. The women's costumes are white, as is that of Solor, the only male in the piece. The setting is a darkly draped empty space with a long ramp running down to the left of the stage at the rear. A simple melody is played repeatedly as the members of the corps de ballet step onto the top of the ramp and proceed downward at a measured pace. At first there is a single dancer who takes three steps forward with the side of her body toward the audience, stretches an arm outward and extends one leg behind her and bends forward tilting herself to the floor before standing to bend backward and then proceed to repeat the same sequence of steps. As she does so, the simple melody continues and a second woman appears at the head of the ramp to replicate the movements of the first. One after another the women continue to appear at the head of the ramp and proceed in the same slow and exquisite manner to descend to the stage level. There the lead dancer continues the variation while leading a file of dancers across the stage to the right. When she reaches the opposite side of the stage, she turns and leads the file back to the left side while continuing to repeat the same steps.

The stage is dense with dancers and still they descend the ramp at the rear, but now the simple repetition of the variation takes on a richly complex look as the dancers give the impression of fluttering lines crossing and recrossing one rank behind the other. The demands on the dancers are extraordinary and require a company of unusual strength to perform this entrance with the stillness of balance and perfection of line that it needs for com-

ALLA OSIPENKO AND SERGE VIKULOV IN *LA BAYADÈRE*

plete satisfaction. As the procession continues, the once empty stage is totally filled with these quietly moving figures whose low bends suggest a certain docile sadness as befits the underworld and whose demeanor shows them to be resigned to their fates. They live in a world beyond passions, a pale zone where they pass back and forth without human anxieties.

When the last member of the corps de ballet has reached the stage, the group lines up in columns facing the audience and together perform a variation that features an extended balance on one leg just before concluding. The group melts away toward the sides of the stage, where they form two long vertical files to frame the space for the entrance of the soloists. It is a piece of virtuoso dancing for a large group of dancers. The number ranges from twenty-eight to thirty-six, depending on stage and other conditions. However, since the music can be repeated as often as is necessary, the effect is the same. This is timeless, classic dance, serene and sure of its conventions, confident of the beauty of the disciplined human body, drawing richness from the most economical means.

Though the corps will not occupy the whole of one's attention as the ballet progresses, it exists as a frame and an echo for the dances of the three principal shades and the *pas de deux* of Solor and Nikia. The solo variations tell us a bit about each of the individuals, but they are muted, not vivid as they would be in another setting. When Solor enters he rushes with a verve that none of the others possess, and stops when he catches sight of Nikia behind a transparent screen at the rear of the stage. He runs off to find her and together they perform one of their most beautiful dances. Using a long scarf, each one holds onto one end, he appearing to pull her to life as he tugs sympathetically on his end. The climax of the ballet occurs with the corps spread in a wide semicircle around the principals, focusing all attention upon them. Solor, despite his betrayal of trust in the world of the living, has descended to the Kingdom of the Shades, if only in a dream, to reclaim his love.

The term *ballets blancs* is used to designate works like this one, which are demonstrations of dancing in which the mood or action is advanced purely through combinations of steps prepared by the ballet master and do not rely for their effect on mimed or dramatic action, to advance the story line. It is nineteenth-century ballet at its purest, and this example is from the hand of Petipa, the greatest master of his time.

The legacy of Petipa belongs to the whole world of ballet, for he set his own individual mark on the way that subsequent generations conceive of ballet perfection. But in a very real sense he is the Kirov's special guiding force. The classic dance in its highest manifestations tends to the clarity of expressive movement that Petipa held out as his personal ideal, in much the same way that poetry is considered the highest form of verbal language. It condenses and strips away incidentals to present the heart of the experience, and it resists "dating" in the way that highly topical ballets do.

The Kirov does its share of ideologically correct and suitable ballets, none of which will be more than a footnote in fifty years' time, but the shape of the human body as extended by Petipa endures through those ballets in which he first demonstrated its possibilities. His school gave Pavlova and Nijinsky their training and produced choreographers like Fokine and Balanchine, both of whom appeared in his productions.

The city that Peter I created to bring Western Europe to Russia has, since the turn of the century, returned the art of ballet to the West, where it came from but where it had fallen on ill days. The first wave of dancers and choreographers who left Russia were fleeing the unbending artistic ways of the czar before the Revolution, and the second wave fled to avoid the unbending ways of the new political ministers spawned by the Revolution. They settled in the West and created the ballet expansion that has seen the establishment of national companies in nations which had forgotten ballet, and in others which had scarcely known it before.

ENGLAND

The Royal Ballet

Two names dominate the history of the Royal Ballet: Ninette de Valois, the iron-willed visionary who established its basic structure; and Frederick Ashton, who formed its style, a style that stresses lyricism, neatness, and a feeling for dramatic nuance. His ballets have been the backbone of the company since it was first established in 1931 and display a range that includes the bucolic and sensuously abstract. With the emergence of Ashton as a choreographer, the company began to shape its own future while drawing upon the Russian school as background.

Ashton was born to English parents living in Guayaquil, Ecuador, and saw England briefly as a child of two when he was taken there on a visit. His family moved to Lima, Peru, where he grew up with Spanish, as much his native language as English. His education was conventional for the time and did not include ballet. Although he fell under the spell of Anna Pavlova when she toured Lima in 1917, he was unable to begin any formal study of dance until much later. Ironically, one of his brothers an excellent social dancer, was invited by Pavlova to join her company, but he refused instantly. Ashton was returned to England to attend public (i.e., private) school and finish his education. The other little boys found his Spanish accent peculiar, and Ashton hated school.

He participated in dramatics and went to the theater in London as often as possible, but had as yet to take a single lesson in ballet. He was not inclined toward diplomacy or business, both of which his father had entered, or higher education, but after his father died he was faced with the necessity of earning a living. His facility with Spanish and French enabled him to work in an export-import firm as a translator. In 1921, at the advanced (for ballet) age of eighteen, he had his first lessons—from Léonide Massine. Massine had been a choreographer with the Diaghilev company and had made an independent career for himself as performer, teacher, and choreographer. Ashton progressed from a single lesson each week to daily lessons with Massine, and also studied with Marie Rambert. She, too, had worked with the Diaghilev company and was now resident in London, as were others who had participated in the various seasons of the Diaghilev company. Ashton studied with several of them as well and arrived at a point where he could begin to function as a dancer, though on a limited scale. He accepted various engagements in music hall and movie theater shows that were given along with the regular features. In 1926 Rambert gave him his first opportunity to choreograph. The ballet, *A Tragedy of Fashion*, was incorporated in a large revue where it was seen by De Valois, who congratulated Ashton on it. For the next several years he arranged one ballet after another, and in 1928 was taken into a company directed by Bronislava Nijinska (Nijinsky's sister) that was resident in Paris. The training and the opportunity to perform were invaluable and a welcome change from the sporadic hit-or-miss productions he had appeared in in London. After a year he returned to work on the incidental dances to a production that Ashley Dukes (Rambert's husband) was preparing, and then to appear with a group of other dancers from Rambert's school in a program of ballets.

Diaghilev's death and the disbanding of his company stirred the scattered world of British ballet into organizing itself. The desire, to emulate what Diaghilev had begun, had, some years previously, resulted in the founding of The Ballet Rambert, which now accelerated its presentations under the name of The Ballet Club. At about the same time, in 1926, De Valois opened her studio-school, The Academy of Choreographic Art, and had started to design ballets for dramatic productions and concert appearances. She began now to teach movement to actors at the Old Vic. By 1931, Lilian Baylis, artistic director of the Old Vic, acquired a newly refurbished theater, Sadler's Wells, and invited De Valois to move her school there.

There were, at the time, a dramatic unit and an opera company operating, and to them was added the Vic-Sadler's Wells Opera Ballet, soon to be known as the Vic-Wells Ballet. De Valois provided divertissements in the operas, designed movement sequences for plays, and choreographed ballets for her own company to perform. The members of the company alternated between the two theaters, and she invited Ashton to create a new work for her company. The association continued steadily until Ashton's retirement as artistic director of the Royal Ballet in 1970.

At the time Ashton created *Regatta* for the Vic-Wells Ballet he had been working for five years and had started to assert his own distinctive creative voice. De Valois had also choreographed a number of ballets but had taken on the additional task of organizing a school and a company. She continued to create ballets for twenty years more, but at a diminishing rate as Ashton blossomed and the administrative side of the ballet began to occupy more and more of her time. She had trained herself for the latter task by studying the Diaghilev company firsthand as a member of it.

Edris Stannus was born in 1898 in Ireland and became Ninette de Valois at her mother's insistence when she appeared onstage. After early lessons in Ireland, she studied with Cecchetti and Espinosa in London, and at the age of sixteen became a dancer in annual pantomimes as well as a performer in music halls and revues. She also danced in the opera ballets at Covent Garden. At about the time that Ashton was taking his first ballet lessons from Massine, she was a member of his small company, and in 1923 was accepted by the Diaghilev company. She remained with it a little over two and a half years, which were among the most instructive and formative of her life. Despite the prestige of being a member of the most famous ballet troupe in Europe, she resigned from it to start her own school and small company. The Academy of Choreographic Art was a grand name for her school, but she wanted to indicate its seriousness and to distinguish it from being just another dance studio.

Teaching in the studio and at the Old Vic became a way of life that provided her the modest income to develop a company.

MARGOT FONTEYN AND RUDOLF NUREYEV IN
SWAN LAKE

She collaborated with William Butler Yeats at the Abbey Theater in staging several of his dance dramas, and also helped to organize a ballet school there. She did almost everything herself, from the most routine administrative task to the complicated business of designing a new ballet and preparing it for the stage. Her talent as a choreographer lay in her ability to sculpt harmonious and flowing tableaus, but her genius lay in her ability to organize people and institutions. "As serious as God and as touchy as hell," was the comment of a contemporary.

As a country without a strong ballet tradition, England had to start virtually from scratch. The Russian teachers came to England by way of the Diaghilev company, and so did many of the dancers in the early years. Tamara Karsavina, Lydia Lopokova, Stanislas Idzikowsky, Leon Woizikovsky, and of course Massine, who restaged his ballets, and the régisseur (rehearsal director) Nicholas Sergeyev, who mounted the Maryinsky versions of several classic full-evening ballets for various companies. There were developing English dancers and also several English stars who had toured and matured with the Diaghilev ballet. Among the best-known of these were Alicia Markova (Alice Marks) and Anton Dolin (Patrick Kay). Among the young English dancers who made their appearances in the early thirties was Margot Fonteyn (Peggy Hookham), who, like Markova and Dolin, had studied with Serafina Astafieva. The latter was a graduate of the Maryinsky school and company and left Diaghilev to found a school in London in 1911. In forming her own school and company, De Valois used and drew upon the skill of the Russian and Russian-trained dancers, but consistently sought a native English choreographer to be the chief artistic voice of her company.

The third important creative influence on the formation of the company that was to become the Royal Ballet was Constant Lambert, a composer and conductor who had created a ballet (*Romeo and Juliet*) for Diaghilev and who was to provide several scores for both Ashton and De Valois. In addition to writing ballet scores, Lambert conducted the first performance of the new company in 1931 and remained as its chief conductor and musical coach for twenty years until his death. Although he composed more frequently in his earlier years with the company, he contributed a score for Ashton in the year of his death. De Valois wanted a first-rate choreographer for her company, and she also wanted a first-rate musical director. When she had them, it was simply a matter of educating the public as to the worth of the developing organization.

It was her intention to create new ballets and also to mount distinguished and historically accurate productions of the great nineteenth-century classics. Her connection with the productions of the Maryinsky was Sergeyev, who had been a régisseur in Russia and was familiar with Stepanov notation. This was a written method of recording choreography developed at the end of the nineteenth century by Vladimir Stepanov, who died tragically young in 1896 at the age of thirty. With the aid of the choreographic notebooks he carried with him out of Russia, Sergeyev was in a position to mount these traditional productions for Western ballet companies. In 1933, De Valois asked him to produce *Coppélia* for the Vic-Wells company, and was so pleased with the results that she asked for productions of *Giselle*, and *The Nutcracker* and *Swan Lake* over the next several seasons. Just prior to the outbreak of World War II in 1939, she had him set *The Sleeping Beauty*, so that the company would have a full complement of the classics, which De Valois felt was necessary to form the dancers in the great tradition. It is a policy from which the company has not deviated.

Another dancer from abroad who played a part in the company's development was Adeline Genée, a product of the Danish school who had a substantial world reputation in the early part of the century. She had danced extensively with companies on the Continent, including the Royal Danish Ballet, and had also appeared on music hall and variety bills prior to the outbreak of World War I. Born in 1878, she made her stage debut in 1888 and retired as an active performer in 1917. She continued, however, to maintain an interest in, and active participation in, the world of ballet.

Another result of Diaghilev's death and the dissolution of his company was the formation of the Camargo Society in London,

RUDOLF NUREYEV AND MERLE PARK
IN *LA FILLE MAL GARDÉE*

named for Marie Camargo, a brilliant dancer of the eighteenth century who shortened the traditional woman's skirt so as to make possible the execution of rapid virtuosic steps. The Camargo Society was organized by dance writers and historians who had no desire to create a ballet company but wished to assist in the creation of ballets and to keep ballet before the public as a living, developing entity, since the Diaghilev company would no longer be doing so. They became a producing organization and on their first evening of ballets, which was performed by members of both the Rambert and De Valois companies, Genée mounted the ballet which embodied the whole Romantic movement in dance. It was the *Ballet of the Nuns* from Meyerbeer's opera *Robert le Diable*. The ballet was created by Filippo Taglioni and the lead role was danced by his daughter Marie, who made an enormous impression in it. Some idea of its impact can be seen in the Degas painting of a production he witnessed forty years later. The ghostly figures of the nuns in their long shrouds have risen from their tombs and are inhabiting a dark vaulted passage. On the same program the dancer-teacher from the Maryinsky, Nicolai Legat, mounted a *pas de deux* which De Valois and Dolin danced. De Valois presented her *Danse Sacrée et Danse Profane* with her company, and Ashton presented his warmly praised *Pomona*. The program celebrated both the past and the present and was an auspicious step for the Camargo Society. The group continued in existence for the next four years, giving encouragement and financial support to the creators of English ballet. Its finances, while precarious, were skillfully managed by John Maynard Keynes, the economist, who was married to Lydia Lopokova and was a firm supporter of the organization.

Adeline Genée, in addition to her efforts at reconstruction, was also the president of the London Association of Operatic Dancing, which later became the Royal Academy of Dancing and is presently headed by Margot Fonteyn. Genée arranged for a selection of English dancers, including the corps from De Valois' company to travel to Copenhagen and give a series of performances there at the Royal Opera House. The high point of the trip was a joint performance with the Royal Danish Ballet in a gala for the King's birthday celebration. At the final performance of the tour, Genée herself appeared with Dolin in a dance tableau, *The Love Song*. The trip was a strong morale booster for the dancers, as foreign touring has traditionally been.

The company also had a young dancer named Antony Tudor, who was to make a strong showing as a choreographer of dramatic ballets. Sergeyev's work with the company was to add the classics to its repertory, as Ashton was contributing those ballets which would become its special heritage. In 1935 Ashton re-mounted *Façade*, a selection of small sketches without any connecting story. The music was first written by William Walton to be played as Edith Sitwell declaimed her poems. These poems played outrageously with language and baroque imagery, and Walton's witty score for small orchestra accompanied them perfectly.

The ballet was commissioned by the Camargo Society in 1931, and for this occasion it was refurbished somewhat; later, Ashton added new episodes, among which is "The Foxtrot" for two couples, the men in Harold Lloyd glasses and baggy trousers, with twenties-clinging dresses for the women. "The Polka" was and is a jaunty flippant solo, and "The Waltz" is played with the vacant expressions and programed movements of a quartet of debutantes. In the "Tango Pasodoble" a gigolo who is hired to teach a young lady to dance, instead makes outrageous passes at her. The part was taken by Ashton himself. "The Popular Song" was a distillation of the two-man dance comedy team that was featured in variety houses all over the world. They are negligently accomplished and go through their pat routine with perfectly straight and slightly bored faces. The ballet was well received when it was first seen and has continued to be, with the dozen or so companies that have presented all or part of it.

Ashton also revived his *Rio Grande* and created *Le Baiser de la Fée*, while De Valois created *The Rake's Progress*, a series of danced episodes based on the Hogarth illustrations for the story of a libertine's descent into madness. In these years Ashton worked with popular revues and operettas, as well as with the Vic-Wells Ballet and consistently produced a stream of good ballets. Another of his most popular productions dates from this time, *Les Patineurs*, with music selected and arranged by Lambert from two of Meyerbeer's operas. The ballet, again, is a series of incidents without a story. The episodes are all related in that they take place on a skating pond where an assortment of people have assembled for relaxation and exercise. There is a flashy young man who performs a whirlwind of leaps and turns, and a steady no-nonsense pair of young women who travel in tandem

LYNN SEYMOUR IN *ROMEO AND JULIET*

very purposefully. Four couples provide the restless and gliding crowd through and against which the various incidents are played. There is also a young couple who are very much in love and very glamorous. One of the distinctions of the piece is the manner in which Ashton selected steps from the classical vocabulary to suggest skating movement. There is a headlong thrust to the production, and the only time that anyone moves backward is either to "fall" or to perform a showy leap. Like *Façade*, the piece has been mounted by companies in various parts of the world with conspicuous success.

The development of television had moved along rapidly enough in Britain for regular telecasts in the mid-thirties, and the Vic-Wells Ballet was invited to present some of its productions over the new medium. *Façade, Les Patineurs,* and *The Nut-cracker* were among the ballets chosen and Ashton created his first and, until now, his last ballet created especially for television. It was a solo for Fonteyn, *First Arabesque,* and was telecast in March 1937. That summer the British Council asked the company to prepare a season to be presented in France as part of Britain's cultural participation in the Paris International Exhibition. It was a flattering invitation, and the Vic-Wells Ballet would go as a unit, not just as part of a larger combined-forces British Ballet. The significance of the company's development since the previous trip to Denmark in 1932, was not lost on outside observers. But while the honor was great, the practical details of the trip were badly mismanaged. Publicity, which is part and parcel of the success of any theatrical venture, was almost nonexistent, and allocation of tickets at the box office negligent. As a result, the company played to poor houses for the most part, and only received proper attention when the run was almost over. As a side benefit the company enjoyed Paris, and many took the opportunity to attend classes in studios run by expatriate Russian teachers like Mathilde Kchessinska, Olga Preobrajenska and Lubov Egorova, all of whom were products of the Imperial schools.

In 1938, Lilian Baylis, who had been a protector and a friend to the company, died. It was a severe blow, as was the necessity of canceling the new production of *The Sleeping Beauty* because of inadequate space. The company was, however, able to mount it the following year and was asked to present selections from it at a command performance at Covent Garden to honor the President of France. Afterward, the company also performed it twice on television in its abbreviated version. The company went on its customary summer tour in the British Isles and gave its final performance on September 2. On September 3, 1939, the country was at war and the company was disbanded. Since all of the London theaters were ordered closed as a precautionary measure because of anticipated bombing attacks, De Valois decided to assemble her dancers elsewhere.

As an experiment the company reunited in Cardiff, well away

from London, and began what was to be a very successful small tour. It returned to London when the bombing attacks had not materialized and the theaters were allowed to reopen. Ashton created *Dante Sonata*, a ballet that seemed to reflect the uncertainty and anxieties of the time, and the company again showed its new production of *The Sleeping Beauty*. Despite the declaration of war by England and France against Germany and Italy, the rest of the Continent was neutral. The government wished to display a business-as-usual face to the neutral nations and dispatched the company on a tour that was to include Holland and Belgium as well as France.

The company began the tour in May, playing in The Hague, then traveled to a border town that was six miles from the Dutch-German border. The preparations for war began to be more and more evident as they approached the border, and the day they performed a general mobilization was ordered. Further performances followed, including a return to The Hague, where the reception was warm and enthusiastic. The Germans invaded Holland and the company was forced to flee, leaving behind everything but the clothes the dancers could wear. A half-dozen productions, including scenery, costumes and music, were abandoned, and the company arrived back in England eight days after it had left, bedraggled, exhausted and discouraged.

The uncertainty and the continued Allied reverses had a deleterious effect on attendance at the performances the company staged during the summer. War preparations were absorbing the men of the company, and air-raid warnings were making regular performances impossible. The company had reached the end of a period when it had developed a strong London following with the establishment of a substantial repertory and something of a reputation on the Continent. For the duration of the war it would have to find another mode of operation to keep going with the dancers it possessed, and to find alternate performing opportunities outside of London.

The company took up residency in a small town in Lancashire, started extensive touring, including outdoor performances, always chancy in damp England, and returned to perform in Lon-

CYGNETS IN *SWAN LAKE*

don when possible. The erosion of men in the company was reflected in the choice of repertory and in the forces used for the standard productions. The larger spectacle-sized ballets were hardest hit and were reduced in scale as best as could be managed. *Les Sylphides*, a ballet requiring only one man, had its fair share of performances, and the company reached out to a wider and wider audience, people who would not ordinarily have been exposed to classical ballet. They weren't seeing it under ideal circumstances, but they were seeing it, and many of them became part of a new postwar audience.

With the company's resident choreographer, Ashton, in the Air Force, De Valois needed someone to provide new ballets for the company and asked Robert Helpmann, the company's leading dancer, to think about choreographing. Helpmann was interested in doing so and over the next several years produced a small body of ballets that were very well received by the public and employed dramatic themes. The most successful of these was *Hamlet*, and Helpmann himself was acclaimed for his portrayal of the central figure. His ballets were done in a style that combined mime, acting and classical balletic steps. It was not the pure classical style that the company had striven for, but survival was more important at the moment.

During this time the work of the school was continued and talented young dancers like Beryl Grey began to emerge and make their places in the company. By the end of the war the company could boast a top rank of ballerinas consisting of Margot Fonteyn, Moira Shearer and Grey. De Valois decided that the reopening of Covent Garden should be celebrated properly with a sumptuous production of *The Sleeping Beauty*. The production was presented in February 1946 and rapidly became a touchstone ballet for the company. In the spring Ashton presented *Symphonic Variations*, his first ballet after being released from the service. It was, and is, a joyous celebration of classic dancing in pure terms. The ballet is performed on a clear stage against a simple light-green backcloth with a few soaring curved and dotted lines, and the three couples dance as if they inhabited a timeless plain. The ballet has no overt story but explores the relationships of the men and women supported by César Franck's variations for piano and orchestra, which give the ballet its title. With Ashton's return to active participation, the company reinforced its own distinctive approach to classicism.

During the next several years the company shifted its operations to Covent Garden for regular spring and fall seasons and made its first triumphant trip to New York. It opened at the Metropolitan Opera House in 1949 and was lauded for its *Sleeping Beauty*, and subsequently for its entire repertory. Its New York appearance was followed by a national tour of the United States, and the company returned to London with the exhilaration that comes after facing and mastering a new challenge. During this time Massine revived several of his most popular ballets for the company, establishing a relationship with the company that had not been possible previously, and Balanchine was asked to mount his *Ballet Imperial*.

In 1951, Lambert, who had been the company's musical conscience, died. He had provided first-rate musical support as composer, conductor and rehearsal pianist besides offering a broadly cultured presence to the operation of the company. A young dancer with the company, John Cranko, produced his first ballet the following year and Ashton mounted a full-evening production of *Sylvia*, which was very well received. Cranko continued to choreograph for the company until he was invited to become the director of the Stuttgart Ballet ten years later. Tours of the United States became as regular a part of the company's year as its seasons at Covent Garden; in 1953 it played throughout the states for four months.

It continued to establish links with the past as well as create new ballets. One of its most successful revivals, Fokine's *Firebird*, had been an enormous favorite of the French audiences for whom it had been created in 1910, and was recostumed and designed in 1926 by the Diaghilev company. The régisseur for that company during its entire existence was Serge Grigoriev, whose exceptional memory and insistence on precise detail insured that the new production would be faithful to the original. It was a tremendous hit and provided a superlative role for Fonteyn. Ashton, who had retired from active performing in the regular repertory, later assumed the character role of the demon Kastchei and demonstrated his special talent for such character parts. In subsequent years he was seen in other such roles.

In 1956 the company was twenty-five years old. Ashton created his beautiful *Birthday Offering*, and the company was given a royal charter which confirmed the obvious—that it was the national company. The name Sadler's Wells Ballet was changed to The Royal Ballet, and the small company which started its struggle for recognition in 1931 became fully vested at The Royal Opera House, Covent Garden. The new name also helped distinguish it from the Sadler's Wells Theater Ballet, which was an offshoot of the parent company. This smaller group toured extensively throughout England especially, though it also appeared abroad and was a training ground for younger dancers and choreographers. Since then the company has maintained a separate identity and performing schedule but with a certain ambiguity. When it, too, changed its name to The Royal Ballet (touring section, or smaller company, as it has been known), its ties to the main group were emphasized and one has never seen a clear profile of the second company emerge. There is a movement of dancers between both companies, switching from one section to another, both draw on the Royal Ballet school graduates for new members, and the smaller section has also performed at Covent Garden when the other has been away. Despite the confusion, however, the second company has performed a service by touring to make ballet available in smaller cities which do not have the facilities to properly produce the major productions of the larger unit, and is a substantial testimony to the growth of the English ballet audience since the first modest beginnings in the mid-twenties.

What was absolutely clear was that, in Ashton, the companies possessed one of the great choreographers in ballet history, and he has continued to demonstrate the fact year after year with a series of first-rate works. One of his masterpieces, *La Fille Mal Gardée*, appeared in 1960 and celebrated a pastoral romance based on an old French ballet which had been lost. The title can be translated in several ways, *The Unchaperoned Daughter* being one of the more common. In a moment of frustration and desperation, the late Sol Hurok advertised it as *The Farmer's Daughter* in an attempt to interest resistant American audiences. It was a ballet that he believed in strongly but one that was neglected by the ticket-buying public in this country. Eventually, after several tours by the Royal Ballet, substantial numbers of the public began to cherish this sunny little masterpiece.

It opens in a farmyard at dawn. No one is evident, and the first dance is that of a rooster leading his clutch of hens from their perches into the yard. He, of course, is blustery and self-important, and they follow him around adoringly as he struts. Soon the young field workers arrive on their way to work and Lise, the daughter in question, is seen with her stern mother, the widow Simone. She is customarily played by a man and spends the best part of the ballet pulling Lise away from her adored Colas. He, too, appears and dances with Lise behind widow Simone's back, but is finally sent packing with all of the other young men to cut the grain that is ripening in the fields. Lise is assigned the task of handing sickles to them as they pass and mischievously tries to slip out the gate at the end of the line, but widow Simone plucks her back and sets her to churning butter while she attends to other tasks in the house.

Colas steals back and they dance together and deftly tie a lover's knot on his staff. At another moment they make a large cat's cradle of a long length of ribbon, and throughout the ballet, ribbons and kerchiefs are featured prominently. Widow Simone soon puts an end to their sport and reminds Lise that she is to marry Alain, the strange and slightly pathetic son of a rich neighboring landowner. Love is not discussed—it is extraneous to the uniting of two large properties. When poor Alain is brought in he carries an umbrella, even though it is a clear day. He and Lise are encouraged to get together, since the parents are resolved that they will marry. Lise has no time for him and Alain is rejected. One has the impression that it is not the first time.

To celebrate the approaching unification of the farms, a picnic is decided upon and all head for the fields. There is singing and dancing and lots of good food and an amusing *pas de trois* in which Colas always manages to slip in to kiss Lise's hand when Alain is dancing with her. All join in the festivities, including widow Simone in a racketing clog dance, but all are halted by a cloudburst which scatters the party. The only one prepared is Alain, who whips out his umbrella and is flown away by means of concealed wires.

The second act is set in the living room-kitchen of the widow's home, where she locks the door to make sure Lise doesn't escape and then sets her to helping at the spinning wheel. The mother falls asleep and Lise tries to steal the key but is caught. While the mother sleeps again, Colas opens the top half of the door and romantically swings Lise off her feet but slips away before widow Simone can catch him. The harvesters return with large bundles of grain which they place in a pyramid in the center of the floor, and Lise is locked in while her mother goes out to make preparations for the signing of the wedding contract. Suddenly Colas bursts from the center of the sheaves of grain and the two dance together after a little hesitation. Lise hears her mother returning and pushes Colas into an upstairs room. Widow Simone looks around suspiciously and decides that the best thing to do with Lise is to shut her in the upstairs room out of harm's way until the contract is well and truly signed. Lise resists but is firmly shoved inside.

Alain, his father and the notaries arrive for the signing, and when it comes time for Lise to affix her name, widow Simone goes upstairs to fetch her. She opens the door and recoils in a faint when she sees her in Colas' arms. The wedding with Alain is called off as the father leaves angrily, but the young couple pledge their fidelity and widow Simone relents from her opposition to their marriage. After all is settled, Alain slips back to retrieve his umbrella and rides it happily away like a hobbyhorse. The ballet is a pure joy and goes from high point to high point without losing its light touch.

De Valois resigned as artistic director of the company in 1963 and was succeeded by Ashton. She continued to devote her energies to the school for the next decade while he concentrated on the company. He continued to produce ballet after ballet of great variety and even a film, *Tales of Beatrix Potter,* which united a dozen animal characters like Peter Rabbit, Squirrel Nutkin, and Jeremy Fisher, who are so much a part of children's stories. He resigned as artistic director in 1970 but continued to prepare ballets for the company as well as for other ballet companies. *A Month in the Country,* choreographed in 1976, represents a special plateau for him in its use of the lyric company style that he created through his works.

He was succeeded by Kenneth MacMillan, who had become the resident choreographer when De Valois retired and Ashton became artistic director. He produced a wide variety of works from full-evening spectacle ballets to dramatic ones like *The Invitation.* In addition to his duties as artistic director, he must preside over various activities that are linked to the Royal Ballet. These include regular choreographing, work with the smaller touring section, consultation with Ballet for All, the education unit of the Royal Ballet, and a speaking acquaintance with the overseeing of the school. Most recently, Norman Morrice has assumed the administrative duties while MacMillan remains as chief choreographer. It is an enormous job and has developed from the small Academy of Choreographic Art studio that De Valois opened in 1926 and transferred, with name changed, to the Old Vic theater in 1931. At the beginning of her career she announced that she was not interested in becoming the first and only director of a company, but wanted to be the first of a line who would succeed her—in effect, that she would establish an institution for the public, not just indulge a personal enthusiasm for a period of time. She has succeeded.

DENMARK

The Royal Danish Ballet

The Danish school has a skimming, twinkling style that is distinctively its own and has preserved it since the middle of the nineteenth century. The company has traditionally been under the patronage of the monarchy, as its title indicates, but its support has now been taken over by the government. The origins of the ballet in Denmark are roughly similar to those in Russia. It was not an indigenous art form but was imported by the court. As in Russia, the model was French with a strong influence from Italian dancers and choreographers.

The acquisition of a dancing master by the royal court had two aspects. To begin with, the instructor was required to teach social dancing and comportment to the royal family and, quite separately, would run a ballet school where the emphasis was on training professional dancers. The most important of the early dancing masters was Pierre Laurent, who set the development of the company through his attention to the school. Prior to this time, most of the dancers who appeared at the opera house were visiting foreign performers.

He was followed by Vincenzo Galeotti in 1775, who had had a successful career as a choreographer and dancer in Italy as well as elsewhere. He remained as head of the company until his death in 1816. He even continued to perform character roles into his late seventies, and created an enormously successful ballet called *The Whims of Cupid and the Ballet Master* in 1786, which is today still in the repertory of the company. It's a humorous ballet in which various contrasting couples find themselves amusingly mismatched by the mischief of Cupid's carefully timed love arrows. Galeotti spent half of his long life (he was eighty-four when he died) touring with his wife choreographing outside of Denmark, but when he was engaged at the Royal Theater he gave his full attention to the development of ballet in Denmark. He was an exceptionally skilled mime, and this dramatic ability persists today in the presentation of the company's works.

Under his direction the popularity of ballet was expanded greatly and the art has remained high in public esteem. While he was engaged in Copenhagen a French ballet master, Antoine Bournonville, was working with the Royal Swedish Ballet in Stockholm. In 1792 he was added to the Royal Danish company, where he danced in many of Galeotti's ballets and succeeded him as ballet master in 1816. Like Galeotti, he had been strongly influenced by the example and theory of dramatic dancing as practiced by Jean-Georges Noverre and Gasparo Angiolini. Unfortunately, he did not have their talent, but he had a son who did.

August Bournonville is the most important name in Danish ballet history both for the ballets he created and for the style of dancing he established. He was himself a classic dancer of excellence, and the choreography of his ballets reflects this. There are, on the whole, more good roles for male dancers in the Danish repertory than there are in any other. He began his training with his father in Copenhagen and Galeotti praised his potential.

His father decided that he had taught him everything he could and that he should continue study in Paris, the center of the ballet world at the time. The Paris Opera had an outstanding company, and the French schools were considered the finest to be found anywhere. There he studied with the phenomenal virtuoso dancer August Vestris, and in 1826 was invited to become a member of the Paris Opera Ballet. The Romantic Era was beginning and Marie Taglioni became the adored dancer of the Parisian public. Bournonville adored her too and was one of her dancing partners.

When he left the Paris Opera, he returned to Copenhagen to perform and, in 1830, to become the court ballet master and choreographer of the Royal Theater. The company had had a succession of directors during the time he had been in Paris, and its condition was highly uncertain. Bournonville established a routine of teaching that he had found beneficial in Paris, began to choreograph, and remained as the leading male dancer of the company for nearly twenty years. His dancing was characterized by manly grace as well as technical accomplishment, particularly in the rapid beating movements of the legs and feet (*batterie*). He devoted himself entirely to teaching and choreography after he retired from active performing.

Twenty-five years after his appointment he resigned to become the ballet master of the Vienna Opera Ballet, a post he retained for only a year before returning to Copenhagen. A few years later he accepted the directorship of the Royal Swedish Ballet and remained there until 1864, at which time he returned to Denmark and the Royal Danish Ballet for good. He retired in 1877 and died two years later. He had many personal triumphs in his performing career, had the satisfaction of seeing his school graduate native-born Lucile Grahn, one of the greatest of the Romantic ballerinas, and established the high artistic level of instruction that has made Denmark notable to this day. When one thinks of Denmark's small population (5,000,000), it is remarkable that the school produces such a steady flow of talented dancers. It has produced as many international male stars since the Second World War as has the Soviet Union, with a population of 240,000,000.

It has produced many female dancers of exceptional talent as

DEMONSTRATION OF BOURNONVILLE TECHNIQUE
BY SORELLA ENGLUND

well, but the numbers of first-rank male dancers is unprecedented anywhere. For reasons that are not quite clear, they tend to be a restless group and can be found dancing in companies throughout Western Europe and the United States as well as in their native Denmark. Paris, Stuttgart, New York and London have all had their share of Danish dancers, some of whom remain and some of whom return to Denmark.

Nothing of any artistic note happened to the Royal Danish Ballet for about fifty years after Bournonville's death. It was almost as if the company were catching its breath. The school continued to function, but there were no choreographers of note to create new ballets. In 1894 Hans Beck, a noted solo dancer with the company, became its artistic director and concentrated on preserving the Bournonville ballets and style, but attempted few ballets of his own. He did choreograph a Hans Christian Andersen* story, "The Little Mermaid," with some success and retired in 1915, although he continued to make himself available for help with the Bournonville ballets almost until the year of his death, 1952.

A characteristic of the Royal Danish company is a tendency to stick close to home and not make many appearances abroad, almost like a close family that doesn't feel the need of outside influences. For fifteen years after Beck's retirement, however, the company was exposed to a series of foreign influences, some of which were instituted by the company director, Gustav Uhlendorff, and others by Mikhail Fokine and George Balanchine, both of whom lived in Denmark for periods of time. With the appointment of Harald Lander, the company entered a new phase in its history.

The repertory was enlarged to include his own ballets as well as those of Balanchine and Fokine, to complement the Bournonville ballets. Lander was known chiefly as a character dancer when he was performing, showing special skill in Spanish and Russian roles. His greatest contributions to the company were, first, his ability to develop dancers (Erik Bruhn, Frank Schaufuss, Toni Lander and Margrethe Schanne among them) and, secondly, bringing the company back into the mainstream of world theater. He left in 1951 after twenty years to become director of the Paris Opera Ballet school for the next decade. He also was invited to stage his ballets there and in various other companies. The best-known of these is *Etudes*, a theatricalized presentation of ballet technique, beginning first with the five positions of the feet and developing into the most spectacular individual variations and *pas de deux.*

---

* Andersen himself had had ballet instruction and appeared in the company as a young man.

That this extraordinary company should be secluded in Denmark, almost unknown to the theater world, is one of the oddities of our time. But until 1950 it remained a quiet secret among the Danes themselves and those few visitors who chanced upon the company when visiting Denmark. Lander, with the aid of the Danish Travel Association, inaugurated a ballet festival in Copenhagen in 1950 which endures to this day and opened the world's eyes to the excellence of the company. Its first trip abroad, to London in 1953, confirmed visitors' good impressions, and the company toured the United States in 1956 to repeat its European successes.

The guiding figure in the school from 1951 until her death in 1975 was Vera Volkova, a former dancer with the Kirov company, whose style in turn had been formed with the aid of Christian Johansson, the brilliant pupil of Bournonville a century before. Since 1965, Flemming Flindt, one of her pupils, has been the artistic director of the company and has introduced many contemporary works into the repertory while keeping a selection of the Bournonville ballets. He has been more daring in his choreography than any of the previous directors and has shown a strong attraction for experimentation. On several occasions modern dance choreographers were invited to stage works for the Royal Danish Ballet, including Paul Taylor, Glen Tetley and Murray Louis. Flindt's own *Triumph of Death* was a series of horrific tableaus that featured mime, elaborate stage apparatuses, and at times nudity.

As with most European companies, the ballet shares performing space with an opera company, and in Copenhagen a dramatic company is also housed in the Royal Theater. There are, however, two performing stages cheek by jowl—the "Old Stage" and the "New Stage"—which alleviates the crowding of schedules somewhat. In addition to its own works, the company also dances the divertissements in the opera productions. The performing year extends from the beginning of September through the end of May, when the now traditional Festival is staged. The company is of substantial size, over ninety dancers, not including the children, who are drawn from the school. These ballet children

AAGE POULSEN IN *NAPOLI*

are one of the unique features of the company, since they travel
and perform with the group, and you will find them listed in any
program of a ballet which calls for children. As is customary,
they are listed alphabetically, the girls preceding the boys. Most
major companies have one or two ballets with parts for children,
and it is an important part of their training to have an opportunity to perform before an audience, but no company travels
their children as consistently as the Royal Danish Ballet does.

The school itself is small compared to other state academies
and normally has less than eighty students. The entrance requirements are the usual ones. The children apply at the age of eight

AAGE POULSEN IN *NAPOLI*

or nine, are given a physical examination, and are then scrutinized for grace and bearing. Those who appear to have the greatest chance for success as professional dancers are accepted into the school. Each year the pupils are given a mandatory test to measure progress. If this is passed, they advance to the next stage of training, which concludes at the age of sixteen. At that point they are taken into the company as "aspirants" for two years. Their education has been totally subsidized by the government, and as trial members of the company they are on the government payroll. At the end of this trial period they are made permanent members of the company and, barring any unforeseen circumstances, will remain with the company until retirement age, which is forty-five for women and forty-eight for men. At that time they can receive a guaranteed pension, which is based on their level within the company. During the year the company makes two or three tours within Denmark and one visit to a country outside Denmark. There is a week's vacation in February and two months' vacation in the summer. The rehearsal period for the coming season begins in August, after which the company starts another performing year.

The Bournonville style, for which the company is famed, is deceptively difficult to master. It demands extreme quickness and nimbleness in the legs and feet and an elegantly composed torso that has a slightly squared look to it. The training is based on the system handed down by Bournonville, who prepared a week's worth of six basic classes designed to develop the whole dancer. There have been changes in the instruction since the end of World War II, but there are still teachers who were trained as dancers in the pure Bournonville style. Students who entered the school up until the beginning of the 1930s took class accompanied by a violin, as it was done in Bournonville's day, rather than with the piano, which is the custom now.

Bournonville would never use just one step if three or four could do the same job. Three or four small rapid steps seldom make the flashy effect that one big bound might, and an appreciation of Bournonville's style must take into account the extraordinary speed required to execute these rapid sequences. The large soaring leaps that draw attention to themselves are less frequently seen in a Bournonville ballet; instead, the viewer is given small waves of movements, precise flurries of steps performed with easy composure, that make their impact slowly but surely. It is a bubbling, sunny style.

One of Bournonville's great masterpieces, *La Sylphide*, is a nearly perfect example of the Romantic ballet and its conventions as experienced by Bournonville when he was a dancer at the Paris Opera. It is a work which has been restaged by many companies and is one of the few authentically Danish ballets that has made an international reputation for itself. Many years later in

1908, Mikhail Fokine created *Les Sylphides*, a ballet about the atmosphere of the Romantic Era which is frequently performed but is quite different from Bournonville's ballet, which was made in 1836 at the height of the Romantic Era. Because of the similarity in names, they can be confused.

Filippo Taglioni, the dancer and choreographer, created the original of this ballet for his daughter, the renowned Marie Taglioni, and it was first performed at the Paris Opera in 1832. Bournonville commissioned a new score from the Danish composer Herman Løvenskjold and created his own version in which he danced the male lead with Lucile Grahn in Copenhagen in 1836. Given Bournonville's skill as a dancer, we can assume that in this version of the ballet the male role was strengthened, but it does present us with an authentic production of a ballet that is saturated with the passions and ethereal complexities of an enchanted land.

The ballet is set in Scotland, a northern country with mists, fogs and mysterious glens. Shakespeare regarded it similarly when he made it the setting for *Macbeth*. The opening scene is the interior of a farmer's cottage with timbered ceiling and a large latticed window at the rear. To the left near a huge fireplace a young man is asleep in an armchair. It is James, the master of the house since his father's death, and across the room another young farmer, Gurn, rests his head on his hands, deeply asleep. A sylph lightly and playfully frolics about James's chair. As she brushes past him, he awakens and is astonished to see such an ethereal creature in his home. He is totally taken with her and follows her around wonderingly. She gives the impression of extreme youth and does not radiate any menace, as one might expect from such a strange creature. She has two little wings attached to her waist and claps with childlike delight at one point. James doesn't know whether he is awake or dreaming after she magically ascends up the chimney of the fireplace.

It is his wedding day and his bride-to-be, Effie, now enters with his mother, and Gurn presents Effie with a small token of his affection. It is easy to see that he is still thinking only of her, though she is to marry James. The latter is distracted with thoughts of the Sylphide, thoughts which would never enter Gurn's rough-hewn head. The room fills with well-wishers and a chandelier of antlers is lowered from the overhead timbers and decorated with flowers. A hideous old woman, Madge, has also entered to warm herself by the fire. She is a fortuneteller but is suspected of being a witch. James wants no part of her and moves to throw her out. He is dissuaded and Gurn pours her

ERIK BRUHN IN *LA VENTANA*

some whiskey before she settles in to tell fortunes. She whispers to one embarrassed young girl that she is pregnant, James's future appears dark, and Gurn is told that he will marry Effie. It is too much for James and he ejects the crone, who departs cursing him.

Effie goes upstairs to dress for her wedding and the other guests drift away, leaving James alone. The Sylphide enters at the window and is distressed that James is marrying. It means that he is deserting her. He impulsively promises not to and, while dancing with her, is observed by Gurn, who happens in. He dashes off to tell what he has seen and James has only a moment to hide the Sylphide. The fire makes it impossible to use the chimney to escape now, so he has her hop lightly into the armchair, where he covers her with his tartan blanket. Gurn returns to mime what he has seen, including a clumsy imitation of flying wings with his arms, and then points accusingly at the armchair. Triumphantly he whips away the blanket and points at the spot where the Sylphide should have been, but she is gone. The others, who have seen nothing, disregard his tale, though James has been acting peculiarly.

The whole group assembles for a wedding celebration, which is to start with Scottish dancing. As they begin, the Sylphide flits in and out of the massed dancers but is seen only by James. He is distracted enough from his dancing that he misses partnering Effie several times but not completely. It only adds to the guests' feeling that he is a bit distracted, but probably because of the impending wedding. He and Gurn each dance a solo variation, and then the group dancing concludes.

Effie is now being dressed in her bridal clothes and the men prepare a toast to the groom. But the groom is dashing away in pursuit of the Sylphide who has thoroughly infatuated him. As she passes out the door she takes his cap from a peg and tosses it to him. At the front where the men have assembled the toast is dramatically offered with a wave of a cup toward the spot where the groom should have been standing. To everyone's consternation, he is not there. Gurn reports seeing him flee into the forest chasing after a sprite. Effie tears her veil off and tries several times to run after him but is restrained. Gurn faithfully stands by as the curtain is lowered on the end of the first act.

The first scene in Act II is a gloomy glade where Madge and her coven of witches dance around a glowing cauldron. They add elements to prepare the lethal brew into which a chiffon scarf is dipped. When it has been thoroughly steeped in the poison they all withdraw.

Scene two is a cleared place in a quiet glen. It is craggy and woody, and elfin sylphs disport as James dashes in. The Sylphide descends to meet him from a rock outcropping as if she were floating down. He is overjoyed to see her and she seems quite happy in the outdoors, which is her natural home. They frolic and are surrounded by a whole band of sylphs, who always seem to form a protective screen about her. He tries to embrace her but in one way or another she eludes his grasp. The circles and diagonal patterns of the corps are beautifully balanced and evaporate only to form and reform in further combinations. When they all vanish he is desolate in the glade. He has left his bride-to-be Effie, only to follow a chimera, and is close to despair. He dashes away to look for the Sylphide.

Members of the wedding party scatter in various directions to search for James. Gurn finds his abandoned cap and is about to notify the others when Madge appears to silence him. She tells him once again that Effie is to be his bride and cautions him about being foolish and finding James. When the distraught Effie inquires after James, Gurn denies any knowledge of his whereabouts. As she sits grieving he reasserts his love for her and asks whether or not she will reconsider. Taken aback at first, she is encouraged to think it over and, in effect, be practical. They all go off to prepare for the impending marriage.

James encounters Madge, who offers him the magic scarf that will bind the Sylphide to him forever. He is pathetically and innocently grateful for her assistance after having been so unkind to her. When the Sylphide returns he holds the scarf behind his back and she is tantalized by it. With a flourish he produces it and entwines it about her shoulders and arms. Abruptly she lurches and falters as the poison does its work. The little wings that were about her waist fall off one by one and flutter to the ground. She sinks down and is attended by her band of sylphs, who then place her on a funeral bier which is borne off in the air. James is distraught, and in the background one hears the sound of a wedding party and sees Gurn with Effie as his bride.

The ballet deals beautifully with the conflict that springs up, when the everyday world of the tangible touches the otherworldly realm of the spirit. The demands of each produce an unbearable tension which is resolved at the expense of the other. Gurn, the down-to-earth man of little imagination but great tenacity, celebrates the happy wedding day that should have been James's. The latter is possessed of a finer sensibility, but it leads him to tragedy. He sees the evil of Madge when others see only the fortuneteller. He is aware of the other realm, which they are not. But like them he is flesh and blood and has no business there. The conflict of actuality and desire tears happiness from him.

The choreographers of the Romantic Era were passionately fond of stage magic and in this production offer several examples of it: the trapeze which hoists the Sylphide up the chimney in the first act, the chair with the movable back which enables her to slip away, the hidden platform which enables her to descend from a high level on the rocky setting to the stage floor, and finally the flying machinery to bear her away. Each in its way contributes to the feeling of otherworldliness which is the Sylphide's natural atmosphere. It is one of the Royal Danish Ballet's finest productions.

The company maintains many of Bournonville's productions as well as contemporary works, but it bears the special stamp of his dance training. They do not clamor for attention but quietly charm audiences by their correct bearing and warm characterizations. It has kept its traditions of the Romantic style and has tried to acquire excellent contemporary works. In a world of hard sell, gimmicks and superficial enthusiasms it is almost an anachronism, but one that we would be the poorer without.

GERMANY

The Stuttgart Ballet

The Stuttgart Ballet, which at home is known as the Stuttgart Württembergische Staatstheater Ballett, is the youngest of the major international companies. It is a fully supported constituent of the State Theater in the county of Württemberg and is located in the city of Stuttgart. It is part of a theater complex which includes opera and theater companies as well as ballet, and is backed by a staff of 750 persons who man the theaters and build everything needed for the productions. All of this has developed since the end of the Second World War. Ballet has now arrived in Germany to stay. But it was not always so.

During the seventeenth century the local aristocracy participated in the court ballets, which were prepared for important celebrations and followed the patterns that were developed in France. Central Europe had its share of political problems, and the Thirty Years' War distracted the nobility from anything except sheer survival. Toward the end of the century, the aristocracy returned to the theater, but the music portions of the productions occupied more of the spectacle than did the dance, which was reduced to informal interludes between vocal or orchestral selections. This pattern was followed until the arrival of Jean-Georges Noverre in the middle of the eighteenth century.

His was one of the leading names in ballet, and his continual difficulties with the Paris Opera directors made him eager to accept appointment to an opera house outside of France. His patron was Duke Carl Eugen, who had a passion for the theater and the means to indulge it. Master of his own private realm, he answered to no one for the way he spent money from the royal treasury. Germany at the time was full of such small kingdoms, each with its own theater and musicians. Because of this, present-day Germany is rich in theaters, even in very small towns. After he had secured an Italian composer to be resident in Stuttgart, Carl Eugen selected a French ballet master to create ballets for his theater. He wanted only the best for his entertainment.

He spent generously, and Noverre was to remain his ballet master for seven years (1759–66), during which time he created some of his most famous works and, almost more importantly, published his *Lettres sur la Danse et sur les Ballets*. The book was a summing up of Noverre's theories on the future development of ballet and was published simultaneously in Lyons and Stuttgart. It was to become the bible of the *ballet d'action* (narrative, dramatic ballet) and is today a valuable text for the wealth of ideas it contains. The volume was dedicated to Carl Eugen, for whom Noverre put his ideas onstage as well as on paper.

It was customary for Carl Eugen to celebrate his birthday with a special entertainment each year, but in 1763 he outdid even his own previously lavish productions. The celebration lasted for two weeks and involved presentations of operas, Voltaire's play *Zayre*, hunts, balls, concerts and ballets. Noverre created one of his most famous and popular ballets, *Jason and Medea*, for the occasion and sent to Paris for the brothers Gaetano and Angiolo Vestris to bolster his cast. The cost was considerable, but the Duke insisted on the best. On the final day of the celebration there was a ballet on horseback in the main square in Stuttgart led by Carl Eugen attended by a dozen spearmen in costumes created for the occasion. The art of dressage (disciplined riding), had been strongly influenced by the development of court ballet, and at this time remained the prerogative of the nobility.

All good things come to an end, and so it was with Noverre's stay in Stuttgart. It became too expensive even for Carl Eugen* to afford, so after seven years of generous support he dismissed Noverre and the expensive guest artists he had brought from France and Italy to grace his stage. He decided to develop local

* He built a new and larger opera house in Ludwigsburg that was large enough to accommodate a troop of horses. The locals resented the expenditure of so much of the Fatherland's money, to which Carl Eugen roared with a Louis XIV hauteur: "What Fatherland? I am the Fatherland."

artists and opened a school, which quietly withered away by the beginning of the nineteenth century, and so did ballet as a separate art in Stuttgart. It became simply a subsidiary of opera, and the few dancers engaged by the court appeared in divertissements during opera productions. From time to time a visiting guest artist like Marie Taglioni would rouse interest in ballet, but it was only a temporary thing. For all intents and purposes, ballet was gone from the opera house as a powerful force for nearly a century and a half.

The second coming of ballet in Stuttgart coincided almost exactly with the two-hundredth anniversary of Noverre's arrival in Carl Eugen's city, only this time it was an Englishman, John Cranko, who was summoned to revive the art. In 1961 he accepted the post of artistic director of the company. He inherited a small group of dancers who put on a few ballet evenings during the course of the year but who did not tour on the international circuit. About the only thing that had drawn attention to dance in Stuttgart in the intervening years was the creation of Oskar Schlemmer's *Triadic Ballet* in 1922. Schlemmer was one of those talented artists who had animated the Bauhaus movement but whose interests extended beyond painting, sculpture and industrial design into designing movement for people and objects. His work was daring and innovative and fed into the expressionist dance movement that was growing in Germany at the time, following the lead of dance experimentalist Rudolf von Laban. It caused considerable excitement but did not result in any significant rise in the dance level of the Stuttgart Opera ballet.

Cranko, on the other hand, was a classically trained dancer who had been a soloist with England's Royal Ballet, and had not only toured foreign countries with that company but could see no reason why Stuttgart should not do so as well. It was simply a question of repertory and dancers. As any wise ballet master knows, a school is essential to the future of any company, and he set out to assemble a staff who could take local pupils and bring them to the level where they would naturally enter into a major company, prepared to dance the most demanding roles. With the

MARCIA HAYDEE AND RICHARD CRAGUN IN
SLEEPING BEAUTY

future blocked out, Cranko began to tend to the immediate present. In 1960 he had staged his *Prince of the Pagodas* for the Stuttgart Ballet when the world was not even aware that there was a ballet company in Stuttgart, which was known mainly as the home of the Mercedes-Benz automobile factory. "Our sister city is Cardiff," he once commented with a smile, referring to another city known for commercial enterprise rather than art.

The pattern which had occurred in every country to which ballet was introduced began to emerge in Germany. A foreign ballet master took up residence, engaged the best foreign teachers to train local children, and invited foreign soloists to lead the company until it was able to feed itself from the students in the school, a process that ordinarily takes about twenty years for full success.

The international personnel of the company were drawn from twenty different countries. They included a graduate of the Royal Danish Ballet, students from the Royal Ballet in London, an American, Richard Cragun, who became the leading male dancer of the company, and a Brazilian ballerina, Marcia Haydée, around whom the repertory of the company was designed. In three years the company had built itself to a complement of three dozen dancers and had scheduled a regular week-long ballet festival. The custom of the ballet week is usual in those European opera houses which have a sufficiently strong ballet company and ballet master to warrant a full week of ballet without any opera productions. Obviously, for a company with international aspirations the ballet week was only the first step in declaring its independent status. In the autumn of 1963 the company made its first major trip abroad when invited to participate in the Edinburgh Festival. This festival, coming early in the autumn, is a showcase for opera, music and drama as well as ballet and is a marked step forward in the life of any company. In addition to having established companies perform, the directors of the festival also invite promising ensembles which deserve a wider audience outside of their own countries. Cranko and Stuttgart had taken the first step.

Cranko had also been busy as the company's chief choreographer, producing fifteen of the twenty-three new ballets or revivals that the company mounted in the first four years of his regime. Cranko had had a successful career in London both as a dancer and choreographer for the Royal Ballet and in the commercial theater, where he staged *Cranks*, a revue that crossed the Atlantic to Broadway for a successful run. He was a choreographer who was not afraid of the entertainment value of ballet and did not exclusively equate seriousness with creativity. He was as at home with the tragedy of *Romeo and Juliet*, which he made into a full-evening ballet, as he was with the comic *Taming of the Shrew*, which he also made into a full-evening ballet. His musical taste was equally varied and included progressive jazz by George Shearing and Stravinsky's *Card Game*. It is estimated that there are about sixty opera houses in Germany with ballet companies, but only Cranko's emerged onto the international scene. It was clearly a case of the right man at the right time. Restless in London, where it was clear that he was not going to be the director of the Royal Ballet because of the senior claim of Frederick Ashton, Cranko traveled to Stuttgart for much the same reason as had his distinguished predecessor Noverre. It offered him an opportunity he did not have at home. His sense of humor was a great aid, since it was inevitable that he would be resented as a foreigner by a certain element of the population. It also helped that he learned German (unlike Petipa, who never learned Russian after he settled in St. Petersburg) and conducted rehearsals in a mixture of German and English. The language of the classroom, however, remained French, as it has in every country in which ballet has taken root.

Cranko's special view of the classic vocabulary was that of a man with a highly developed dramatic sense. He had plotless, "abstract," ballets in his repertory and even created several fine ones himself, notably *Opus One*, but his deepest sympathies were engaged by story ballets. The style of movement most necessary to the realization of these ballets was one that required classical schooling but also the dramatic strength to show clear characterizations. He needed dramatically oriented dancers who understood the nuances of character development and could project them effectively.

Cranko's ability to portray motivation and character through classic dance clearly emerged as he created ballet after ballet with a strong story line that required a full evening for its telling. He is ,unmatched in keeping the narrative line clear and advancing it surely, no matter how many characters are presented in the actual working out of the plot. One of his most effective full-evening ballets was based on Pushkin's great poem *Eugene Onegin.* Tchaikovsky even wrote an opera based on the story, but when it came to selecting music for his version, Cranko did not choose the existing operatic score but went instead to lesser-known works by Tchaikovsky and had them orchestrated as a single score. The plot involves a proud nobleman, Onegin, who decides that a vacation in the country will offer him some diversion from the dull life of the city. While there, on a hunting trip with a friend, he encounters a romantically inclined young woman, Tatiana, who immediately falls in love with him but whom he finds too simple and country-bumpkinish for his sophisticated tastes. She, of course, being hopelessly in love, writes him a passionate letter, and it is interesting to see how deftly Cranko uses the simple act of jotting down words to show the whole of Tatiana's hopeless infatuation.

Her friend Olga, whose fiancé, Lensky, introduced Onegin into the household, also likes him but intends to marry Lensky. At Tatiana's birthday party Onegin is obviously bored to distraction by the ways of country society and is particularly cruel to Tatiana. He draws her aside but not, as she hopes, to declare his own love for her, but to ridicule her infatuation as schoolgirl silliness and to tear up her letter as being ridiculous. A somewhat older man, Prince Gremin, is also at the party, and it is the secret hope of the hostess that he will make a suitable match for Tatiana. The latter is so distressed that she cannot even entertain the idea. Onegin, still bored, flirts with Olga to tease Lensky but rouses an unexpected anger in Lensky, who challenges him to a duel. It was not Onegin's intention to go that far but, since he is a man of honor, he must accept the challenge. The motto of his crest is "When I am not honorable, then honor no longer exists."

He is, of course, a far better duelist than Lensky, who barely knows how to handle pistols and inevitably spurns all attempts by Tatiana and Olga to dissuade him from going through with the duel. He has been wounded deeply by Olga's innocent betrayal and recklessly pushes ahead. He is clumsy handling his weapon, and Onegin quite calmly kills him with his shot. He might have fired harmlessly over the young man's head but does not. The horror of it reaches even him after he has done it, and it of course turns Tatiana away from any romantic thoughts she had had about this visitor from St. Petersburg. Onegin is a cold, self-centered person who does not have a scrap of feeling for anyone in the world except himself. After he has "won" the duel, he hastily leaves and begins to travel to rid himself of the unhappy thoughts of the ill-fated country trip.

We next encounter Onegin at a fashionable ball in St. Petersburg, where he has returned after several years of travel. The host is the same Prince Gremin who was at the party in the country years ago. Now he is entertaining in his own magnificent home, with his Princess, Tatiana, whom he has married. Onegin's surprise is evident as he assesses the changes that have taken place in the young woman since he had so coolly dismissed her. She is the center of attention and has a demonstrable air of self-possession. He is severely shocked at his own blindness and tries to interest her in himself. He writes her a letter.

The final letter scene is full of irony; here is Onegin pleading with someone he has rejected, and she refuses him. The man who was once so proud of his honor is reduced to making a dishonorable attempt at a liaison. Tatiana, who still feels a passionate attachment for him, does the honorable thing and sends him away as if she were putting her childhood behind her. She is now truly a woman of position and cannot entertain Onegin, who represents a closed chapter in her life.

Even when drawn to an established classic ballet such as *Swan Lake*, Cranko always sharpened the story line of the ballet. There are literally hundreds of productions of *Swan Lake*, and none of them are exactly alike, though all of them stem from the wonderful score that Tchaikovsky prepared for the ballet. Choreographers, in general, have tended to retain certain portions of the ballet, as they were set by Petipa or his co-choreographer Ivanov, but have felt free to alter other sections so that the story conforms more closely to their own personal view of the essential tale. Like most mythical narratives, the story can be understood in various ways. Contemporary Soviet productions tend to see love as the powerful conquering force that routs the evil magician Rotbart, while others see the tale as essentially a tragedy, and still others see the Prince rather than the Swan Queen as the victim. As might be expected, when Cranko examined the story he brought his own particular viewpoint to bear.

"I am always surprised by productions of *Swan Lake* that claim to have used all the music," he wrote. "Such a production would last about as long as *Die Meistersinger*. While opera lovers can take this length, balletomanes tend to enjoy shorter fare. Something must go, and I have therefore cut the well-known waltzes and *pas de trois* from Act I and put in their place the equally beautiful but seldom performed *pas de six*. This gives Siegfried the opportunity to dance and also to develop the character. The Black Swan *pas de deux* remains in the place Tchaikovsky intended, and in the fourth act the Drigo *pas de deux*, which always seemed too slight for the situation, has been replaced by the beautiful *Elegy for Strings*. I have tried to base my own work on the classic Romantic style of Petipa, working freely and in my own manner, but not losing sight of the great man's direction.

"Consequently, most of the second act has been retained in its usual form. For the opening of the fourth act and the famous elegiac entry of the swans I have 'borrowed' from various Soviet productions. However, all the musical repetitions have been cut and the drama has been strengthened accordingly, so that the Prince emerges as a living person who experiences a tragic ordeal, rather than being a human crane who simply lifts the ballerina.

"The national dances have been woven into an overall dramatic arrangement instead of being pointless divertissements. What of the ending? There have been many 'happy endings,' where the lovers are reunited after death in 'fairyland,' but I believe that Tchaikovsky intended to write a tragic ballet. Consider the situation: Siegfried proves unworthy, he breaks his vow and unselfconsciously confuses outward appearances with inner reality . . . he is a tragic hero and must be vanquished. The tone of the music, especially in the fourth act, is tragic. In the imperial theater the Czar (surrounded by so many tragedies) made it an unwritten rule that everything must close happily. But Odette and Siegfried are not the sort of lovers who can 'live happily ever after.' "

As can be seen from these brief remarks, Cranko instinctively went for the dramatic elements of the production and sought to strengthen them with a clearer delineation of the character of the hero, even if he had to play down the role of the Swan Queen a bit to do so. Musical values in terms of repeats are eliminated to keep the story moving at a strong, clear pace. Considering others of his productions, it was an inevitable decision.

The story of *Romeo and Juliet* has proved an irresistible subject for ballets, and Prokofiev's full-evening score has been equally magnetic to choreographers. The first Soviet production of the ballet to this music, that of Leonid Lavrovsky, was first given in 1940 by the Kirov Ballet, which continues to present the ballet to this day. Since then there have been a dozen others, among which Cranko's has achieved considerable prominence. All of the ballets have used the Shakespearean story as the basis for the ballet, as did Prokofiev for his score. It is therefore strongly programatic music, and Cranko, who found its structure much to his liking, retained it essentially as written.

The tragedy of the lovers takes place inside the confines of the boisterous and rough-edged society of Renaissance Italy. The fate of the lovers inevitably crosses the collision course of the two proud houses of which they are members. Cranko effectively shows the dueling and the carousing of the men of the Capulet and Montague families with the combination of lightheartedness and deadly seriousness that probably was the daily temper of the times. Skillfully he introduces the infatuated lovers, who discover one another in the course of their family comings and goings. They try to elude the inevitable conflict but cannot and are destroyed by their families hostilities. The story has had a wide appeal, but it is significant to see the power it has exercised over English choreographers. Frederick Ashton produced a three-act version for the Royal Danish Ballet in 1956; John Cranko's production was first seen in 1962; three years later Kenneth Mac-Millan, who succeeded Ashton as artistic director of the Royal Ballet, produced a third, using the Prokofiev score; and Antony Tudor, using the music of Frederick Delius, showed his one-act version of the story in 1943. The latter production was mounted for American Ballet Theater.

Shakespeare again proved a useful source for Cranko when he adapted *The Taming of the Shrew*. There was no extant music for the ballet, so he commissioned a score tailored to his dramatic needs. The resultant ballet is somewhat of a rarity in that it is humorous all the way through as Petruchio "tames" the terrible-tempered Bianca amidst the swirl of amorous foolishness that forms the background to their story.

It was a terrible blow to the company when Cranko died of a heart attack while returning from a successful tour of the United States in 1973. He had so clearly put his mark on the company that it was exceptionally difficult to find a suitable replacement for him. Glen Tetley, who succeeded him a year later, is an American choreographer who had worked both in the United States and extensively in Europe. It was significant that the company elected to invite an active choreographer, since it indicated that the creative impetus it had received from Cranko was still the overriding concern. Originally Tetley had trained as a modern dancer but had also been a member of a ballet company. He had choreographed works for his own independent modern dance company and also for Ballet Rambert and the Netherlands Dance Theater. He was versed in several styles but had a distinct preference for "abstract," plotless works that were somewhat at variance with the repertory that had been created by Cranko. In 1976 he left the Stuttgart Ballet, and the direction was provided by members of the company headed by Marcia Haydée, its leading ballerina. In the nature of artistic enterprises, however, there is always a tendency for a single creative personality to emerge and assume direction of the company. Until such a figure appears, the company invites visiting choreographers to provide new ballets and carefully nurtures the works that Cranko created and used to set its individual style.

CHAPTER SIX

Teachers and steps

The studios, where dancers learn to do the superlatively exciting things that they regularly demonstrate on glamorous stages, are, by contrast, rather ordinary places; sometimes downright drab. Occasionally one encounters a really smart-looking studio, but it is the rare exception. No matter what its decor, though, the ballet studio has a broad, uncluttered wooden or linoleum-topped wooden floor, a barre (wooden railing) affixed to the wall a little below shoulder height running along three sides of the room, and a wall-to-wall mirror on the fourth side. In one corner of the room is a piano, and during class the accompanist plays selections that are rhythmically appropriate to the exercise being performed.

The classes are to a great extent repetitive, as in any regimen of exercise, and they are also strenuous, but the music is exceptionally helpful in keeping the class moving along. A good accompanist will immediately select the proper music to support the beat that the teacher wants the exercise performed to, and can also provide a little musical commentary for the benefit of the class. For example, in a particularly strenuous portion of the class the accompanist may humorously play one of dolorous themes from *Swan Lake*, or at a lighter moment may select something from outside the classic ballet repertory such as a Joplin "rag" or a familiar and perenially popular song. The class, made up of professional dancers, has a wide familiarity with music and is able to appreciate these supportive selections.

These little musical jokes, though, are side issues, since the main thing is to provide the required rhythmic base for the various portions of the class as it develops. A good accompanist, however, adds important variety to the class, which should at all costs be kept from being routine. The routine class easily degenerates into a comfortable class, which ends up being of little real use to the dancers. The goal is always for perfection, to go a little bit beyond present accomplishment, an ideal which may never be achieved but which is the aim of the course of instruction. Success is measured in inches or fractions of inches, in the proper curve of the foot, the lift of the torso, the angle of the head, or the spacing of the arms. In every step there are dozens of things that have to be attended to in order to produce the harmonious look that distinguishes correct execution. Feet, legs, hips, chest, arms and head must always be placed in stylized relation to one another for the proper "look." They also have to be placed there instantly while moving at high speed, so that the positions become instinctive. There simply isn't any time for the brain to think; the muscles themselves have to do the "thinking" automatically. Just as great pianists talk about having the music "in the fingers," dancers have to have the ballet technique and its particular choreographic shaping "in the body." Class is the basis for all subsequent development.

There are all sorts of classes, which are graded according to the achievement level of those taking them. These range from the amateur "adult beginner" to the final *classe de perfection* (polishing), where professionals receive artistic coaching. Teachers come in all sizes, shapes and temperaments, from indulgent to vaguely hostile. Unfortunately they come in varying degrees of qualification also, from superb to incompetent. Anyone, literally anyone, can open a dance school, and through stupidity can permanently injure young children when their bones are soft. There are no licensing requirements! REPEAT: NONE, NOT ONE! The state won't let a barber cut your hair without registering, but it will permit an incompetent dance teacher to hurt children. And many young children whose bones are still soft are injured or given completely erroneous training. Maria Tallchief, who was for years the reigning ballerina with the New York City Ballet, had taken early training in her native Oklahoma and had been incorrectly taught. When it became apparent that she had great potential despite the poor training, she had to go back to the basics and start to learn the correct placement and positioning all over again. She succeeded because she had a strong gift and desire. With less desire many would have bitterly chalked it off and forgotten completely about a performing career.

In lieu of a national licensing system to attest to a teacher's qualifications, there are a few basic rules that one can follow in choosing a school for a child. The first would be to have the child attend the official school of a professional ballet company. Obviously this is possible only in cities which have a professional ballet company. There are, however, hundreds of ballet companies today in the United States. One easy way to make up your mind about the company and its stature is the number of performances it gives during a year. If it gives only one performance a year, it is a showcase company for the school and not a serious performing ensemble. Do not be fooled by the charm of the ballet master or mistress; keep a clear head. It is your child; make a logical assessment of the school, not an emotional one.

It is reassuring when the head of the school has had a substantial performing career with one or another of the major companies. It is also reassuring when the school will not accept very young children. It is an indication of their seriousness. You may want your child to start at the age of four, but you're wrong and the person who tells you so is right. It may make you angry to be thwarted, but it's for your child's good. Remember, it would be very easy and profitable for the person running the school to accept your child as a fee-paying student, but the honorable and

SECOND POSITION AT THE BARRE: COLLEEN NEARY

professional thing to do is to refuse. Training should begin for children at about the age of eight or nine. The best professional schools, those which supply dancers to the major companies, do not consider children below this age. They know the right way to train dancers. They have the track record to prove it. Some of them, however, have created beginners' classes for children which are clearly preparatory and not as demanding and may suggest these "pre-ballet" lessons.

It is always reassuring when a particular dance school has had graduates who have appeared with major companies. Many dancers who have retired from performing open dance studios

DEMI-PLIÉ IN SECOND POSITION: COLLEEN NEARY

and recommend their best pupils to the companies with which they themselves have performed. It is an informal but real measure, since students attest to their teacher's skill. Lacking any of these other guidelines, it is best to avoid the school that promises instant results. The proper development of children takes time and patience. Be selective, look around and never decide on a school only because it happens to be located conveniently.

A basic dance class, whether it is for the most advanced professionals or for beginners, has the same core structure. It begins with each of the dancers spaced around the room standing with one hand on the barre, which functions as a support for the first part of the class. The exercises begin slowly and are designed to loosen and warm up the muscles, beginning with the feet and then progressing to all parts of the body. It is a total workout from the instep to the neck. During this part of the class there is little jumping, and only gradually is work *en l'air* (in the air) introduced; it is almost completely *á terre* (on the ground) at the beginning. The exercises are given in sets—so many repetitions to the front, to the side and to the back. When they have been satisfactorily completed, the dancer does an about-face, grasps the barre with the other hand and repeats the exercises in the same sequence on the other leg. The supporting leg is always closest to the barre, and the working leg is in the direction of the center of the studio. It is very measured and symmetrical. The last thing in the world a teacher wants to do is produce little injuries by putting demands on muscles that have not reached the proper state of elasticity. The actual time that it takes to achieve this adequately loosened state differs according to the individual teachers; some spend more time on this portion of the class than do others, but all commence with barre work.

The small movements of the feet which begin the class are enlarged into big movements of the legs. All of the exercises start and finish in one of the five positions of the feet and are accompanied by the proper placement of the arms. The basic thrust of all the exercises is to lengthen muscles, to stretch them a little more than they already are. It is not designed to build bulk muscle, although the legs in particular do develop substantially. While at the barre, all of the exercises are done with the foot either flat or relevè (heel) raised slightly, weight on the ball of the foot). Point work (on the tips of the toes) is quite separate. As the students perform the exercises the teacher stresses certain things in general about the execution of the step, the particular quality he wishes to see emphasized, and proceeds constantly around the class looking at individuals and making corrections. Roughly half the class is spent at the barre before the next part begins. This next portion is called center floor work.

With a word or two the teacher brings the class to the center of the studio and begins to arrange the pupils in lines, making

BATTEMENT TENDU FRONT: COLLEEN NEARY

sure that each one has an unobstructed view of the mirror. In addition to listening to the corrections of the teacher, they will be able to view themselves to see how closely they are approximating the step being practiced. The dancers stare at themselves in the mirror in a curiously detached way, as if they were looking at someone other than themselves. In a way, they are. They are looking at their bodies as artistic instruments. There is little self-admiration involved, but rather a cool, appraising glance. If the image is good, there is satisfaction; if it is not, there is more work to be done. Dancers look at themselves in this evaluating way every day.

BATTEMENT TENDU SIDE: COLLEEN NEARY

Once the body has been warmed up, it is time to perform steps that begin to approximate the feeling of dancing. The supporting barre is gone and the dancers must now rely on their own balance as they perform steps and combinations of steps. Each teacher styles a class in an individual manner, so that there is no set standard. Some emphasize balance, others the shift of weight, still others the line of the body. With this in mind, each assembles combinations of steps that will produce the desired effect. These combinations are *enchaînements* (a stringing together of various steps into a short passage of dancing). They do not have the artistic quality of a choreographed ballet, but essentially they

BATTEMENT TENDU BACK: COLLEEN NEARY

follow the same procedure. Some teachers are known for their imagination in framing these combinations and give a very "dancy" class, while others place less emphasis on this aspect of center floor work. All, however, open up the movement more and more from the relatively restricted exercises at the barre.

The class tempo accelerates as the students work on jumps and turns. Since these steps require more space, such combinations are done by small groups following one after another. They begin at one of the far corners and progress down to the mirror wall on the diagonal, then return to the opposite corner at the rear of the room, where they wait for everyone in the class to finish the combination. Then, in order, they perform it again, moving down to the mirror wall on the diagonal, showing the other side of their bodies. As in the barre exercises where the whole body was involved in a symmetrical way, so too in center floor work, the body is exercised first to one side and then the other. At the end of the class there is a *révérence*, which is nothing more than a courtly bow involving graceful configurations of the arms. When the hour or hour and a half is finished, normally there is a bow to the class by the teacher and polite applause from the class members. In some companies it is the practice to have male and female members of the company take class together. In other companies they are separated. The Russians generally adhere to the latter custom. Point class is universally reserved for women only.

In the course of ballet history there have been many noted teachers, both men and women, but one of the most celebrated was Christian Johansson, who taught at the Maryinsky school in St. Petersburg for over forty years. He was born in Stockholm in 1817, danced with the great Romantic ballerina Marie Taglioni, and was hired to perform with the Maryinsky Ballet as a lead dancer. He began to teach in 1860 while still performing and when he retired from the stage he continued to do so well into his eighties. He died in 1903, the year that Petipa retired.

Among his pupils were many of that legendary generation who at the turn of the century so dramatically brought ballet back into Western Europe from St. Petersburg—Tamara Karsavina, Mathilde Kchessinska and Olga Preobrajenska, all of whom subsequently went on to teach the next generation. Johansson was noted for the difficulty of his classes, his strong vocabulary and all-seeing eye. He became partially blind toward the end of his life, but he never missed anything with the one good eye remaining to him. He had been educated by Bournonville and was molded by the principals that that master had developed from the French school of dance in the early nineteenth century. It amused him that his pupils in Russia were taught the French style, while France's own dancing legacy had been lost in France itself.

STRETCHES AT THE BARRE: COLLEEN NEARY

STRETCHES AT THE BARRE: COLLEEN NEARY

He maintained the old custom of accompanying the dance class by himself on a miniature violin called a *pochette* and rarely had a word of praise for any of his students. He accelerated and slowed his tempos radically, so that even the best were hard-pressed to keep up and when something pleased him he would mutter, "Now you can show that to the public," the implication being that all the rest was best hidden from public view. The glorious Karsavina he called a "cow on ice" and "idiot" while throwing his bow at her, and lamented when she made a mistake, "Pity you are weak-minded; what a dancer I could have made of you but for that." He was most assuredly of the old school. But with Enrico Cecchetti produced the dancers, later the teachers, who have created the efflorescence of ballet in our time. The anger he showed was always prompted by his driving concern to bring out the best in his pupils. He himself did not rest and would not allow them to do so either.

The Imperial system was dictatorial and the boys and girls who studied in the Maryinsky school lived a strictly controlled life, boarding in dormitories and being driven to and from the theater in special carriages. It was the classic academy where the child was prepared for a professional career with the finest teachers available, while being given instruction concurrently in the humanities. The system exists in Russia today, as it does also in Denmark.

The system in the United States is quite a bit different. There exist numbers of good teachers, but to a great extent the schools are dependent on the revenue from their classes to support themselves. They can offer some scholarship help but they must accept fee-paying students for the most part, no matter how much they feel constrained by the system. The one major exception to this rule is the School of American Ballet, which is the school of the New York City Ballet and which has for several years been able to offer extensive scholarship assistance to talented students regardless of their ability to pay. This was made possible by a substantial grant from the Ford Foundation and is a step toward creating a true academy in the traditional sense, as a training ground for professionals. It is, however, a far cry from the state-supported academies of Europe whose continuity is assured through government subsidy. Until the arts are regarded as part of the same family of humane endeavors as universal health care and quality education, it is unlikely that such support will be forthcoming.

Historically, the traditions of the various styles of dancing within the broad ballet vocabulary are developed through an interplay between the dancers and the teachers. The former react and emphasize a certain carriage of the body almost instinctively, and the teachers make a system out of it. The style we associate with the Maryinsky/Kirov dancer is the product of French grace, Italian virtuosity and Russian temperament. One of the great Russian teachers, Nicolai Legat, who was a product of the training commented: *"Epaulement* [the carriage of the shoulders in relation to the head and legs], though it can be reduced to technique, is essentially a feeling with regard to line and posture. The sense of *epaulement* came to Russians instinctively, but with such conviction that we introduced and adopted it in our art as a principal." In this brief comment one can hear both Legat the dancer and Legat the teacher speaking. After retiring from active performing he devoted himself to teaching and in time developed a class for each day of the training week (six days), which would be given in turn. He conducted class seated at the piano which he played to accompany the exercises, and gave instructions to the students through a combination of finger gestures and French phrases. The late André Eglevsky, whose school and company is located on Long Island, described how students would periodically dash up to the piano to examine his finger movements closely for the exact combination of steps and then return to the floor to do them. It was regarded as an odd way to teach, but Legat was so respected that all the first-rate dancers passing through London studied with him. His old studios at Baron's Court are today the studios of the Royal Ballet.

August Bournonville, who set the style of the Royal Danish Ballet, also developed a class for each day of the week. These would be given in turn and then repeated, so that the dancer would have a fully rounded workout by the end of the week.

Asaf Messerer, ballet master and choreographer of the Bolshoi, also developed his classes in a set of six to be given at the rate of one a day. The most influential figure in this century in the Soviet Union was the ballerina teacher Agrippina Vaganova, who had studied under both Johansson and Cecchetti and learned elements of her art from both. She was highly dissatisfied with her own progress as a dancer, though she attained the rank of ballerina. She retired from the stage in 1918 and began teaching immediately, constantly searching for the ideal course of instruction that would combine both the French and Italian schools in a formal way. The proof of her success was the emergence of a new generation of phenomenal dancers in the twenties and thirties, including Marina Semyonova, Galina Ulanova and Natalia Dudinskaya among others. Her book of instruction, *Basic Principles of Classical Ballet*, gained wide acceptance throughout the Soviet Union and has had an influence abroad as well. One of her talented pupils, Vera Volkova, worked extensively in the forties with the dancers of the Sadler's Wells Ballet (now the Royal Ballet) and subsequently with the dancers in the Royal Danish Ballet school.

Vaganova never felt that her system would remain totally unchanged and she herself altered things as she went along, but she did lay the firm basis for development. When she began to codify her system in postrevolutionary Russia, everything was questioned, especially anything that had to do with traditional practice. Her quiet good sense enabled her to make her way through the potential political tangles with great skill. As a simple example, she defended the use of French in ballet instruction with the observation that it was international and had universal acceptance and that it should be used in the same practical unself-conscious way that Latin is used in medicine and English is used in sports. By the time she died in 1951, she had lived to see her concept of the expressiveness of the whole body and her insistence on the importance of the back accepted throughout the Soviet Union.

She was meticulous in her attention to detail but did not insist that any teacher using her system be restricted to one particular format. She did not create a separate, unchanging class for each day but allowed her disciples to evolve exactly the sort of class that they needed, following her broad general principles. There is no telling where great teachers come from. Some of them have had outstanding careers as pure classical dancers, and others have had more modest success as demi-character dancers. What they all share is a systematic approach to the question of movement, so that they break down steps into their component elements and logically strengthen the students in their development of good habits.

The several hundred basic balletic steps can be started from any of the five positions of the feet and directed forward or back, to the right side or the left, resulting in thousands of variations, but basically they are all aspects of seven simple types of movement. Again, they are given in French because many of the steps take their names directly from the action that these words describe. When you see dancers lower their torsos toward the stage (with the back held upright) and keep their feet in place, they are doing a *plié*—from the verb *plier*, "to bend." If they lower halfway, it is a *demi-plié*, and if they go all the way down, it is a *grand plié*. Ideally they should keep their heels on the stage for as long as possible in order to give the correct look. To do so requires that the tendons in the heels are nicely stretched, which is what regular class does. There are all sorts of gliding steps along the floor connecting sequences, and *glisser* (to slide) is one of the basic movements. The step called the *glissade* is used frequently by men to get into a jumping position. *Sauter* (to jump) describes a family of jumping movements, some of which go straight up and down and others of which shift the weight from one leg to another. These "thrown" jumps can be done in a variety of ways and are the traditional strength of the male dancer. When a darting movement is used, *élancer* (to dart) describes the action.

Another basic action is to raise the body without jumping, and the family of *relever* (to raise) steps is very large. The simple action of lifting the heels from the floor and placing the weight on the ball of the foot is known as the *relevé*. It is an action that enters into performing any of the other steps. *Étendre* (to extend or stretch) describes those actions which are developed slowly. One of them is the *développé* (the unfolding action of the leg as it is drawn up along the front of the supporting leg and then stretched out to the side at waist level). Many female dancers develop such extensions to ear level. The last of the basic actions is *tourner* (to turn) and the many types of turns *à terre* and *en l'air* provide some of the most exciting moments in ballet.

These, then, are the basic movements of the body from the five positions of the feet with the legs in the balletic turnout. Why there are just five positions and not more or fewer is a mystery. Ballet masters and dancers have experimented to see whether there are others, but the consensus is that the five are totally adequate. It is like the situation in mapmaking, where cartographers have found that they never need more than five colors to clearly identify different countries, even when they are dealing with as compact a collection of countries as one finds in Western Europe. The same holds true for any map of the continental United States, where five colors are perfectly adequate to separate the individual states.

The most obvious thing that distinguishes male dancing from female dancing is the use of the toe. In classical ballet point work is the exclusive prerogative of the female dancer. It is basically a *relevé* taken to its maximum degree of development. There is no further way to extend the line of the leg once you have reduced the area of contact with the stage to a tiny cluster of toes. Ideally, the dancer should not rest all of the weight on the big toe but spread it across the others as well. Depending on the shape of the foot, this is done to a greater or lesser degree. In the point class teachers will work with individual dancers to achieve as much spread as is anatomically possible.

Before the development of point work, the footwear of male and female dancers was similar, but the point shoe demanded something extra in the way of support for the foot and ankle. Thus it was that the "blocked" point shoe was developed. When women first danced on point during the era of the Romantic ballet there was no special shoe with a reinforced shank and a padded tip. The women pressed wool into the tips of their regular shoes and darned the ends to give themselves cushioning and a little more support. Eventually the reinforced shoe was made, but women still darn and prepare their shoes in individual ways so as to achieve the greatest support with the greatest flexibility. It is a balance that each must find for herself, although they all start with the same basic shoe.

The performing life of these shoes is quite short despite all of the preparation that goes into each one. A professional dancer with a major company will use eight pairs a week on average when performing. The shoe bill is a problem for all companies, who would like to cut down on the high cost of shoes. Even with mass-buying discounts, they cost from eight to ten dollars a pair,

FIFTH POSITION AT THE BARRE: COLLEEN NEARY

FIFTH POSITION ON POINT: COLLEEN NEARY

and simple arithmetic will show that the bill for a company which has fifty female dancers and performs forty weeks a year is staggering. It's probably only a problem of engineering, but no one has been able to come up with a shoe that combines lightness, flexibility and support with durability.

The shoe that the male dancer wears is considerably simpler and consists of a firm leather sole and a soft leather upper. Normally a bit of elastic is sewn across the instep to make the shoe cling to the foot. There is no need for reinforcement in the male shoe, since point work is not choreographed into ballets for the male. Many male dancers can go on point, which is really nothing more than the next hitch upward in a high *relevé*, and very occasionally a choreographer will use this ability when choreographing a character role such as the enchanted donkey Bottom in *A Midsummer Night's Dream*. Frederick Ashton, who created a ballet called *The Dream* based on Shakespeare's play, made a point about the braying pride of the transformed rustic by creating a short variation for the male dancer on point. For the variation specially blocked shoes were used. In Soviet Georgia the men perform several folk dances on point, but these are isolated instances. Point work remains a prerogative of the female dancer in 999 cases out of 1,000.

Some of the most beautiful moments in female variations occur when the dancer is on point, with only one small portion of her body touching the floor and supporting her. It is at these moments that balance, which the female dancer must have above all other qualities, can be seen with utmost clarity. To stand in *relevé* (on the ball of the foot) requires a great deal of balance as well, but there is something extraordinarily special about the delicacy of the point in such poses.

While the male dancer must also demonstrate great balance in everything he does, he is especially judged on the quality of his jumps. There are two aspects to the jump, the first is elevation (the height achieved) and the second is ballon (lightness). Ballon is achieved with the most minute adjustments of the body and though a quality of extreme subtlety, is unmistakable. It imparts to any jump, whether low or high, a floating quality. It, of course, makes its major impact when combined with great elevation, but is very effective even in jumps with lesser height. The secret seems to lie in the ability of the dancer to create the illusion of calmness and stillness which is maintained through a soft return to the surface of the stage.

There are various ways in which one can classify the basic steps. The most fundamental of these are the categories of bending, sliding, jumping and so forth which describe the action but not its quality. Dance manuals have different ways of desig-

SAUT DE BASQUE: KIRK PETERSON

nating steps, but most often it is by grouping jumps, turns, beats and the like into related families of movement. Marius Petipa regarded them from still another aspect, a qualitative one that assigned an expressive weight to each step rather than a mere description. He never codified all of the material into a teachable system but the elements of it show that he considered movement in seven broad categories with certain emotional or dramatic qualities. Poses such as the *attitude* he thought of as particularly useful to show climactic moments such as the Rose Adagio in *The Sleeping Beauty*. *Batterie* (beaten steps of the legs and feet) he thought added sparkle; lightness he associated with jumps; flow was enhanced by the *port de bras* (positions of the arms); pirouettes could give speed; preparatory steps linked movements; and point work added a finishing touch. In his own mind he associated emotional qualities with the academic steps in the way a composer finds emotional coloration in various instruments of keys. Painters use their colors in a similar fashion. None of the assigned designations is absolutely perfect, but in general they do describe a very real and logical ordering of the materials of classical dance. There is no reason to think that a talented choreographer could not achieve the quality of lightness in a ballet drawing mainly on movements of the arms rather than jumps. Nor is it at all inconceivable that a painter could take a violent color like red and tame it in a composition. But these changes would not alter the basic thrust of the movement or color, merely show an exception to a general rule.

The final step in any dancer's career, after learning how to dance well alone, is to learn to dance well with another person. Theoretically, any qualified male and female dancer can perform together, but the reality is quite different. Leaving aside any great disparity in height, which automatically rules out any pairing except for comic effect, there are subtle degrees of movement and configuration that favor any pair of dancers. To the public they "look well together"; to the dancers themselves they have a feeling of sympathetic movement. They are able to anticipate one another's actions and gracefully aid one another in performance. The principles of partnering can be taught, but the great teams of dancers give something extra to one another which is not achieved in other pairings.

In the course of any ballet you will see men and women dancing together, with the man supporting or lifting the woman. The support can be offered in a number of ways, but basically it is designed to extend the velocity or the number of turns in a sequence, to provide a secure anchor for balance, or to extend the height and length of a jump. The idea is to enhance what the dancer could do alone. This requires enormous confidence between the partners, because the female is going to go beyond her normal physical limits. In a turning sequence she will initiate the step, but then rely on her partner to keep her turning smoothly after the initial impetus for the turn has run down. He stands behind her and, with his hands on her waist, maintains the turn, or perhaps she rises to point and places an extended hand in his while he walks slowly around her so that she is turned in a full circle. In a jump she springs to the side with her legs extended while he firmly grasps her waist and walks several steps to deposit her lightly far from where she started. This type of lift is normally assisted by the jumping strength of the female, so that in effect the male does not have to lift as much as he has to steer the live weight of the female. The size of the female has little to do with the amount of weight she presents to the male, but the spring of her jump does. A very famous ballerina, now retired, was noted for the ethereal quality she achieved during these lifts, but her partners paid the price. "She was ninety pounds and she weighed two hundred when you lifted her," remarked one of the most famous. The reason was simple: she didn't jump! There was no assistance from the female. All of the strength had to be supplied by the male, who in the course of a ballet would have to lift her dozens of times. If you have ever lifted someone who was unconscious, you know what the meaning of dead weight is. The female who does not jump is dead weight.

While basic instruction in partnering is given to all male dancers, the real work of the partnership is developed between the dancers themselves. There is no short or easy route to a great partnership; it is the product of continual work. The female is enhanced in the *pas de deux* by the graceful skill of her partner. He must be acutely aware of her balance and correct unobtrusively and surely. The male can be instructed what to do and how to do it in general terms, but the specifics differ from one pair to the next. The teacher can bring the dancers only to a certain stage; they must progress beyond that to artistry. The qualities of the human body are as various as the timbre and pitch of the human voice. Though trained to move within the defined steps of the classical vocabulary, the individual always has a special way of articulating a step, pausing before going on to something else, phrasing, or any of a dozen other things. These are subtle nuances of movement which are recognizable with familiarity. These qualities of movement are the personality of the dancer expressed in the vocabulary of classic dance. The words we use every day to talk to one another take on the intonation of the individual and, though they are the same in meaning, receive a special quality from the voice uttering them. To the trained ear, all sorts of differences can be heard within any particular language. It is no trick at all for a native speaker to detect a variety of accents in his own language while remaining completely oblivious of equally strong differences in a language he does not understand. The "language" of the classic dance has many regional accents and, within these, varieties of expressiveness, depending on the individual dancer. The eye has to be trained to distinguish them by repeated viewing. It's only a question of familiarity.

CHAPTER SEVEN

Critics and publications

The best way to find about about ballet companies is to buy tickets and watch them yourself. The next best way is to go a movie or watch a television program about a company and get some feel for it. The third way is to read about ballet. There are a variety of publications that carry articles and reviews on ballet, and they can be most conveniently grouped as appearing daily, weekly, monthly, quarterly, or on special occasions. Each has its value, and one should be aware of them all so as to select the ones that will be most helpful.

The publication most frequently encountered is the daily newspaper, which may have a special dance critic or one critic who writes on various cultural subjects. No matter how they differ in other respects, daily newspapers have one thing in common: their desire to be responsive to the interests of their readers. In terms of criticism, this might include covering ballet performances not up to professional standards simply because a substantial number of people in the town have children in ballet class who are appearing in the yearly production. This would be more in the nature of a news story than a strictly critical evaluation. Major papers have a general policy against reviewing school performances on the grounds that they do not meet the standards that would be demanded of any visiting company from outside the community. An exception is made in New York for the School of American Ballet performances in the spring, since some of its graduates have already been accepted into New York City Ballet, and also for the High School of Performing Arts, some of whose graduates are already in professional companies. Several years ago one young woman went by limousine directly from her late-afternoon graduation performance to the theater where she was scheduleld to appear that evening. Again, these are exceptional situations.

The critic who is writing for the following day must go to the performance, note what was of merit in it and try to highlight its good points for the general audience. In general, he must try to enlarge an audience's appreciation of what is to be seen. If, as a side matter, he convinces people to see something they would not ordinarily have attended, or if he says something that is of use to the choreographer or the individual performer, that is by way of an added bonus. The thrust of his commentary should be directed to what has been presented onstage, with an eye toward opening up aspects of its worth for the audience. The critic sits on the same side of the footlights as everyone else, and it is as an audience member that he finds his frame of reference.

Critics differ in their reactions, as do most people. They have their likes and dislikes but do not allow them to degenerate into prejudices. If they do, they cease to be trustworthy guides, as would a food writer who announced that he did not like fish and ignored that aspect of the great cuisines. Critics are of two sorts basically: they are dancers or dance students whose career ambitions were thwarted as far as performing is concerned, or they are people who have followed the field as members of the audience for a number of years and developed personal standards. Both share an enthusiasm for the art form. Some begin writing early for college newspapers, others find writing outlets later in the professional world of publications. In my own case, I did not write a word about dance until fourteen years after I had started attending performances. Dance critics do not develop in a vacuum; they tend to appear in centers where there is a substantial amount of dance activity in the course of a year. An active critic in New York will attend four or five performances a week on average throughout the year. It adds up to a great deal of viewing, but it is necessary to maintain contact with the present dance explosion.

Critics are useful to you inasmuch as they provide information which is not contradicted by your own feelings after seeing the same event. You will not always agree with a particular critic, but he is a useful guide if you find that in two out of three cases his reactions are verified by your own. If you cannot tell from one occasion to the next whether your opinion will coincide with that of the critic you are reading, then you cannot rely on his judgment and must find another source of information. This is not to say that he is right and you are wrong or vice versa, but only that you cannot count on his enthusiasms to match your own. In some cases you may find that you never agree with a local critic, so that he becomes reliable as a negative guidepost.

Following is a short selection of reviews and comments that have been published about the New York City Ballet production of *A Midsummer Night's Dream*. The ballet is a full-evening work with elaborate sets and costumes and tunefully familiar music, including Mendelssohn's famous "Wedding March." The reviews range from good to bad in their appraisal of the work, with a selection of mixed reviews which combine some favorable and some unfavorable comments. The thing to remember is that all of the writers saw the same production and came away with different opinions. Again, this doesn't mean that one is right and the other wrong, merely that in artistic matters there is a great deal of room for individual taste.

The first one is quite clearly a rave: "Magnificent is the word for the impression the New York City Ballet made in its formal debut Friday night." It hit another reviewer in a similar way: "It looks as though the New York City Ballet performance of *A Midsummer Night's Dream* exemplifies the poet's observation that 'a thing of beauty is a joy forever.'" A third writer liked it but found it a little lacking in its feel for Shakespeare's original play: "With a flutter of moonbeams and a quiver of quavers Balanchine's magical realization of Mendelssohn's *A Midsummer Night's Dream* flitted into the New York State Theater last night at Lincoln Center. It is a lovely iridescent thing, full of gentle dancing and sweet music . . . but there is little Shakespearean feeling in the ballet." Yet another commented enthusiastically upon "the ballet in which he unfolds the Shakespearean plot with uncommon clarity (and that takes some doing)." Some reserve was shown after initial enthusiasm in this notice: "Certainly everybody got his money's worth, for it is a large and sumptuous production visually beautiful in high degree and full of originality and invention. That it is not as good yet as it will be after it has had a few more performances, is not surprising." One man was not at all pleased: "The fantasy is a bit of a strain at the present period, and not the least tribute to this evening-long event is that it nearly, not quite, manages to keep boredom at bay."

Critics who write for weekly publications normally concentrate on the most significant events of the preceding week and have considerably more space in which to discuss them. There one can expect to find a more elaborate discussion of the merits of more of the members of the cast or of details of production or music. Weekly criticism is ordinarily concerned with the same scope of events as daily criticism, but the critic has more time and space to editorialize on his reactions. One rarely changes one's first impression of a new work, but time gives an added opportunity to orchestrate or fine-tune the initial reaction into its component parts.

Critics who write for monthly magazines normally take a wider view of things and will cover a group of similar events in one review or will take an overview of a whole season that a company has presented. Opinions may be offered on the direction a company is taking rather than concentrating only on a particular production or dancer at a given performance. It is also possible, with a larger body of events, to write about one dancer's approach to a variety of roles, to compare a company's present season with past ones, or to comment on the development of a company's technical prowess as an ensemble. These sorts of comments are not possible to make until a number of performances have been seen and the company or the dancers have been allowed to display the full range of their skills.

Quarterly criticism can take an even broader view of things and may include discussion of an entire season in which many companies have appeared, balancing one against the other. Or it may examine the work of a particular choreographer or company in some depth. One does not read quarterly criticism for a checklist of individual performances but for consideration of trends. The farther away in time one is from a specific performance, the more one expects in thoughtfulness about overall matters, either about an individual performing talent or about a choreographer or a full company. One expects a sense of historical significance to come into play, since there is time to separate the significant from the everyday occurrence. Daily criticism is restricted to a single event and is hot from the fire, while time allows a tempering of judgment. Both are valuable, though they have separate roles to play in one's appreciation of performances.

Outside of impartial criticism there is another source of information about companies which is partisan, since it is produced by the companies themselves, but nevertheless useful. This type of information consists of publicity materials, which include advertisements with quotations, souvenir books on sale at performances, and the program one receives when being seated. All of these have to be recognized for what they are—information about the companies which is totally controlled by the companies. It is highly unlikely that one would ever find an adverse word in any of them.

Selecting judicious quotes about the merit of companies is basically a word game that is played by the publicity office. The governing rule is that there is no review, however bad, that cannot provide at least one favorable quote. My own personal favorite occurred after the disastrous appearance of a small ballet company that was poorly trained, oddly sized (tall women and short men, and vice versa), with a repertory of inept ballets by the company director, and music of dismal modernity or cloying sweetness. A colleague of mine excoriated this hapless group for nearly a column, pointing out all of its deficiencies, and ironically concluded with the phrase that the company "can certainly put on a show." Of course the last phrase appeared in the publicity, but nothing else did. In judging quotes be wary of such isolated snippets, especially of single words isolated by lines of dots fore and aft. However, if sentences, paragraphs or entire reviews are reprinted, one gains confidence in the advertisement in which the assessment is offered.

The souvenir book is an art form in and of itself, with its bright-colored cover, glossy photographs and feeling of luxury. It too has its rules, but it can often be a valuable guide to the company's artistic direction, history, stars and administrative hierarchy. Souvenir books are generally sold from little stands in the lobby of the theater where the company is playing, and the people who buy them rarely have a chance to read them before seeing the company, which is when they are most valuable. They are normally read afterward when their usefulness is lessened. Try, if possible, to secure a copy of the souvenir book beforehand and look it over carefully before going to the theater. In the case of major ballet companies, one can write to the publicity office and ask to be sent one as soon as they are available. Since this is at least a week before the opening of any season, if not more, it gives one plenty of time to learn about the company on its own terms. One could enclose a separate check for two or three dollars when sending in for tickets, which is usually well in advance of the actual date. If you have to buy it the day of the performance, glance through it before the houselights dim.

The cover of a typical souvenir book has a photograph of a ballet or a performer that the company is particularly proud of and wants to draw your attention to. Or it will have an illustration that tells you something about the occasion itself or the tone of the company—a period lithograph to conjure up a Romantic mood for a company that specializes in nineteenth-century classics, or a large, bold number to indicate an anniversary year or the like. The possibilities are as extensive as the moods or occasions, but in each case the company wants to inform the audience of the significance of its season.

Inside there is usually a long article by a critic or historian who has followed the company over a period of time and recounts the development of the company and indicates those special things that set it apart from others. These essays, though written by friendly observers, contain a great deal of information which one cannot easily come by except from extensive reading in a variety of outside publications. There will not be a harsh word sounded about the company, but then in matters of record there need not be. Frequently there is a second article about one of the company members which is complimentary, discusses some related aspect of the season and may have a more anecdotal tone. These are harmless and may even provide some additional information.

Close to the front of the book it is customary to show a listing of the dancers grouped according to their relative importance in the company, along with the names of the artistic director, designers, conductors and other technical staff. These names will turn up in the actual performance program, where once again the ranking of the dancers will tell you which are the most important to the company and who to be on the lookout for. A few companies list the dancers alphabetically without dividing them into graded categories of accomplishment. In these cases one does not derive much from the list, but further back in the book there are usually brief biographical sketches, and these will be about the major figures in the company. Ordinarily they are accompanied by photographs.

This portion of the book is most useful, since it enables one to identify individual performers by sight rather than trying to figure out who they are during the course of a ballet. A good rule of thumb is to judge the importance of the individual by the amount of space devoted to him in terms of the length of the entry and the size of the photograph. These books are a form of advertising, and in advertising one always gives most emphasis by placement and size. The people one comes across first in this section are considered to be of major importance to the company. At times it may be a choreographer rather than a dancer; but whoever it is, is a figure of special note. Customarily, female members of the company are presented before the men, but this is not inflexible. These top-level dancers are also usually presented in alphabetical order, but if they are not it is an indication that the company wishes to draw your attention to those listed first.

The entries on the individual dancers will mention aspects of their training, when they joined the company, and roles with which they have had a special success. They will also mention any honors they have received or international prizes they have won. At times they may give a brief commentary upon the particular qualities that characterize their performance. These little biographies can frequently be very helpful in guiding one as to what to watch for when the performer is featured in a ballet. At the very least, if you buy a souvenir book just before the performance, a quick glance at the photographs will help you to identify the dancers you will see in the major roles to be performed that afternoon or evening.

One other significant section of the souvenir books is devoted to photographs of the various ballets one will see during the course of the season. Along with these photographs, which show the featured dancers and portions of the supporting corps de ballet, there will be a commentary on the story of the ballet; if it has a dramatic plot line, this will be summarized; and if it does not, the mood of the piece will be characterized. These photographs are taken during a performance or a dress rehearsal of the ballet, so one can see what the costumes look like. Frequently these photographs are in color and are thus even more useful as an aid to identify the individual performers. The large portrait pictures of the dancers may or may not show them in costume.

The souvenir book is not an impartial critical platform like a newspaper or magazine; it is a form of advertising that is controlled by the company, and as such reflects the company's own image of itself. That is its strength and also its shortcoming. It will not be critical of any aspect of its operation or any of its ballets, and if one were to read all of the souvenir books the impression would be that all of the companies are equally marvelous, though perhaps in different ways. That isn't true any more than all advertised products are equally good, but it would be bizarre for a man to take out an advertisement to tell you what was wrong or lacking in his product.

The souvenir book concentrates on what is right with a company and is scrupulously accurate about the administrative directors of the company, the ranking of the dancers, the dates of first performances, and other official historical information. In one unusual case, the appointment of a new ballet master for a foreign touring company was revealed in its administrative listing for a tour of the United States before the announcement appeared in his own country's press. Admittedly, one doesn't read souvenir books for news stories, but they are accurate about such information. Considering the time and energy that companies expend on every aspect of these books, they are a bargain. Nothing in them appears by chance—the size of every picture and the weight of every word is carefully measured.

While you must pay for the souvenir book, the program given away at each performance can be very useful. Its essential purpose is to identify the ballets to be performed in order that evening or matinee, and to list the names of the dancers who will perform them. It also indicates when there will be an intermission, either between shorter ballets or between the acts of a full-evening ballet. Between some sections of longer ballets or even between shorter ballets there is a pause rather than an intermission to allow for a scene change or the like. These are normally brief and the lights in the auditorium will be brought up to half strength so that the audience is not left waiting and wondering in the dark. As soon as some people see house lights turned up, they assume it indicates an intermission and bolt for the lobby. No sooner do they get there than the lights lower, indicating the continuance of the performance and they have to scramble back and waste time clambering into their seats. A glance at the program would have saved them the trouble.

Sometimes a performer will be injured and another dancer familiar with the role will perform it, or a whole ballet may be substituted. An announcement of this is normally made in the program by means of a small slip of paper inserted with the name of the ballet and the dancer. If by some chance there is a last-minute accident which does not permit the printing of an insert for the program, an announcement must be made from the stage. Companies are careful about this, since it is required in the dancers' contract. From time to time there is a change in the listed running order of the ballets and the audience is informed of this in the same manner.

On a mixed program of shorter ballets it is important to know which one is being performed and to be familiar with the dancers who perform it. The program has this information. It's surprising how often one hears this desperate whisper as the lights are lowered: "Which one is next?" It also enhances the pleasure of watching when one can identify the various dancers. It not only enables you to watch for your favorites but contributes to the understanding of ballets which do not have an overt story line. The repertories of nearly every ballet company now contain works which do not tell a story in terms of specific characters or a dramatic incident, but rely on the interplay of the dancers without any identification as "a young girl," "her father," "the soldier," and the like. In these ballets it is particularly important to be aware of the individual dancers so that their comings and goings and involvements are not baffling surprises but recognizable parts of an emerging development.

The great difficulty is that, at first, all of the dancers look alike, unless they have striking physical characteristics which make them stand out. The fact is that few dancers are instantly recognizable, but with a little care one can verify their identity by consulting the program. An example would be *The Four Temperaments*, choreographed by George Balanchine and performed by New York City Ballet. The ballet does not distinguish between the dancers in terms of costume. It is performed in practice clothes—a white T-shirt and black tights for the men, a black leotard and white tights for the women. Despite the uniformity of the costuming, it is divided in such a way as to make the identification relatively easy with the use of the program.

As can be seen from the heavy black typeface, the ballet is divided into five sections starting with "Theme" and concluding with "Fourth Variation: Choleric." Each of the four variations is characterized by a descriptive word which identifies the mood of the section and gives one a clue as to its general flavor. Beneath each of the five sections are the names of the solo dancers and the members of the corps who will make an appearance in that section. For the final movement the words "and Ensemble" indicate that everyone who has appeared previously will join in the finale. In this ballet that means twenty-five dancers, as a quick count will reveal. Out of that number you will be able to identify nearly half of them quite readily. In the "Theme" three couples are listed in order of appearance—"1," "2" and "3"—and the dancers whose names appear side by side will be dancing with one another, so that indeed the first *pas de deux* will be danced by Marjorie Spohn and Stephen Caras. Since there are no names listed in smaller type, they will not be framed by members of the corps de ballet and one can concentrate on them.

The "First Variation: Melancholic" will feature a male solo, since only Bart Cook's name is listed in large print. As all of the assisting members of the corps, who are listed, are women in this instance, he will be the only male onstage. Just below his name two members of the corps are connected in a slightly special way —"Judith Fugate and Delia Peters"—so that you know they will play a slightly more prominent part in the action than the other four, who are listed in the same typeface but without the distin-

The Four Temperaments

Music by Paul Hindemith
(By arrangement with Belwin-Mills Publishing Corp., sole U.S. agents for B. Schotts Soehne, Mainz, Publishers and copyright owners)
Choreography by George Balanchine
Lighting by Ronald Bates
Piano Solo: JERRY ZIMMERMAN
THEME
1. MARJORIE SPOHN, STEPHEN CARAS
2. WILHELMINA FRANKFURT, JAY JOLLEY
3. HEATHER WATTS, NOLAN T'SANI
FIRST VARIATION: MELANCHOLIC
BART COOK
Judith Fugate and Delia Peters
Victoria Bromberg, Dolores Houston, Lourdes Lopez, Catherine Morris
SECOND VARIATION: SANGUINIC
MERRILL ASHLEY and DANIEL DUELL
Elyse Borne, Laura Flagg, Nichol Hlinka, Sandra Zigars
THIRD VARIATION: PHLEGMATIC
JEAN-PIERRE BONNEFOUS
Maria Calegari, Nina Fedorova, Linda Homek, Garielle Whittle
FOURTH VARIATION: CHOLERIC
COLLEEN NEARY and Ensemble
Music Composed: 1940
Ballet Premiere: November 20, 1946
This work for solo piano and strings together with the opera *L'Enfant et les Sortilèges* by Ravel constituted the first Ballet Society (the direct predecessor of the New York City Ballet) program given November 20, 1946. The popularity of this ballet has increased greatly both here and in Europe through successive performances. It has always been a favorite of the dancers in the company.

PROGRAM LISTING: *THE FOUR TEMPERAMENTS*

guishing "and." As is customary, all members of the corps are listed alphabetically, with a comma separating their names. (If there were male dancers in the corps they would be listed on a separate line in the same size type but customarily below the female dancers.) As can be seen in the listing of the solo dancers "Marjorie Spohn, Stephen Caras"—the woman's name ordinarily precedes the man's. If a man's name is listed first it is for a specific reason, perhaps to show that he will be onstage before the others, or perhaps the choreographer wishes to make a point about the construction or casting of the ballet. It is, in any case, done for a specific reason and is out of the ordinary. Ballet tends to be very careful in its observance of traditional courtesies.

The "Second Variation: Sanguinic" is a *pas de deux* with four different members of the corps assisting. The "Third Variation: Phlegmatic" features a male soloist again with four more members of the corps, and the "Fourth Variation: Choleric" will be for a solo female dancer who will be joined by the rest of the dancers in the ballet. Like all of the other soloists she will be identifiable by the way she is featured in the ballet.

Another useful aspect of the program is the information that is conveyed in the program notes. These are found in a small paragraph either before or after the listing of the dancers and give a little background so that one learns a bit about the ballet before seeing it. To use the program to its fullest takes a bit of time, but intermissions (fifteen minutes ordinarily) give one sufficient time to chat as well as to look at the program. In many programs there are also articles about the company which help to give one an idea of the things it considers important. Sometimes these articles comment on a production you will see at that performance, and sometimes not. There is no hard-and-fast rule.

Another example of a typical program entry is this one for *La Bayadère* as it is performed by American Ballet Theater. The names of the five dancers who will perform away from the corps de ballet are listed, and the first two, Nikia and Solor, are clearly identified. If you have read the program note you will see that Solor and Nikia were lovers, so she is the one he will pursue. Since he is the only male dancer listed, his partner, the "pursued" Nikia, will have to be Marianna Tcherkassky. "The Shadows," however, are listed together and though, in fact, they do dance together they also dance solo variations. In this case the company has not listed them in alphabetical order, departing from the practice in order to alert you to something. Here they are telling you the order in which the three will appear for the variations, so that you now know that the first one of them to do a solo will be Rebecca Wright, the second Nanette Glushak, and the third will be Jolinda Menendez. With this information you will have identified all of the solo dancers. The corps is listed, as usual, in alphabetical order, not in the order of appearance.

La Bayadere

Choreography by Marius Petipa   *Staged by* Natalia Makarova

Music by Ludwig Minkus

Costumes by Marcos Paredes   *Lighting by* Nananne Porcher

The Kingdom of the Shades is the last act of *La Bayadère* by Marius Petipa. Nikiya, a bayadère or East Indian temple dancer, was in love with Solor. A rival for his love presented her with a basket of flowers in which was hidden a venomous snake. Nikiya was bitten and died. In a dream, Solor visits the Kingdom of the Shades and among the ghosts of other bayadères discovers Nikiya and vows never again to forsake her.

Miss Makarova considers this passage to be one of Petipa's finest creations and a perfect example of symphonic choreography. As with a symphony, a theme is stated, developed, re-stated and resolved in a final coda. The spirits of the bayadères emerge one by one and in an attenuated line, wind and unwind in an infinitely repeating pattern. The continuing series of canteleva arabesques can be compared with the seemingly endless repetition of the single theme in Ravel's *Bolero* and as with the *Bolero* the repetition causes an almost unbearable mounting of tension. This melodic and changing pattern of dance serves as a background for the rather playful variations of the three soloists and for the more forceful, virtuoso solos of Nikiya and Solor. Though no definite meaning can be ascribed to a single movement, the sum total of movements conveys an emotional feeling of sadness, remorse, and reconciliation as the two lovers are once more joined together.

Nikiya Marianna Tcherkassky

Solor Ivan Nagy

The Shadows Rebecca Wright, Nanette Glushak, Jolinda Menendez

and

Elizabeth Ashton, Carmen Barth, Amy Blaisdell, Nina Brzorad, Susan Frazer, Melissa Hale, Aurea Hammerli, Cynthia Harvey, Janne Jackson, Marie Johansson, Francia Kovak, Linda Kuchera, Elaine Kudo, Lisa Lockwood, Sara Maule, Ruth Mayer, Christine O'Neal, Janet Popeleski, Berthica Prieto, Leigh Provancha, Cathryn Rhodes, Lisa Rinehart, Janet Shibata, Christine Spizzo, Denise Warner   Patricia Wesche   Sandall Whitaker   Cheryl Yeager

PROGRAM LISTING: *LA BAYADÈRE*

Romeo and Juliet

Narrative Ballet in one act by Antony Tudor
based on the play by William Shakespeare

Music by:	Frederick Delius
	arranged by Antal Dorati
Scenery and costumes by:	Eugene Berman
Lighting by:	Nananne Porcher
First presented at the	Metropolitan Opera House in
	New York City on April 6, 1943

Heads of two houses at variance with each other:	
Montague	Rodney Gustafson
Capulet	William Carter
Romeo, son to Montague	John Prinz
Mercutio, friend to Romeo	Dennis Nahat
Benvolio	George de la Pena
Kinsmen of the Montagues	Peter Fonseca, Charles Maple, Raymond Serrano
Tybalt, nephew of Lady Capulet	Marcos Paredes
Kinsmen of the Capulets	Victor Barbee, Miguel Campaneria, Michael Owen, Miguel Sanchez
Friar Lawrence, a Franciscan	Frank Smith
Paris, a young Nobleman	Richard Schafer
Lady Montague, wife to Montague	Nina Brzorad
Lady Capulet, wife to Capulet	Sandall Whitaker
Juliet, daughter to Capulet	Hilda Morales
Nurse to Juliet	Ruth Mayer
Rosaline	Nanette Glushak
Ladies at the Ball	Misses Blaisdell, Frazer, Hale, Harvey, Maule, O'Neal, Prieto, Rhodes, Wesche
Townspeople:	
Candle-Seller	Christine O'Neal
Trading Woman	Janne Jackson
Cripple	Roman Jasinski
Blind Man	Buddy Balough
The Girl	Aurea Hammerli
Handmaidens to Juliet	Misses Ashton, Hammerli, Kudo, Rinehart, Spizzo, Warner,
The Attendants	Susan Jones, Carmen Barth
Conductor:	Akira Endo
Assistant to Mr. Tudor:	Hugh Laing

Romeo and Juliet
The scene is Verona

Prologue—Ball at the House for the Capulets—Romeo and his Kinsmen leave the ball—Romeo woos Juliet in the Capulet orchard—Betrothal of Romeo and Juliet by the Friar—Street scene, the deaths of Mercutio and Tybalt and the flight of Romeo—Romeo's farewell to Juliet—Preparations for the wedding of Juliet to Paris—Procession to the tomb—Scene in the vault of the Capulets and deaths of the lovers—Epilogue.

William Shakespeare (b. 1564 at Stratford-on-Avon, England): Romeo and Juliet, one of his earliest plays (circa 1596), was based upon a popular story of the same name by Luigi da Porto, published in 1530.

Frederick Delius (b. 1862 at Bradford, England): The music for *Romeo and Juliet* has been drawn from various orchestra pieces including *Eventyr, Over the Hills and Far Away, Briggs Fair*, and others.

PROGRAM LISTING: *ROMEO AND JULIET*

The program listing for *Romeo and Juliet* is of a different structure altogether, since it is a story ballet with a host of characters. Just below the title of the piece a note explains that it is a ballet in one act indicating that with this many characters it will be very compact and you will have to be on the alert to identify each of them in order to derive the full impact of the story as it unfolds. Since the note also characterizes the ballet as a narrative, it will relate specific incidents and generally follow the line of the play, though, being a ballet, certain things will be altered to accommodate the demands of dancing and music.

The characters are listed pretty much as they are identified in the original play. The title tells us that the two principals are Romeo, of the house of Montague, and Juliet, a Capulet. Since the story revolves around them (John Prinz and Hilda Morales), one can identify many of the other characters by their relationship to the principals. Each of the characters will have a different costume, so it will be relatively easy to keep track of them once they have been identified. The description of Montague and Capulet as "Heads of two houses at variance with one another" immediately alerts us to the fact that there is a conflict, even if the story were not familiar from past reading. Mercutio, who is described as a "friend to Romeo," can be expected to

253

demonstrate this friendship clearly, and Romeo should, by his behavior, indicate who Montague is, since he is his son. The "Kinsmen of the Montagues" will obviously ally themselves with the principals of the house, and the "Kinsmen of the Capulets" will line up on the opposite side. The monk "Friar Lawrence" should be easy to pick out because of his habit, and the "Nurse to Juliet" should be found attending her. Lady Montague will obviously be at the side of the head of that house, as Lady Capulet will be her opposite number in the house of Capulet. Other characters, such as the "Blind Man," "Cripple," "Candle-Seller," and "Trading Woman," will identify themselves by their actions. The ballet is outstanding and it is worth taking a few moments to look over the program so as to derive full satisfaction from the recounting of the story.

The Joffrey Ballet, which frequently revives excellent ballets, selected Kurt Jooss's *The Green Table* one year, and its program listing and notes are a very useful guide to the ballet. No individual characters are identified by name but only as types: the "Standard Bearer," Robert Thomas; the "Profiteer," Gary Chryst; and even "Death," Christian Holder. Below these listings are descriptions of the seven scenes, which give you the various characters in the order of appearance and even a physical description of the costume of "Death," who is "in the panoply of the War God." Reading the contents of the seven scenes also makes very clear that "Death" is the central character and that the ballet is cyclical, since the first and last scenes are the same. The setting of the last scene, the "Peace Table," is ironically put in quotation marks, which indicates the choreographer's melancholy attitude to the actions of the men who are on the left and right sides of the table.

This does not exhaust the possibilities of the usefulness of the printed program but it does at least indicate how it can be of help. The basic attitude of the company with regard to the ultimate reader of the program is to provide as much factual information as possible. One thing that is scrupulously avoided is any type of commentary that would express an artistic judgment on

CRITICS AND PUBLICATIONS

THE GREEN TABLE*
Danse Macabre in Eight Scenes
(Created between two wars as a memorial for the Unknown)

Choreography by Kurt Jooss	Music by Frederic Cohen
Lighting by Thomas Skelton	Conducted by Sung Kwak
Set and costumes after the originals	Pianists: Stanley Babin and Mary Roark
by Hein Heckroth	Masks by Hermann Markard

(American Supervision by William Pitkin)

This production was made possible by a grant from the New York State Council on the Arts.

THE CHARACTERS

Death .... Christian Holder
Standard Bearer .... Robert Thomas
Young Soldier .... William Whitener
Young Girl .... Charthel Arthur
Old Soldier .... Gregory Huffman
Guerilla Woman .... Diana Cartier
Old Mother .... Trinette Singleton
Profiteer .... Gary Chryst
Women .... Ingrid Fraley, Jan Hanniford, Beatriz Rodriguez, Krystyna Jurkowski
Ann Marie DeAngelo
Soldiers .... Robert Estner, Richard Colton, Donn Edwards

THE GENTLEMEN IN BLACK:

LEFT SIDE OF THE GREEN TABLE:	RIGHT SIDE OF THE GREEN TABLE:
Gary Chryst	Robert Estner
Richard Colton	Philip Jerry
Russell Sultzbach	Jeffrey Hughes
Kevin McKenzie	Tom Fowler
Donn Edwards	William Whitener

Scene I: The Gentlemen in Black, around The Green Table — The Diplomats at a Peace Conference. The result is War.
Scene II: The Farewell — Death (in the panoply of the War God) summons The Standard Bearer, who calls the men to arms. The Profiteer appears.
Scene III: War
Scene IV: The Refugees — Confronted suddenly by Death, they break and flee — all save the Old Mother, who, unafraid, finds deliverance in his arms.
Scene V: The Guerilla — A woman, distracted by grief and rage, kills one of the enemy. She, too, is taken by Death.
Scene VI: The Brothel — In which Death finally saves The Young Girl from the misery of her existence.
Scene VII: The Aftermath.
Scene VIII: The Gentlemen in Black — again at the "Peace Table."
* First Prize, International Congress of the Dance, organized by Les Archives Internationales de la Danse, Paris, July 3rd, 1932, Theatre des Champs-Elysees.

THE GREEN TABLE—First performance by Ballets Jooss on July 3, 1932 in Paris, France. First performance by the City Center Joffrey Ballet on February 27, 1967 in Toronto, Canada.

PROGRAM LISTING: *THE GREEN TABLE*

the piece you are about to see. It would be presumptuous of the company to attempt to sway audience opinion in that fashion before the ballet has had a chance to make a case for itself on its own terms—i.e., well costumed and well lit with a group of skilled dancers on an appropriate stage. The company will, however, try to supply you with any factual material that can be of use and then let you make up your own mind. And the more frequently you attend ballet performances, the more confident you will be in that opinion.

CHAPTER EIGHT

Chronology of significant events

IN BALLET	IN CONTEMPORARY SOCIETY

1469

Marriage of Lorenzo de Medici to Clarice Orsini celebrated with a masque as well as sporting competition and processions.

1475

Giuliano de Medici Pageants painted by Botticelli, as was the custom in Florence of using the finest painters for such entertainments.

1492

Christopher Columbus' first voyage of discovery to the Western Hemisphere.

1493

Leonardo da Vinci's *Paradiso* performed.

Columbus' second voyage to the New World.

1512

Henry VIII introduces court productions to England patterned after Italian models.

1513

Vasco de Balboa crosses the Isthmus of Panama and discovers the Pacific Ocean.

1552

Marked expansion of court theaters in Italy.

Expanded exploration and settlement of North America by French and English navigators.

1580

Francis Drake becomes first English explorer to circumnavigate the globe.

1581

Ballet Comique de la Reine by Beaujoyeux (Baldassare di Belgiojoso) at the behest of

Catherine de Medici for the marriage of her sister. The production, including music and recitation as well as dancing, is considered the first clear modern ballet. It combined French court dance with Italian staging, which set the pattern for development over the next two centuries.

1588

Thoinot Arbeau (Jehan Tabourot) publishes his *L'Orchésographie*, the first modern treatise codifying ballet steps.

Privateers and pirates continue to ply the Spanish Main. One of these, Thomas Cavendish, becomes the second Englishman to circumnavigate the globe.

1626

Peter Minuit purchases Manhattan Island for $24 and founds New Amsterdam.

1651

Louis XIV, "The Sun King," makes his first appearance in a court ballet, at the age of thirteen.

Massachusetts Colony continues to expand.

1661

Louis XIV founds Académie Royale de Danse in the Louvre.

1664

Louis XIV appears in *Le Mariage Forcé* by Lully and Molière.

New Amsterdam surrenders to the English, who change the name to New York.

1673

Pierre Beauchamps made Maître de Ballet of the Académie Royale de Musique et de Danse.

Dutch retake New York temporarily.

1681

Professional female dancers make first appearance on French stage.

William Penn granted a charter for the Pennsylvania colony.

c. 1700

Beauchamps describes the five basic positions of the feet.

1711

Tuscaroras massacre 200 settlers in North Carolina.

1726

Marie Camargo makes her debut at the Paris Opera.

Increasing hostility between French and English in western New York.

1733

Georgia, last of the thirteen original colonies, founded.

1738

Jean-Baptiste Landé establishes ballet school in St. Petersburg at the invitation of Empress Anna.

1760

Publication of Jean-Georges Noverre's *Letters on Dancing and Ballets*.

The French and Indian War; Montreal surrenders and all Canada is under English control.

1775

Noverre's *Jason and Medea* performed. Bolshoi Theater in Moscow opens.

Start of the Revolutionary War.

1783

Successful conclusion of war and final peace treaty, ending hostilities with England, signed.

1803

The Louisiana Purchase of New Orleans, plus the land between the Mississippi and the Rocky Mountains, from France, doubles the size of the United States.

1812

Salvatore Viganò becomes ballet master of La Scala in Milan.

War of 1812 with England.

1820

Renowned teacher Carlo Blasis publishes in Milan, his *Elementary Treatise on the Theory and Practice of the Art of Dancing*, a fundamental text still in use today.

The Missouri Compromise admits Maine as a "free" state and Missouri as a "slave" state to the Union.

1822

Marius Petipa, shaper of Russian classical style, born in France.

1823

The Monroe Doctrine enunciates United States rejection of European colonization efforts in the Western Hemisphere.

1825

Augusta Maywood, first American ballerina to achieve international reputation, born.

Erie Canal completed.

1829

August Bournonville appointed ballet master of the Royal Danish Ballet and sets the definitive development that characterized his long tenure.

Andrew Jackson becomes President and nationalizes the "Spoils System" of rewarding loyal political party workers.

1832

Marie Taglioni dances in *La Sylphide*, ushering in the Romantic ballet.

Jackson begins attack on the Second Bank of the United States by removing government deposits and redepositing them in "pet banks."

1836

Samuel Colt patents his "six-shooter."

1841

First performance of *Giselle* by Paris Opera Ballet.

1845

Pas de Quatre performed with the leading Romantic ballerinas Taglioni, Cerrito, Grisi and Grahn.

Joint resolution of the Congress to annex Texas.

1846

Giselle danced in United States for the first time by Mary Ann Lee and George Washington Smith.

War with Mexico provoked by the annexation of Texas.

1847

Marius Petipa engaged by Bolshoi Ballet.

General Winfield Scott captures Mexico City.

1861

Start of the Civil War.

1862

Petipa stages *Daughter of Pharaoh*, becomes ballet master of the Imperial Theater in St. Petersburg.

1867

Sylvia presented by Paris Opera Ballet.

George Armstrong Custer and his troop of cavalry annihilated at the Little Big Horn by Sitting Bull.

1872

Serge Diaghilev is born.

President Ulysses S. Grant is re-elected to a second term.

1879

Thomas Edison invents the incandescent electric light.

1880

Mikhail Fokine is born.

1890

Petipa stages The Sleeping Beauty.

The Sherman Antitrust Law, designed to discourage the formation of monopolies, passed.

1892

Lev Ivanov stages The Nutcracker.

1895

Petipa-Ivanov production of Swan Lake.

The first attempt to legislate a personal income tax declared unconstitutional.

1898

Fokine proposes reforms in ballet emphasizing dramatic

Battleship Maine sunk in Havana, and the Spanish-

interpretation rather than virtuoso display and uniform blending of choreography, music, decor and costuming.

American War results.

1904

Theodore Roosevelt announces the Roosevelt corollary of the Monroe Doctrine, giving the United States international police power in the Western Hemisphere.

1906

Anna Pavlova becomes prima ballerina of the Maryinsky.

The Pure Food and Drug Act passed.

1908

Vaslav Nijinsky graduates from the Maryinsky school.

1909

Diaghilev presents the first season of Les Ballet Russes in Paris to tumultuous reception.

Henry Ford mass-produces the Model T.

1910

Petipa dies in retirement.

1914

Panama Canal opened. World War I begins in Europe.

1915

First tour of Diaghilev's Ballets Russes in the United States.

1916

Second U.S. tour of Diaghilevs Ballets Russes.

1917

Declaration of War against Germany brings United States into World War I.

1918

World War I ended.

1929

Diaghilev dies in Venice; members of the Ballets Russes disperse.

The stock market crash in New York begins a worldwide depression.

1931

First full evening of ballet given by the Vic-Wells Ballet, under the direction of Ninette de Valois, at Sadler's Wells Theater.

Wiley Post and Harold Gatty fly around the world in 8 days, 15 hours and 51 minutes.

1934

The School of American Ballet established in New York by George Balanchine and Lincoln Kirstein.

Civil Works Emergency Relief Act continues program with $950,000,000 appropriation.

1935

First season of the American Ballet, for which Balanchine choreographed *Serenade*, his first ballet in America.

Social Security Act passed.

1935

Catherine Littlefield organizes the Littlefield Ballet in Philadelphia.

1937

San Francisco Ballet and school founded by William Christensen.

Neutrality Act affirms United States non-involvement in wars outside the Americas.

1938

Page-Stone Ballet Company formed in Chicago by Ruth Page and Bentley Stone.

1939

American Ballet Theater (then Ballet Theater) organized by Richard Pleasant and Lucia Chase around members of the Mordkin Ballet.

FDR asks for assurances from Hitler and Mussolini to refrain from aggression.
World War II begins in Europe.

1941

The American Ballet tours South America.

Japanese attack on Pearl Harbor draws United States into World War II.

1945

World War II ends.

1946

Sadler's Wells Ballet reopens the Royal Opera House, Covent Garden, with a performance of *The Sleeping Beauty*.
Ballet Society formed under the direction of Kirstein and Balanchine.
American Ballet Theater becomes first American ballet company to visit England ˙after World War II.

College enrollments swell with returning veterans attending on government grants, part of the "GI Bill" enacted by the Congress.

1948

New York City Ballet formed by Ballet Society as constituent company of the New York City Center of Music and Drama.
Dance Collection of the New York Public Library formed. (In the thirty ensuing years it has become the leading dance research center in the world.)

Social policies of the New Deal continued by Harry S Truman, who wins an upset victory in the presidential election.

1949

The Sadler's Wells Ballet makes its first appearance in the United States and begins a series of appearances that continues to the present.
Jerome Robbins becomes associate director of New York City Ballet.

1950

New York City Ballet makes its first visit to London.

U.N. police action involves U.S. military intervention in South Korea.

1951

American Ballet Theater School opens.

1956

Robert Joffrey Ballet Founded and makes first major U.S. tour.

President Dwight D. Eisenhower re-elected for second term.

1957

Royal Danish Ballet makes first tour of the United States.
San Francisco Ballet makes its first overseas tour.
Bolshoi Ballet makes first American tour.

1960

American Ballet Theater tours U.S.S.R. for the first time.

1961

Kirov Ballet makes first American tour.

New York State Council on the Arts founded.

1962

New York City Ballet tours U.S.S.R.

1963

The Robert Joffrey Ballet tours U.S.S.R.

A ten-year staged grant made by the Ford Foundation to assist the long-range development of ballet in the U.S.

1964

New York City Ballet becomes resident dance company of New York State Theater.

Opening of New York State Theater at Lincoln Center, the first major auditorium designed for dance.

1965

National Foundation of the Arts and Humanities established as a federal agency.

1967

Association of American Dance Companies founded.

1968

American Ballet Theater tours Japan.

1969

New York City Ballet celebrates its thirtieth anniversary.
Stuttgart Ballet has successful season in New York.
American choreographer John Neumeier named director of Frankfurt State Opera Ballet.

American astronauts explore the surface of the moon.
Around this time, press references are made about New York being the dance capital of the world.

1971

American Ballet Theater makes first appearance at the newly completed Kennedy Center in Washington, D.C.

American Ballet Theater signs a new union contract substantially raising dancers' salaries.

1972

New York City Ballet honors Stravinsky with its week-long Stravinsky Festival.

Ford Foundation makes a staged grant of $1,000,000 to American Ballet Theater.

1974

American choreographer Glen Tetley named director of Stuttgart Ballet.

1976

Bicentennial celebration ballets prepared by all the major companies.

Official celebration year of the two hundredth anniversary of the founding of the Republic.

1977

Increasing financial pressures felt by all the major companies.

Largest Performing Arts budget ever submitted, approved by Congress.

CHAPTER NINE

Glossary of ballet terms

ADAGIO   As in music, a slow tempo: a dance in a slow tempo. The word is derived from the Italian *ad agio*, meaning at ease or in a leisurely manner. Adagios are danced by ballerinas and their partners. Adagios may occur in a ballet when the drama of the piece so dictates (*Swan Lake*, Act Two), as the central portion of *grand pas de deux* (*Swan Lake*, Act Three), or simply as the music demands (*Symphony in C*, second movement). In adagio, the ballerina displays her beauty in slow, unfolding movements and sustained graceful poses. The principal quality of adagio is control.

Adagio is also the name for a section of any ballet class. Here the dancers practice—in the center of the room—slow, sustained exercises designed to give ease in the performance of dances that require balance, perfect line, and unquestionable authority in those who execute them.

The great Italian ballet master Carlo Blasis regarded the correct execution of adagio as the "touchstone of the dancer."

ALLEGRO   Dancing that is lively and fast, in comparison to adagio. All steps of elevation—jumps, *entrechats*, turns in the air, etc., are forms of allegro. An important quality of allegro is *ballon*, the ease with which a dancer remains in the air during a step in elevation and the ease with which he takes off and lands from a jump.

ARABESQUE Set pose. In the most common form of arabesque, the dancer stands on one leg, with the other leg raised behind her and extended fully. The height of the raised leg is variable, as is the position of the arms.

ASSEMBLÉ Literally, together. A step in which the dancer rises low off the floor, straightens both legs in the air, and returns to Fifth Position.

À TERRE On the ground. *Par terre* is synonymous. Some dancers are called *terre à terre* dancers because they succeed best in steps that require no elevation, steps performed on the stage.

ATTITUDE Basic pose of the classic dance, first described by Carlo Blasis (1829), who modeled it after the famous statue of Mercury by Bologna. In the basic attitude, the dancer stands on one leg and brings the other leg up behind at an angle of ninety degrees, with the knee bent.

BALLET From the Italian *ballare*, to dance, via *balleti*, the diminutive form of *balle*, a dance-song.

BALLET BLANC (white ballet) Ballet in which girls wear long white gossamer costumes: *Les Sylphides*, *Giselle* (Act Two), etc.

BALLET D'ACTION Literally, a ballet in which something happens: a ballet with a plot.

BALLET MASTER In the early days of ballet, the ballet master was a choreographer, a man who designed or composed dances for a ballet company. In France and in Russia today, this is still the case. In England and America, the ballet master (or ballet mistress) is the person responsible for company instruction and discipline, the person who gives classes to all the company dancers, rehearses them in all ballets in the repertory, and assigns parts. He may or may not be a choreographer as well, though this is often the case. The name artistic director combines the jobs of ballet master and choreographer.

BALLETOMANE A ballet enthusiast: a person who attends the ballet regularly, has decided opinions about dancers, and is partisan about the type of ballet, music, etc., to be preferred above all others. In the ideal sense, the balletomane is one whose great love for ballet as an art transcends partisanship for the individual dancer and choreographer. It is to be regretted that the loud and long demonstrations of some balletomanes are sufficient to drive the newcomer from the theatre. Marian Eames has written: "Exactly who coined the word *balletomane* is not known. It would seem reasonable to assume that the behavior of the dance enthusiast was to blame for the selection of the ending *mane* rather than *phile*. Indeed, the dance enthusiast appears to have been frenzied to a degree in his devotion and often absurd. Yet his frenetic outbursts lacked the embarrassing hollowness of contemporary movie madness, for the idolatry lavished upon individual dancers was not born of a mere susceptibility to physical 'allure.' The adorer was moved by qualities and style which he could analyze and discuss; furthermore, his obsession with the art itself should not be confused with the easily bought allegiance of zealots who are beguiled less by the avowed object of their enthusiasm than by the glorious trappings which surround it."[*]

BALLON   A characteristic of *elevation* (dance in the air). The ease with which a dancer maintains in the air a position he normally holds on the ground; the ability to ascend lightly into the air and to land softly and smoothly.

BARRE (or bar)   The round horizontal bar secured around the walls of a ballet classroom or rehearsal hall at a height of about three-and-a-half feet. The bar is usually placed opposite the long mirrors in which the dancer can watch what he is doing. Every ballet class begins with exercises at the bar, the dancer holding the bar for support as the daily elementary and constantly repeated exercises are performed; the lesson continues with exercises in the center of the room.

BATTEMENT   A nickname for an action of the leg. For example, the *battement tendu* (stretched beating), where the dancer—in the simplest form of this exercise—stands at the bar and extends her foot in front of her on the floor, or sideways, or back.

BATTERIE   The master term that applies to all movements in ballet in which one foot beats against the other, or in which the two feet beat together. Two types of this movement are distinguished: *grande batterie* (large, high beating steps) and *petite batterie* (small beating steps executed at a lower elevation).

BRISÉ   Literally, a broken movement. A beating step of elevation in which the dancer rises from the floor, beats one leg against the other, and returns to the same Fifth Position—distinguishable from the *entrechat* in that only one leg beats.

CABRIOLE   A movement of *grande batterie*. The cabriole develops the *battement*—in which one leg moves away from the supporting leg and returns—into a brilliant step of elevation: here both legs beat together in the air. One leg swings up to an angle of ninety degrees, the other leg rises, meets it, and both calves are beaten together (the feet do not cross); the legs are fully extended, knees straight, toes pointed. Cabrioles are also executed

[*] Foreword to "Russian Balletomania" by Anatole Chujoy, *Dance Index*, Vol. VII, No. 3.

at an angle of forty-five degrees from the floor; they can be performed in any direction—front, back, and to the side.

CARACTÉRE   The character dancer, or the dancer *en caractère*, performs national or folk dances—mazurkas, polkas, etc.—dances that are not performed on point. The dancer *en demi-caractère* performs popular dances such as the cancan, but may dance these on point; these are comic or semiserious dances, in other words, performed with some classical technique.

CHANGEMENT DE PIEDS (changing of the feet)   Small jump from Fifth Position in which the dancer changes the position of both feet in the air.

CHASSÉ   Literally, chased. A sliding step: the dancer jumps low off the floor, lands, and the working foot chases the landing foot out of position. A *chassé* embodies the same mechanical principle we see when we watch a horse canter. There the hind legs, moving together, displace the front legs.

CHOREOGRAPHER   Someone who makes dances. The word means, etymologically, someone who records dances. It has come to mean simply the person responsible for the design of movement in a ballet. It is inaccurate to say that a choreographer "writes" a new ballet—for no choreographer sets down on paper what he wishes dancers to do from one moment to the next—but this is sometimes said.

All good choreographers have been good dancers. But to be a good dancer, of course, is not necessarily to be a choreographer. The dancer wishes *to be moved*, the choreographer wishes *to move*. To combine the two inclinations successfully is rare, but rare indeed are great choreographers. The choreographer is best compared to the poet: he is a man who uses the material of the classic dance that has been developed over hundreds of years, just as the poet uses the language he writes in. Like the poet, the choreographer finds new ways of saying things.

CLASSIC   The word classic when applied to ballet is not the contrary of romantic. It applies to a rigorous basic vocabulary of steps and movements capable of infinite variation and a system of instruction that makes such variation possible for individual dancers. Classic ballets can be romantic, realistic, or mythological in subject matter. The classic dance is the dictionary of ballet and, as a method of instruction, it is also its grammar: basic steps and movements that must be learned and mastered if the student is to become an instrument of its possibilities. The classic dance is the fundamental material out of which new ballets are made; it constitutes the basic, instinctive knowledge that permits the dancer to perform them. As a system of instruction, the classic dance has been perfected through centuries of innovation and experiment. We know what is anatomically sound and physically possible. We know what must be taught first, how that must be learned so well that it becomes instinctive, what to teach next. We learn all this in schools, as dancers and teachers before us have learned it. Properly speaking, what we call the classic dance might be more easily understood if it were called the academic dance, after the academies in which it was evolved; but the word *classic* has come down to us, along with the tradition of the developed academic dance, and is now universally accepted. When we go to the ballet and see a ballet described as *classic* in the program, we know that the word doesn't imply something that is serious and perhaps not entertaining: classicism in dance is the basis for the finest entertainment.

CORPS DE BALLET Dancers who appear only in large groups: the chorus, the backbone of every ballet company. Jean-Georges Noverre (1759) advised the ballet master to "make your *corps de ballet* dance, but when it does so, let each member of it express an emotion or contribute to form a picture; let them mime while dancing so that the sentiments with which they are imbued might cause their sentiment to be changed at every moment." Until the present century, the function of the *corps de ballet* was merely decorative: as a group they embellished with their poses and did not distract from the performances of principal dancers. In dramatic ballets, they reacted with appropriate emotion to the dramatic situation (the death of Giselle, the huntsmen in *Swan Lake*).

The New Ballet of Mikhail Fokine, as he himself expressed it in 1914, "in developing the principle of expressiveness, advances from the expressiveness of face to the expressiveness of the whole body, and from the expressiveness of the individual body to the expressiveness of a group of bodies and the expressiveness of the combined dancing of a crowd." Every dancer in the crowd scene in the original production of *Petrouchka* (1911) had something to do at every moment, and each dancer was related in both action and reaction to the principals on stage. Ballet prior to Fokine was essentially linear: the stage was divided into parts where the *corps de ballet* danced, where the soloists danced, where the ballerinas danced, and these established patterns were seldom violated. With Fokine, movement on stage became orchestrated: each dancer on stage was an instrument contributing vitally to the general impression. Formerly it was only possible for a soloist to dance diagonally across the stage; now this is done by large groups of dancers: every dancer in such a group must be a soloist. Although every *corps de ballet* contains dancers of great talent who may eventually become principal dancers, and although it is wise for every soloist to have had experience in a *corps de ballet*, it is always possible in large state schools to discover talent early and not to permit it to idle long in the *corps*. This is the practice today with our ballet companies that are attached to schools. Talent is discovered early and used as soon as possible in appropriate roles. In ballet companies where the directors must first observe their new dancers in the *corps de ballet*, the *corps* itself becomes a kind of school, a testing ground, where talent is discovered. Experience in a *corps de ballet* gives a dancer invaluable lessons which are difficult to learn in any other way. Here she learns timing and precision; she learns also her relation to other dancers and other groupings of dancers on the stage. She learns, in fact, all the things that she must know to become a star.

DANCE (and danse) From the old high-German *danson*, meaning to drag or stretch.

DANSE D'ÉCOLE Literally, dance of the school. The classic dance, the academic dance based on the Five Positions and turn-out (*see* Classic).

DANSEUR NOBLE A classical male dancer; partner of the ballerina in classical roles (Albrecht in *Giselle*, Siegfried in *Swan Lake*, etc.).

DÉVELOPPÉ From the French word that means, literally, to develop or to unfold. A gradual unfolding of the leg as it rises from the floor and is extended fully in the air. As it is raised toward complete extension, the foot of the working leg passes (*passé*) the knee of the supporting leg.

DIVERTISSEMENT A dance or a series of dances for simple diversion and pleasure. A *divertissement* may be a whole number, like *Aurora's Wedding*, which contains plotless dance excerpts from *The Sleeping Beauty*, or it may be part of a whole ballet, like the folk dances that celebrate Prince Siegfried's birthday in the third act of *Swan Lake* or the series of character dances that come in the last act of *Coppélia*. A *grand pas de deux* taken out of a ballet and performed alone without its surrounding plot is a *divertissement*.

ÉCHAPPÉ (from *échapper*, to escape or slip) A step in which the dancer's feet escape from a closed position to an open position as she jumps upward. The movement is brisk and vigorous.

ELEVATION The ability of a dancer to rise from the floor to perform jumps, and the capacity to remain in the air in the midst of these movements. The *danse d'élévation* was first popularized by

Marie Taglioni (active 1822–48); within living memory, Vaslav Nijinksy (active 1908–19) still serves as a model conqueror of the air.

EN ARRIÈRE Backward.

EN AVANT Forward.

EN DEDANS Inward.

EN DEHORS Outward.

ENTRECHAT Probably derived from the Italian *intrecciare*, to weave or braid. A beating step of elevation in which the dancer jumps straight into the air from *plié* and crosses his feet a number of times, making a weaving motion in the air. The term *entrechat* is compounded with numerals to indicate the number of movements of the legs: *entrechat-trois, entrechat-quatre, entrechat-cinq, entrechat-six, entrechat-sept, entrechat-huit*. Each leg moves once in a crossing: hence the term *entrechat-six* means six movements—counting both legs—or three crossings. *Entrechats* up to *entrechat-six* are movements of *petite batterie*, small beatings; *entrechat-six* and above are movements of *grande batterie*, large beatings.

FOUETTÉ (from *fouetter*, to whip) In *fouetté en tournant*, a whipping motion of the free leg which propels the dancer around the supporting leg.

GLISSADE (glide) A gliding movement from Fifth Position to an open position and back to fifth position—usually seen as a preparatory step for jumps.

JETÉ (from *jeter*, to throw) The word is derived from *jeter* rather than *sauter* (the French word for jump) because in this movement, the dancer *throws* one leg away and up in the air. This is a jump in which the weight of the body is thrown from one foot to the other. There are small jumps in ballet (*assemblés, changements, échappés*, etc.), but these are all preparations for the large aerial jumps in which the dancer's body describes a swift, high trajectory in the air. In *grand jeté* the dancer pushes off from the floor with one foot in a variety of preparatory positions, holds a fleeting pose in flight, and lands softly on the other foot.

LIBRETTO The story line of a ballet; in a ballet without a plot, the idea on which the ballet is based. The ideal ballet story can be seen plainly and requires no extraneous explanation. The story of the *Prodigal Son* is a good example: once there was a boy who had everything, then he had nothing, then again he had everything.

NOTATION The writing down of dances in a form sufficiently intelligible for their accurate reproduction. Dances were written

PAS D'ACTION   Action in dancing—that part of a dramatic ballet, for example, where the relation of the characters is clarified. A *pas d'action* is not pure dancing and not pure mime, but a combination of the two, an integral part of the ballet spectacle. It's similar to many moments in opera where characters—after suspending the action for a while and singing a quintet—turn again to each other and resume their dramatic relation.

PAS DE DEUX   A dance for two people. Although a *pas de deux* is any dance for two people, the usual, standard *pas de deux* consists of four parts: the adagio, in which the *danseur* supports the ballerina in a slow, graceful dance; a variation of the ballerina; a variation of the *danseur;* and the coda, a concluding passage for both ballerina and *danseur* in which the dance is brought to a felicitous conclusion.

PAS DE TROIS   A dance for three people. *Pas de quatre* is a dance for four people; *pas de cinq,* a dance for five; *pas de six,* for six; and so forth.

PIROUETTE   A complete turn of the body on one foot. *Pirouette* used to be applied only to turns by men, while the term *tour* was reserved for turns by women. The terms are synonymous. Girls turn in pirouettes on *pointe,* boys on *demi-pointe.* Ideally, the body is vertical in pirouettes; the foot of the supporting leg remains in one place. The free leg can be lifted slightly off the floor, the knee bent, as in the most common form of pirouette; it can be raised in back, the knee straight, as in *pirouettes en arabesque;* or it can be raised in back, the knee bent, as in *pirouettes en attitude;* and so forth. Pirouettes have dazzled audiences since the history of ballet began, but multiple pirouettes were not introduced until 1766. At that time, three turns by a boy and two by a girl were considered spectacular. Turns performed off the floor are called *tours en l'air.*

PLIÉ (from *plier,* to bend)   In the classic dance, this is a bending of the knees, the knees wide open, the feet turned outward. The function of the *plié* in the dancer's body is like the function of springs in an automobile: it is necessary for the development of elasticity. *Demi-plié* is a half, or small, bending; *grand plié* is a deep bending of the knees.

POINTE   The dancer *sur les pointes* dances on her toes. This innovation of the Romantic ballet (c. 1820) is now universally used by female dancers in ballet: men stand on their toes only in certain Russian folk dances. If the dancer has been properly trained, dancing on point is neither painful nor uncomfortable nor damaging. Although the classic ballet is the only form of dance that uses toe dancing consistently, ballet existed long before toe steps were introduced; dancing on *pointes* cannot be called the single hallmark of ballet. Dancing on *pointes* is actually an extension of a basic feature of the classic dance: the straight line formed by the stretched leg and the pointing foot when the free leg moves from the floor. The ballet slippers of Marie Taglioni, who popularized toe dancing were unblocked. The toes of ballet slippers were later blocked with glue, as they are today, to give the dancer additional support. Every dancer darns the exterior of the toe of her ballet slipper—not for support, but to provide security of position while she dances and to prevent slipping. Dancing *sur la demi-pointe* is on the half-toe, where the dancer is supported high on the ball of the foot and under the toes.

PORT DE BRAS   Movement or carriage of the arms.

RÉGISSEUR   A stage manager, a person who has direct supervision over the presentation and the responsibility for the smooth running of a ballet performance.

RELEVÉ (from *relever*, to lift again)   In ballet, the raising of the body onto *pointe* or *demi-pointe*.

RÉVÉRENCE   A deep bow.

ROMANTIC   Ballets that we call Romantic are a *kind* of classical ballet. *La Sylphide* (1832), which epitomized—until the masterpiece *Giselle* (1841)—what we recognize as Romanticism in ballet, was romantic in subject, temper, and mood; but both ballets expressed this, with innovations, in the vocabulary of the *classic* dance. Similarly, *Les Sylphides* (1909)—which embodies Romanticism in name, substance, and music—consists of classical steps and movements. What is classic in ballet is what has been developed over the years; what is romantic is a period through which that development passed. Romanticism in ballet, in other words, is not the opposite of classicism.

Romanticism was responsible for revolutionary innovations in classic technique and in the subject matter of ballets. Its desire for ethereal creatures caused dancers for the first time to rise on their toes, introduced the white ballet costume so familiar to us in *Giselle, Swan Lake,* and *Les Sylphides,* and caused the expansion of the dance vocabulary to meet the expressive requirements of elfin, unattainable heroines and heroes who aimed at—and so seldom secured—permanent happiness. As it contrasted real life with fantasy, the Romantic Ballet naturalized the pastoral theme that dominated earlier ballet. Where previously nymphs and shepherds were potential gods and goddesses, these pastoral characters now became realistic, only to escape later from realism's cruelty to supernatural kingdoms (Act Two of *La Sylphide* and *Giselle*).

The heroes of the Romantic movement in ballet are: Théophile Gautier (1811–72), French poet, critic, and novelist, the librettist of *Giselle;* Jules Perrot (1810–92), dancer and choreographer, collaborator on *Giselle* and creator of the *Pas de Quatre.* Its heroine is its great ballerina Marie Taglioni (1804–84), creator of *La Sylphide.* The Romantic Ballet dominated the classic dance from about 1820 to 1870.

After this time, what we recognize as the great classical ballets—*Swan Lake, The Sleeping Beauty*, etc.—were created on the basis of a new uncovered, unconcealed technique and a more exacting dance discipline. Thus, unlike literature, music, and the other arts, ballet's great period of classicism came *after* the development of Romanticism.

ROND DE JAMBE A rotary movement of the leg; the dancer describes circles in the air, or on the floor, with the pointed toe of the working foot. The *rond de jambe* is a basic exercise in the ballet class and a ballet step seen frequently on stage. The *rond de jambe en l'air* is executed away from the floor.

SAUTÉ (from *sauter*, to jump) The word is used as a modifier to explain that a jump is involved in a step or prose: *sauté en arabesque, échappé sauté*, and so forth.

TOUR *See* Pirouette.

TOUR EN L'AIR A turn in the air. The dancer, standing in Fifth Position, rises from the floor from a *demi-plié*, executes a complete turn, and returns to original position. *Tours* may be doubled or tripled for spectacular effect, but three complete turns in the air is the maximum.

TURNOUT The distinguishing characteristic of the classic dance: knees that face frontward in a normal standing position are turned out from the hip at an angle of ninety degrees. Because dancers wore heels on their shoes at the time the five absolute positions were established, the complete ninety-degree turnout was not perfect until sometime later. Complete turnout is not forced in beginning students.

TUTU Ballet skirt; a nickname for *tunique*, tunic. The so-called Romantic tutu, which reaches to about twelve inches above the floor, was made famous by Marie Taglioni in the first famous Romantic ballet, *La Sylphide;* it is still familiar to us in *Giselle* (Act Two) and *Les Sylphides*. Gradually, however, with the perfection of dance technique, the tutu has been shortened to make the whole leg visible.

VARIATION A solo, a dance for one person. Synonym: *pas seul*.

Index

(Page citations appearing in italics refer to illustrations)

INDEX

INDEX

INDEX